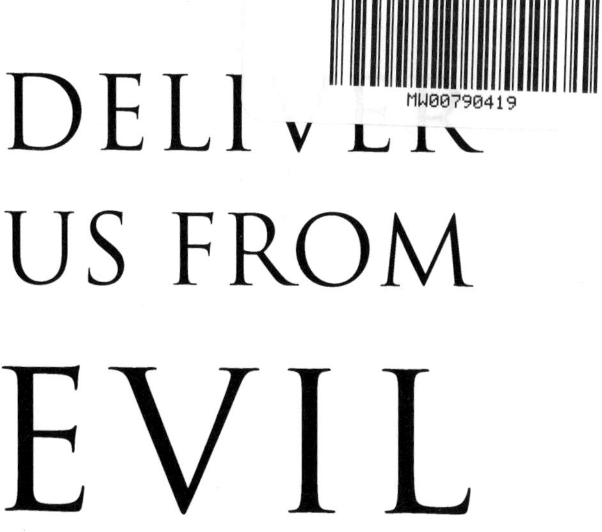

DELIVER US FROM EVIL

DEBORAH HUNTER-MARSH, MSW

eLectio Publishing
Little Elm, TX
www.eLectioPublishing.com

Deliver Us From Evil

By Deborah Hunter-Marsh

Cover Design by eLectio Publishing and Ned Hoste

ISBN-13: 978-1-63213-196-6

Published by eLectio Publishing, LLC

Little Elm, Texas

http://www.eLectioPublishing.com

Printed in the United States of America

Publisher's Note

The publisher does not have any control over and does not assume any responsibility for author or third-party websites or their content.

The author has made every attempt to present events, locales, and conversations as accurately as feasible. When possible, details have been confirmed with the individuals involved, with accounts included in commercially made video tapes, and with publicly available documents filed in court. Any inaccuracies and discrepancies are unintentional. To promote anonymity, in some instances, names of individuals have been altered.

This book is dedicated to my children,
who taught me more
than I taught them.

CONTENTS

ACKNOWLEDGMENTS

To my niece, Niki Vandover, for her support and assistance with this book.

To my sister, Rebecca, also my roommate; if we had to go through our rough childhoods, at least we had each other. You are my friend and I love you.

To my coach, editor, and now good friend, Kathie Giorgio from AllWriters' Workplace & Workshop, for your watchful eyes. The high quality of this book is because of you. See you in class.

To Dr. Ellsworth, thank you for your assistance and guidance in teaching me to not die dumb and for the beautiful Foreword for this book. You saved my life!

To my once-in-a-lifetime love and constant companion, Pierre; without your motivating support and assistance, I could not have written this book. Your continuous love and support are unimaginable. You are my best friend!

FOREWORD

By Sterling G. Ellsworth, PhD

This book is a dramatic account of survival and learning from severe betrayal trauma. Since 1964, I have interviewed thousands of beautiful people, helping them to recover from and make sense of their emotional suffering. Deborah is one of these people.

As a psychologist, I am often amazed at how people get through emotional injuries that would destroy most of us! Deborah is again one of these people. In addition to her emotional trauma, she is pretty much homebound with intense daily physical pain from a knee surgery gone wrong. I admire her courage and am thankful she has still been able to write this book that will inspire everyone who reads it. It will help all of us to count our blessings, to see the big picture and learn from being a student in the earth school.

Many people have been sexually abused, usually by someone they know. Betrayed by friends and relatives, they often lose any hope of trust in human beings. Their lights go out. Their hope for significance and meaning in life are dashed to pieces. Depression, anxiety, and a host of other fear-based thoughts and feelings plague their lives. This is especially true when their abuse is early on and repeated through the years. When the perpetrator is a parent who should have been trusted and respected, it is very devastating. When it is also an authority figure in the person's religious value system, it is life-wrenching. When it is life-threatening, including a near-death experience, it is nearly incomprehensible. Deborah's story has all three of these factors. Not only is it high drama, but it teaches us the amazing power in each of us to survive, to repress, to look for meaning in our suffering, and to assign blame.

Deborah continues to grow today. I tell her often, "You won't die dumb," or "You will be one of the wisest people in heaven." She still gains support from her weekly sessions with me.

I admire her for seeing the great truth, "Never judge an instrument by the user." She doesn't hate any church. She doesn't hate all pastors, priests, or bishops. She knows most of them to be good, hard-working helpers in their churches. She is a great example for all of us. Don't throw out all hammers because a few users hit their thumbs while driving a nail. Churches can be like hammers—good instruments for giving us purpose and meaning in life. Deborah's bishop father abused this instrument repeatedly. It's not the instrument's fault.

Deborah's story moves us all closer to the great truths available in betrayal trauma. It is a good read for all students in the "earth school."

DELIVER US FROM EVIL

INTRODUCTION

They say it takes a village to raise a child. Having had three children, I know that to be true. It also takes a village to write a book. Besides all the people I have thanked, there are also teachers who helped me in my travels to get to be an author. A book is an endeavor that takes longer than a child to produce and when you hand it over to the publisher, you are as exhausted mentally as you are physically with a baby.

Chapter 14 talks about coping skills for the long-term problems of being sexually abused. It offers an immense amount of information on therapy. Therapy is my support system. Without therapists who genuinely cared about me, I also would not have been able to cope emotionally with telling my readers about such intimate details of my and the other individuals' abuse.

One thing I want to impress on your mind is the complete and total shattered character of my father. What made my father a sociopath? He had no conscience. There were many other things he did that were negative which you will see as you read this story, but he never felt remorse for them. If he had, he would have stopped molesting and raping all the people he did. Yet he felt no guilt or he would have controlled his behaviors long before he did near his death. The only thing that stopped my molester was poor health, lack of opportunity, and, finally, his death.

Dad was very narcissistic and he didn't want to go through life obeying any of the societal or religious rules, which made him antisocial. These two diagnoses most often lead to someone being sociopathic. As you read the book, you will see all the signs and deviant symptoms that were there for my father.

I recently asked Dr. Ellsworth, "Are all fathers, uncles, or brothers who molest or rape a child sociopathic?" He told me there are many causes for pedophiles both in and out of the immediate family. He has interviewed fathers and they tell him various answers. "It is a complex issue with a variety of answers. Whole books have been written and so I can't give you one answer," Dr. Ellsworth said.

I also want to mention that since we were a Mormon family, there is a lot of Mormon terminology. I have created an appendix with the simplest definitions I could think of and as the church defines them. Let me make it perfectly clear my sister Rebecca is active in her beliefs of the Mormon teaching, and I believe some of the concepts, but not all of these teachings. We are not against the Mormon faith. In fact, I quote from some of the talks and teachings that the leaders have offered. We feel our dad knew the gospel better than most and yet he allowed Satan to guide his steps instead of the Lord's teaching and rules. This story is not the LDS Church's fault. They could not have known the secret life my father kept.

We hope you will read the whole book to gain insight and knowledge that you are not alone. There are millions of victims and survivors in this world. If this book helps you in any way, please spread the word to others and leave reviews where appropriate, especially on Amazon.

You can find me on Facebook, Twitter, Pinterest, our website and blog (deliverusfromevil.us) and my email (marshahunter2000@gmail.com). I look forward to hearing from you.

CHAPTER ONE

Innocence

Dead at age seventy-five. Praise the Lord! Free at last! The daughter who is free at last! There is one less pedophile walking the streets at night. His obituary reads:

> *Walton W. Hunter died at his home in Huntington Beach, California after a long, lingering illness. Born October 25, 1920, in Enoch, Texas. Served in the Air Force. Served two missions for the Church of Jesus Christ of Latter-day Saints. Mormon Bishop twice for 17 years. Dedicated to missionary work, loved teaching and expounding the gospel, counseled church members in times of stress. Prominent businessman. Hunter Motor Company.*

What they forgot to add was, "Charming sociopath, conniving pedophile, master manipulator, controlled people with money."

More of his obituary:

> *Loving husband to June B. Hunter and devoted father to four children: Wayne Hunter (Utah); Rebecca Hunter-Rapp (California); Deborah Hunter-Marsh (Oregon); Cynthia Hunter-Steele (California). Also, he was a devoted grandfather to 21 grandchildren and two great-grandchildren.*

Sounds like a normal obituary, but my father and family were as sick and twisted as they came back in 1995. You won't hear much about Wayne, our older brother, or Cynthia, our little sister, in Rebecca's and my book because of a little family dispute: they don't believe that this story ever happened. They believe the fairytale that ours was the perfect Mormon family, where everyone was happy. Theirs was a childhood of hot rods and after-school snacks, riotous jokes and trips to Disneyland. Everything would still be great for them—except for those pesky sisters, Rebecca and Deborah, who keep making up outlandish lies about our father raping and molesting them and their children.

We also disagree about poor little anxious Mom, how she cleaned up sheets from our beds without even seeing the blood or body fluids on them. Furthermore, we have been unable to agree about our mother's part in the abuse of their grandchild, Alexander. So we disagree a little—what family doesn't? If Wayne and Cynthia were writing this book, they would stomp their feet and urge us to quiet down and go away. But it is our story and our book, and we are going to tell the family secrets.

Hopefully, this story will help other men and women who have been abused, who are too traumatized to speak and have decided to bear their family secrets in silence. As my therapist, Dr. Sterling Ellsworth, always told me, "Ye shall know the truth and the truth shall set you free. But first, it may make you miserable!" How true this turned out to be.

So let's hold on to our hats, buy a bookmark, and hide under the covers if need be, because the trip we'll take with our story may be scary at times. It may be graphic at times, but we promise it will be true.

As they say on *Law and Order*: "We have the evidence." In fact, we are the evidence!

—1959—

I was five years old and would be starting kindergarten soon. Today was my special day because it was the first time I got to go alone with Dad to the car lot and I had been looking forward to it for a long time. He agreed to take me with him, and that made it my special day. As we drove the shiny blue Buick to the car lot, I recognized many landmarks in Salt Lake City along the way: Natter's Market, Conoco gas stations, and finally, Liberty Park. I knew we were getting close. We passed Sears on the right, and as the light turned green, we arrived at Hunter Motor Company. The sign, in all its glory with the royal blue background and golden lettering, made me feel special that I was going there for the day. It was a small mom-and-pop car lot on State Street and is no longer there, but in 1959, it did a fair amount of business.

"Uncle Elvan," I said as I gave him a big hug, "you smell like spices."

"New cologne, kid. Gotta close a deal. See you inside," Elvan said as he turned and quickly walked away.

Uncle Elvan was my dad's older brother and that made him my uncle. He had greased black hair like my dad's, but otherwise, he didn't look like my dad at all. He looked like Grandpa Hunter with his turned-up pixie nose and his weak little chin. He worked for Dad at the car lot, selling cars, and he looked sharp today with his crisp white shirt, black suit, and red and black tie with a little pioneer tie tack. I remembered Mom telling us that the Mormon pioneers settled here in the Salt Lake Valley.

Dad wanted to put up some signs he picked up at the sign shop yesterday on a couple of cars on the lot before going inside the office.

"Louie, Louie!" I said as I walked further into the car lot and started to run to give him a high-five.

"Debbie," Dad said, "you're not greeting him with a big hug. Hi, Louie. Mom would die…" and I immediately knew what Dad meant by that with the grease and my clothes. They were not new, but still in good condition, and Louie was covered in grease.

Louie worked on the cars if they were broken and he was always covered in grease and oil. Dad said he was a Negro and his folks were colored people. All I knew was he had darker skin and played Go Fish with me and I always won and he always went and got lunch for all of us, or at least, every time I had been there.

"Well, it still smells the same as usual," I said to Dad. "Dirt, oil, and gasoline, that's what the car lot smells like." I didn't like the smell again this time at the beginning of my visit, but I grew used to it as the day went on. That was what happened each time I came to the car lot, either with Mom and/or my other siblings. At first, I didn't like the smell, but soon, I found it intoxicating.

"Hey, kid," Chuck Van Dam, one of the lead salesmen, said to me as he rolled his eyes. "Why are you here today?" He made clicking noises with his gum.

"Mom had a church luncheon, the other kids are somewhere else, and I get to come with Dad to the car lot without my brother or sisters, just me and my dad," I said as happily as I could. I wasn't crazy about Chuck either and he passed by me and up the stairs, probably to see his wife. There was a one-bedroom apartment connected above the car lot where Chuck and his wife lived. It was a dilapidated old building, but it served its purpose. Dad often talked of the days when he would have a second car lot with a fancy, new, and modern office building.

"I am going up to my apartment to see if the little wifey has lunch ready or if she's going to be my lunch today. You know what I mean, kid?"

No, I do not know what you mean, I said to myself. I'm only five.

My father said that his office was mine for most of the day, so I gathered my toys and entertained myself in the hot and dusty room. Dad told me that I needed to stay in there most of the day. After entering the office with Dad carrying some of my books, I climbed up into his big brown swivel office chair, where I felt so small while coloring and looking at my books. My favorite books were picture books, as I could not read yet; at least, not very many words. I was through coloring and playing with my toys around lunchtime when Louie was sent to get some hamburgers for everyone. It wasn't often that I got a hamburger from Dee's drive-through. We almost always ate at home.

After we had eaten, Dad could tell I was bored, so he gave me a green pad of paper and a special white pen with black, blue, and red inks. You could choose the color. He asked me to write down all of the license plates' numbers and letters, which kept me busy for another couple of hours. I knew my ABCs and 123s but didn't know how to write them all, so the sheets of paper looked more like chicken scratches than an ordered list. I was dying to jump in the rainbow-colored puddles, but I knew they were oil and gasoline and I would get in big trouble if I splashed in them, so I didn't.

It was hot and the sun beat down. By the time I returned to the office, a pink sunburn kissed my shoulders in the places my flowered playdress didn't cover. My father commented that Mother wasn't going to be happy and spread some lotion on the pink areas.

We then took our traditional walk across the street to Sears, this time just me and Dad, to get some chocolate-covered jelly rings. We crossed in the middle of the street with cars whizzing by. I learned that you should always cross at corners in the crosswalk with a stoplight. Maybe Daddy knew of a different rule. And you always do what Mommy and Daddy tell you to do or they get very angry at you.

Buying these chocolate-covered jelly rings was one of the fun things my father did with his kids whenever we came to the car lot. Today, I got to do it without the other kids—just Daddy and me.

When we returned to the car lot, I was very tired and my father told me to lie down in his office for a while. It felt good to take my sandals off and feel my yellow butterfly blankie, so soft and cool. It only took a few seconds and I was out like a light for a long nap.

I awoke suddenly to find my father's fingers fondling my pee pee area and a car salesman entering the room to get something out of the desk. I think he saw Dad taking his hand out of my panties because I heard Dad explain to the salesman that he thought I wet my panties during my nap. As I rubbed my eyes open to come out of the fog of sleep, I was confused and asked Daddy if he was playing the "secret game" when I just woke up because my panties were still down by my knees. I started to cry and was overwhelmed with sadness that Daddy would play the secret game with me asleep. He had done this before and I had woken up to his feeling my pee pee at home, but never anywhere else. I started crying because I was asleep and I didn't know what he had been doing.

I asked through my tears if we had to play the secret game at the car lot. I didn't want to, but again, Dad got to decide when and now where we had to play that. I was a smart cookie; someone had called me one time and I liked the name cookie. I knew Daddy wasn't supposed to touch me there. I asked my Sunday School teacher, Sister Lambert, and she said only mommies can help you when you go to the bathroom when you are three or four years old. Daddy had been playing the secret game with me since I was in big girl panties. He said it came with the territory, whatever that meant.

Dad was in no mood to answer anyone's questions. I continued to cry for a few more minutes as Dad was gathering my toys and trying to soothe me at the same time.

I was inconsolable at times, but when he told me to be quiet, I cried all the harder. My family always called me the melodramatic child, but I just expressed my feelings out loud. The man I called father tried to comfort me, but I pushed him away. How could a daddy do such a horrible thing to his little girl? I wanted to scream, but just then, my father told me, "Deborah, why are you crying? Did you have a bad dream? I just came in and found you sitting up and crying. You must have had a terrible dream while you were napping." He thought he had me awake when he checked my panties and I was wrong about the secret game happening then. That's why he told the salesman what he was doing. The salesman didn't realize Daddy was just checking to see if I peed because I was all sweaty and wet.

"Do you remember what your dream was about?" he asked.

"You!" I rubbed my eyes with the blanket.

"It's my fault you had a bad dream?" Daddy said. "What do I have to do with you having a nightmare?"

"Never mind." I was confused. "Can we just go home now?"

By the time we gathered up my picture books and my toys and the chocolate jelly rings to share with my brother and sisters, I still did not remember what my dream or nightmare was about. I still felt angry at my father but didn't quite remember why.

On the way home, Dad didn't say much and my mood was lifting a little. The dream Dad thought I had began to fade from my mind. My father said, "Let's not tell your mother that you had such a bad dream. It might ruin her day or upset her, and she'll be very tired."

I replied, "What dream, Dad?"

He told me to forget it, and it was never spoken of again.

When we arrived at home, I gave Mom a kiss and showed her the new pen Daddy gave me. I went to my bedroom and drew monsters with sharp teeth and reaching arms until dinner was ready. I made a book out of the monster drawings and kept it in a secret place that not even Mother would find.

It seemed as if Dad had been touching me forever. Somehow, I knew it was wrong for daddies to touch their children down there, but I thought all or most of them did that. They didn't do it on television, so I thought it was not right, and Sister Lambert said it was a sin and none of our parents would dare do something like that. On other occasions, when Dad touched me, he swore that if I told anyone about our secret games together, he would say I was crazy and wouldn't be believed—it was my word against his. And I was just a little girl.

"The men in white doctor coats will come and take you away and you will be locked away forever," said Daddy, "because you would be crazy."

I did what my father said in order to protect him, the family, and myself. The memory of being molested at the car lot was now buried.

* * *

My very first body memory came when I visited Hawaii with my husband, Steve, in 1982. He went on a business trip, and I accompanied him as we rarely had the opportunity to travel together. And what a wonderful trip it was! The sun was bright in the sky, and I tanned and napped by the pool while Steve taught or attended classes. For once, we didn't fight and got along great.

On the hotel bed, we played, wrestled, and teased each other.

"Remember, I'm not ticklish," Steve said, "but I know who is." He began to tickle me.

I grabbed both of his hands and said, "Oh, honey, honey, you didn't come—now stop that—you didn't come all the way to Hawaii to tickle me, did you?"

"Well, it's a fun thing to do because you are so…" Steve replied.

"I know, I know, but let's think of something we both like that's a little like tickling," and I gave him a nice, romantic kiss on the lips. "Something along these lines," I said and I kissed him again. He started kissing me back and then pinned me and my body on the bed. I asked, "What are you doing? Wasn't the kiss enough of a hint?"

He stated, "Yes, but I'd rather tickle and wrestle with you right now," and he pinned my arms down.

When I tried to pull away, I could not with all my might get loose. I said, "Steve, this isn't funny anymore. If you don't get off of me, I'll

have to scream." I began to shout and that's when he put his hand over my mouth and accidentally covered my nose as well.

I flipped out and he saw that tears were welling up in my eyes and he let go of me. I flew into the bathroom and locked the door and hid between the toilet and the bathtub in the fetal position, rocking myself back and forth.

"Honey, oh, honey, what's wrong? I was just kidding around. Did I hurt you? Are you all right?" He begged for any answer.

All I could do was rock back and forth and cover my ears and close my eyes.

"Sweetheart, tell me what I did?" Steve asked for the tenth time.

"You tried to hurt me, you meant to hurt me, I know you did," I said and it echoed loudly in the bathroom. "Why would you want to hurt me?" and I rocked and cried until I fell asleep a couple of hours later.

Steve pleaded and apologized most of the night for whatever he did, but I did not emerge until I woke up in the morning with dried tears on my face. I apologized, and I cried, and I begged him to understand that I didn't know what happened. The event was a mystery to both of us. It was my first body memory, but I didn't understand why I was so upset.

When we arrived home a few days later, I remembered that I had an appointment with a new therapist, Dr. Sterling Ellsworth. I was tempted to skip the appointment—I had been to many therapists, and my depression and anxiety were as bad as ever. I did keep the appointment, and I asked Dr. Ellsworth why I became so angry at my husband in Hawaii when we were just playfully wrestling. He said that he would need to have more sessions with both of us to understand that reaction. When couples come to him wanting marital counseling, he insists on meeting with each individual separately in the beginning and then he brings both of them back together to work on the marriage at some future point. What he didn't tell me was that he already suspected that my anger could be traced to a suppressed memory, perhaps from childhood. We would just have to wait and see.

It wasn't long before I woke up one morning and the day at the car lot returned to me. I shook my head at my bizarre dream that I had been molested as a child. I lay back down and sank into the bed, surrounded by the covers and the pillow. Suddenly, I knew beyond a shadow of a doubt that I had been molested. It was not just a dream, but a fact that I no longer could deny. Whether it was by my father or someone else, I was still unsure. But I was positive that somewhere in my past, the happy moments were tainted by a dark shadow. We discussed it with Dr. Ellsworth at the next session, and our wrestling in Hawaii fit clearly into my coming memories.

"If someone was going to sexually molest a little child, wouldn't a hand over the mouth silence her?" Dr. Ellsworth asked.

I agreed with that part, but I was having an increasingly difficult time with the idea that it was my father. I just couldn't fathom that. I prayed that God would help me know who it was, and if it was my father, that I could somehow accept that knowledge. I described my father as seductive, charming, and handsome, and by the second and third sessions, I revealed to Dr. Ellsworth that my father had affairs with other women. He wasn't surprised.

I had no more dreams, memories, or thoughts about it until Steve and I prepared for our next appointment. Dr. Ellsworth lived two hours away from our home. This might sound ludicrous, but he was a remarkable therapist who was the same religion, and two or three of my close friends went to him also and gave him rave reviews, so he seemed like a perfect fit to help with my pain and depression. I fell asleep on the way down to Dr. Ellsworth's office and was startled awake by a car horn honking.

"Debbie. Debbie, are you awake? You're crying, honey. Why are you crying?" Steve said as he gently rubbed my shoulder.

"Oh, I'm awake now. Who was honking? Why are there tears all over my face? Why am I so upset?" I said as I wiped the tears off.

"I don't know why you are so upset. You started saying 'No, no, no,' and then you said 'Daddy' in your sleep, and that's when someone honked their horn and you woke up crying. Did you have a bad dream?" Steve said and then I really started crying and Steve had to pull the car over to get me calmed down.

I was wailing and shaking my head, saying, "NO, NO, NO! It can't be! It just can't be my father. I have to get to Dr. Ellsworth. I have to tell him it was my father. AND HE RAPED ME! He didn't just molest me at the car lot, there were other times he molested me and then he raped me. I can't believe it. Hurry, get to Dr. E's office so I can tell him. He just won't believe it. Can you believe it, Steve?" I said as I grabbed his hand and squeezed it tight.

I sobbed for the next hour as Steve tried to console me. We spent our entire appointment processing the fact that I was now positive it was my own father who molested and raped me. It wasn't a dream—it was a memory. I knew that God revealed the truth to me, no matter how horrible and awful that truth was.

I had more nightmares and dreams about being raped, and each time these thoughts invaded my mind, I would cry out, scream, or become violent with rage. One night, I went into my closet with some scissors to cut my legs. The decision to cut my legs was completely impulsive and irrational, leaning on the side of being mentally ill. But that's the place I was at for now. By cutting my legs, not deep or long, it allowed me to focus on the physical pain and not the emotional pain, which was overwhelming.

Steve was outside my closet door, saying, "Honey, please, can I come in and console you in some way?"

"No," I whimpered, trying to get a breath in between sobs.

He kept begging me. "But honey, please don't cut your legs again, you don't deserve that kind of treatment."

"That and worse; I must have done something very bad to warrant that severe of abuse from my Mormon bishop father. I do deserve it."

"Shred a picture of your dad, the one on the wall of your dad and mom. I'll get it."

I screamed back, "No, I'll tell you what I'm going to shred," and Steve could hear the scissors tear at some kind of cloth. He opened the closet door just enough to see what I was shredding.

"Not your wedding dress. You love that dress," he said, trying to open the closet door now all the way. He couldn't as I had put a wooden dowel at the bottom part of the doorway so it would only allow Steve or anyone six inches to open the closet door. I needed a lot of control at this time. "Remember, honey, that's the dress that made you feel like Cinderella at the ball, only in Southern style. You love the big hat made of chiffon and silk like the dress," Steve pleaded.

"But I wasn't good enough to get a white dress, not a white dress, it had to be a beige dress to match my tainted body," I said as I gasped for air. Just as I started to cut my leg again, Steve took the closet door off its hinges and grabbed the scissors out of my hand just before my strength completely wore out and I was on the floor in a heap like a ragdoll, with sweat pouring down me one way and tears all over my face and down my neck another way. I was wrung out. I could have still cut my legs, but I awoke from my crazy state to realize cutting my legs didn't help as much as I hoped it would. I fell completely to the floor, exhausted and all cried out for the moment.

Steve took me in his arms and said, "No more, no more. You've done enough damage to yourself."

"But not as much as my father did to me. He ruined my life."

And Steve rocked me slowly back and forth, saying, "I know, I know."

Steve was a six-foot-three-inch burly type of guy. He had thick wavy unruly black hair and he could be very loving to me and I truly needed it at this particular point. He told me later when I was handling the sexual abuse better, that if I had killed myself, he would have dressed me in a little girl's dress, pink with ruffles, and would have told my parents, "There is the child you destroyed. There is little seven- or nine-year-old Debbie. Now you live with her death on your hands." I loved him all the more for it.

Knowing the truth, I often hid in my closet underneath the clothes, where no one could come in and touch me. Steve sat at the closet door and soothed me with positive reassurances. I was suicidal at this time, and Steve watched carefully to see that I didn't take an overdose of my medications. The anger raged inside of me, and I continued to want to cut my legs, but I didn't. If I cut my legs, it seemed to relieve some of the pain I felt inside, but it was only a temporary solution with a permanent scar. I felt like a ragdoll thrown upon the dirt; used, abused, and thrown away as garbage.

For months, there were counseling appointments where I received empathy, kindness, and acceptance from Dr. Ellsworth. He gave me a gentle hug, encouraging words, validation, the tools to understand my memories, and coping skills. Most of all, he didn't try to control me. He said, "Well, if you can't cope with some of the tools I've given you, like journal writing, artwork, or driving to your safe place and crying or screaming, then you can call me. But try two other coping mechanisms first."

I never did have one memory come back to me in Dr. Ellsworth's office. They mostly came in dreams, but dreams that were unusually vivid and followed by a surety throughout the day that the "dream" was the truth. They became clearer and stronger every day after that. We processed the newest or most troubling memories at each appointment by talking, crying, left-hand writing to try to get at repressed memories, and artwork. He was so patient, kind, and encouraging, despite the fact that I was such a wreck.

Dr. Ellsworth invited my parents to come to Oregon for therapy with me to help us all heal from this tragic experience and become a closer, more open family. I begged them to come. At my next counseling session, I stepped into Dr. Ellsworth's newly decorated therapy office, noticing the new wallpaper. There was a sunset motif on the west wall and a sunrise motif on the opposite wall. There were cute knickknacks from beaches and lakes he and his wife had been to with his sailboat.

"I like your office, especially the sunset scene on that wall," I said, trying to make small talk when what I really wanted to do was lie on the floor in the fetal position and cry my little heart out. "They're not…not coming," I sobbed.

"Who's not coming?" Dr. Ellsworth said, leaning forward.

"My parents, my stupid, stupid parents. They think I've had a total break from reality or it's a false memory that you caused," I replied.

Dr. Ellsworth sat back in his high-backed white recliner and said, "Did you tell them that all your memories have happened elsewhere than my office and that you started getting memories back even before we met?"

"Yes, I did." I began sobbing uncontrollably. "It's true, it's coming true. My father said when I was a little girl, that if I told what he was doing to me, no one would believe me. It's coming true, they don't believe me, the whole family has written me off, even some friends too."

"Let me send them another letter, urging them to come and 'save' their daughter from me. You get my drift, Debbie?" Dr. Ellsworth clasped his hands around my mine, which were in one big fist. "Maybe I can convince them into coming, using the Lord's words from the Bible to soften their hearts. Then maybe we might get somewhere with them. Any loving parents would want to come help their daughter and knock some sense back into her head," he said, smiling with a special twinkle in his eye. "Now what do you think about that, Deb?"

I stopped crying and wiped away my tears. "Yeah, they're really into using the Lord's words to convince me 'out of this trance' I'm in." This was the first bit of hope I felt in a long, long time.

He was antsy in his chair. "We'll have to do it that way, but in a professional manner. Debbie, if your own daughter flipped her wig—I use the term gently with love and empathy—and was telling people that you beat her up twice weekly when she was growing up, wouldn't you go to therapy with her to find out what made her think that? Because you love your daughter unconditionally?"

"Well, yes, I would. I have nothing to hide…"

He stopped writing in my chart to say to me, "Exactly my point. They don't want to come because they do have something hide." He threw his pen onto the coffee table and leaned back in his chair. "I've written in your chart to send another letter to your parents, pleading with them to come and work this out as other families have."

"Have other patients and their parents really come and worked through this kind of stuff?"

"Not many, but some have. Now, what else is going on with you?" Dr. Ellsworth said, winking at me.

I began to cry again.

I kept the letters, proving that we did invite them; I so hoped they would do it for me. But once again, I was abandoned. Here are some of the letters, although Mom (June) just makes excuses for not coming, that they and Dr. Ellsworth wrote:

CLINICAL COUNSELING PSYCHOLOGY
STERLING G. ELLSWORTH, PH.D., P.C.
202 EAST BEACON DRIVE, EUGENE, OREGON 97404
TELEPHONE 503-688-1520

Oct. 25, 1989

Mr. & Mrs. Walton Hunter
406 Avenida Palamas
San Jose, Ca. 95123

Dear Mr. & Mrs. Hunter

Thank you for your concern regarding Debbie. It is always good to see parents who are willing to take an active role in their child's healing process.

Debbie says she has presented our idea to you that you both come to Oregon in the near future to participate in therapy. I feel it is a very appropriate time for this to take place. I would like to discuss in person your concerns and feelings regarding the current situation. I would like to meet with the two of you alone first and then jointly with Debbie. Many of my clients who are concerned and wish to help their children participate in this manner.

I have the following weeks when our session could take place. They are the week of Dec. 18, 1989 or anytime after that. Please let my secretary know as soon as possible which time would be convenient for you so we can get the time scheduled.

I feel that you will both find it very beneficial to participate in this manner and look forward to meeting with you.

Sincerely,

Sterling G. Ellwworth, Ph.D. P.C.

14 November 1989
406 Avenida Palmas
San Jose, CA 95123
Tel #408-225-5941

Dr. Sterling G. Ellsworth
202 East Beacon Drive
Eugene, Oregon 97404

Dear Dr. Ellsworth:

Thank you for your recent letter concerning our daughter, Debbie Marsh.

At the time Debbie suggested we come to Oregon sometime soon and participate in therapy with her, we both thought this might be very worthwhile. However, I have recently received two letters from Debbie which are so full of animosity toward us that we feel meeting with her right away would only bring on more hurt for all of us.

As you are probably aware, our problem with Debbie and Steven is two-fold: one, emotional and the other, financial. As soon as we are able to put an end to the financial problem, then we hope there can be a meeting with Debbie which would help all three of us to heal and bring our whole family back together again.

For the moment, we feel we have lost our daughter and her family, but through our faith and prayers, our relationship can eventually be mended.

Sincerely,

June Hunter

June Hunter

May 8, 1992

Dr. Ellsworth,

In the recent general conference of the church, Elder Richard G. Scott spoke on "Healing the Tragic Scars of Abuse". His talk was excellent - he spoke not only to those who have been abused by others, but also to those who have been wrongly accused and the injustice and pain which results. The following is a quote from the text of his speech:

"I caution you not to participate in two improper therapeutic practices that may cause you more harm than good. They are: Excessive probing into every minute detail of your past experiences, particularly when this involves penetrating dialogue in group discussion; and blaming the abuser for every difficulty in your life............There is another danger. Detailed leading questions that probe your past may unwittingly trigger thoughts that are more imagination or fantasy than reality. They could lead to condemnation of another for acts that were not committed. While likely few in number, I know of cases where such therapy has caused great injustice to the innocent from unwittingly stimulated accusations that were later proven false. Memory, particularly adult memory of childhood experiences is fallible. Remember false accusation is also a sin."

The above quotation explains exactly what happened in the therapy of our daughter, Debbie Marsh. You and other psychologists were not aware of the circumstances and people involved which helped persuade Debbie to accuse us. You also are not aware, and apparently do not care, that the accusations are not true and that the effect of her accusations has split our family apart and helped in destroying my husband's physical health. We have lost our daughter and her family, except for an occasional phone call from the girls. However, the most painful thing to me is that our daughter, who needed family so much, has withdrawn herself from all of us, except our daughter-in-law who dislikes us and has encouraged her in accusing us.

My last thoughts and prayers every night and every morning are for Debbie and her family and I continually ask for a miracle which will reveal the truth to her. My husband and I are getting older and will not have to live with the painful results of your therapy too much longer; however, Debbie and the girls will suffer the rest of their lives - this is what makes me the most unhappy.

My reason, therefore, for writing to you is to implore with you and your colleagues to abandon this philosophy which was used with Debbie so that other families will not have to endure this terrible pain.

Sincerely,

June B. Hunter

Mrs. June B. Hunter

STERLING G. ELLSWORTH, PH.D., P.C.
PSYCHOLOGIST
COUNSELING AND PSYCHOTHERAPY
1675 N. FREEDOM BLVD., VILLAGE GREEN BLDG. 4, PROVO, UTAH 84604
TELEPHONE 801-377-3131

May 20, 1992

Mrs. June B. Hunter
9026 Summerhill Point
Alpine, CA 91901

Dear Mrs. Hunter,

I am sorry there is so much pain in your family. You evidently blame everyone but yourself for this pain. This makes you feel better, but it is not the truth.

You assume that all therapists do the two things Brother Scott cautioned against. You have no knowledge of what any therapist does, only your own assumption which comes from your intense need to externalize blame.

I know exactly what happened in my therapy with Debbie. I can state without any reservation whatsoever that none of these things or any other leading techniques happened in her therapy. I never do any of those things nor have done in all my 30 years of practice. The last thing I want is for people to have been sexually abused!

She told me this after barely four interviews. No one had a chance to do any of those probing leading things. I agree there are therapists who do, but I am not one.

She has been to other counselors, therapists and groups besides myself, and probably was aware before seeing me of her feelings.

Sister Hunter, have you ever wondered deep down, if a daughter did make up false accusations of sex abuse toward her father, why she would do such a thing? The motivation is anger. You should be looking at causes of her anger in yourself, and your husband should be looking too. Instead, both of you refused to join in therapy to help her with her pain and anger. You persist in blaming everyone but yourself for your family problems. When parents spend all their time defending themselves and thinking of themselves only, instead of helping resolve the child's pain and anguish, is what splits families apart, not the accusation of sexual abuse.

I have worked with many families where this has occurred and in each case where parents do all they can to aid in the "victim's"

Page 2

pain, depression, and anger, the situation has healed and the family is closer than ever.

You left out the main body of Elder Scott's remarks. "To say forget it (or it didn't happen) does not help." "Serious cases require professional help." Jesus said, "Know the truth and the truth will set you free": Debbie has tried gallantly to discover the truth in her life and as a result enjoys more peace and happiness.

I have no influence over my 52,000 colleagues in the country. Besides I cannot implore them or myself to abandon a philosophy which we never abscribed to nor practiced in the first place. Your false accusations to me and other therapists will never heal the pain in your family. Isn't it odd that people who so easily make false accusations of others reap what they sow?

No family has to endure any unnecessary pain if they are unselfish and come to the aid of a suffering child as we invited you to do by special letter, and you refused.

I pray that you and all people like you will wake up and be willing to look, investigate, and humbly be open to a child's feelings and see <u>why</u> she would feel this way and to help her if she were deluded, rather than rebuke, castigate, cut her off, etc. and then pray for a miracle,that <u>she</u> will come to her senses!

I have taken the liberty of sending your letter as well as a copy of this one to Debbie.

If I can be of any help to you or if you have any questions, please contact me.

Faithfully,

Sterling G. Ellsworth, Ph.D.

SGE/mc

cc: Debbie Marsh

I was disappointed and relieved at the same time. I was hurt that financial matters were the top priority. No matter how we asked or how many times Dr. Ellsworth asked them, they would not come to Oregon and meet with Dr. Ellsworth and Steve and me. I knew things would never be good or even tolerable between us again and I was sad.

Over time, I remembered an event that happened during the rape many years ago that soothed me. As I recall, my father appeared in the middle of the night and climbed onto my body, hurting my body and soul. I remembered wondering how he could do this to me. My father was a bishop in the Grant 9th Ward and he only did what God told him to do, so if he was raping me, I must be very bad. I was a bad, bad person. My father was covering my mouth and nose tightly with his big hand and I could not breathe or cry out for help. I tried moving and scratching his hand away. The words blazed through my mind—he wanted to kill me. I couldn't get any air, and I silently begged him to let me breathe. At that moment, I felt nothing apart from my father violently raping me and not letting me breathe. I knew I was dying.

All of these thoughts raced through my mind as my father was raping me for the first time. I thought I was a very bad girl that God would have told my dad to do these things to me. It made sense to cover my mouth so I couldn't make noise during the rape—which was violent and quick because I left my body so fast—mostly because I slept on the bottom bunk bed, I had no bedroom door, and my room was only twenty feet away from my mother's ears. I thought God wanted me dead and if he did, what a horrible little girl I was in God's eyes and in my father's eyes as well. YOU ARE BAD! My spiritual being took that message to heart and repeated it every day and every time I was in trouble.

Soon, I found myself floating up to the ceiling and looking at my dad's partially naked body covering my body—in the bunk beds my sister Cynthia and I shared, with only my dainty foot protruding. A soft, warm light filled the room. I saw a male angel dressed in white. He held me in his arms and I pressed my cheek against his soft, silky robes. There are no words to describe his brightness and warmth. Pure joy, love, and euphoria are the closest words I can think of to describe what I felt that night. Even though this hideous monster, my father, was violating my body in every way, I felt safe. I was rescued by a heavenly angel, and he held me for quite some time with no words passing between us. To communicate, we used thoughts and I asked him why my father was doing this to me. The angel explained that my father might have gotten to my body, but he did not truly get to my soul.

I want to stay here with you forever, I thought. *I want to feel this joy and love always.*

Come with me and I will show you why you cannot stay, why you must go back.

The angel thought of where he wanted us to go and we were there, at a low stone wall overlooking a green valley, the lushest and greenest shades of color, overflowing with trees of every kind, birds that were all different colors, and luscious fruit and flowers beyond description.

He said, *This is why you must return back to your body.*

I do not remember what he showed me after that, but I know it was something wonderful, perhaps my life's mission, such as raising my children or being influential in different ways. He said I would be safe now, now that it was time to go back, but I clung to him. I couldn't get enough of his energy, his love, and I think I was with him until morning.

The first thing I heard on the morning after my rape was my mother waking me for school. On my older sister's radio, Skeeter Davis sang her new song, "The End of the World."

Why does the sun go on shining, why do these eyes of mine cry, don't they know it's the end of the world 'cause you don't love me anymore.

It was the end of my world, for I was no longer Daddy's little girl. The molestation stopped, so being raped came as a surprise. He treated me differently. After that, he would bring me grown-up gifts like a pearl necklace. The rapes happened two more times—that's somewhat foggy—and then stopped. He even told me I was his lover. That's why I was not Daddy's little girl anymore.

My world as I knew it was over and I lay back down and cried. I couldn't even sit up the morning of the first rape in my bunk bed because my body ached so horribly, let alone go to school. Every part of my body was throbbing the first time it happened and my eyes were almost swollen shut from crying. I ended up staying home from school because Mom was convinced that I had a fever. I remained in bed most of the day. Although there was blood on the sheets, Mom said nothing about it—she just changed them in silence. When I asked Dr. Ellsworth much later why she didn't gasp in horror or ask me about them, he said it was her form of denial.

I didn't remember the angel, the rape, or the suffocation for several decades, but now in 1989, my rage and anger made them feel immediate. I also remember the near-death experience, and it still soothes my anger and rage. I still don't know whether to thank God for sending an angel to love and care for me on that horrible night, or whether to be angry that he made me return to my body and suffer through years of torment, depression, and family dysfunction. I choose to thank Him. I would have been alone and even more frightened were it not for my angel. I might have died!

CHAPTER TWO

Walton W. Hunter (The Younger Years)

My ancestors on my father's side are pretty famous. There are books written about them and news clippings from decades ago written about the Sullivan clan. My great-great-great-grandfather was Tom Sullivan. Tom Sullivan moved from Georgia to Mississippi just to find a place that was beautiful to farm on, a place that was also private so he and relatives could make moonshine—whiskey. He brought his two wives and five children with him to Sullivan's Hollow, Mississippi, and settled that beautiful land.

No, this is not going to be a genealogy history lesson about the Hunter side of the family, but the Sullivans prove that murder, rape, theft, and drinking have long been inbred into this side of the family and that my father could have come by his ways of sin through example set forth by each generation that gave those attributes to their sons and daughters. From news clippings, genealogy records, and Chester Sullivan's book on Sullivan's Hollow and the gunfights, I introduce you to my ancestors.

Once, Wild Bill Sullivan came as close as any Sullivan ever came to being hanged in Sullivan's Hollow. He and his brother Wils (short for Wilson) were neighbors. Their wives visited back and forth, and their children played together. But, as the Sullivans say, the children "fell out," then the mothers, and presently the brothers "fell out" too. This was not what ol' Tom Sullivan settled this country for, but this was what the town came to those days.

They say that one night, during a church social at Old Zion Church, Wild Bill Sullivan and Jack Sullivan stabbed poor Wils to death. Some of the witnesses ran to Wils' home, calling out, "Boys, Wild Bill jest stabbed yuh daddy dead." Wils' eldest boy grabbed a shotgun and shot Wild Bill's mule out from under him as he was getting away, but Wild Bill escaped through the brush.

Eventually, Wild Bill and Jack were arrested and charged with their brother's murder. Wild Bill soon found out it was one thing to shoot a cousin, but quite another to kill your own brother. Feelings mounted against him. Folks who fed him now wanted a rope around his neck. At the trial, nobody could prove, though everybody believed, that Bill and Jack Sullivan stabbed Wils Sullivan. In the end, they were given long prison terms anyway for all the past times they couldn't be caught for bootlegging moonshine whiskey, theft, raping young ladies, and a murder or two that couldn't be proven, but everyone was certain it was them. However, they served only a short time, when they were pardoned by the "Great White Father," Governor Vardaman.

Perhaps I should explain about killing in Sullivan's Hollow. Everyone was against it, and as church-going Baptists, the Sullivans didn't urge it. Yet killing was something a man could do to obtain immediate personal justice for some wrong. Thus, among these hill-bound folk in 1850, killing was not nearly as bad as robbing. No one would kill without good cause, according to this line of thought, and no Sullivan, they said with pride, was ever hanged.

But for the most part, the Sullivans were wonderful people. Chester Sullivan's book states, "The people of Sullivan's Hollow were hospitable and helpful, they were great storytellers and better jokers than Bob Hope. We say this because they are proud of their land, their family, and want to be photographed in a clean shirt."

Why are the Sullivans and Sullivan's Hollow important to this memoir? Because that's the furthest back I can trace my father's ancestors and it's also where the shame began for my father. With raping and robbing, bootlegging and murdering going on at a man's discretion, it's no wonder it was called the "meanest part of America." Some of my Sullivan ancestors left Sullivan's Hollow in 1892 to find a better, more productive life and to be free to live without all the violence and lawlessness that went on in Sullivan's Hollow. They became like gypsies. They moved about every year or two to different states, settling at one point in Enoch, Texas, just long enough for

Verna Hall, now Verna Hunter, to have their second child, my father, Walton W. Hunter, on October 25, 1920.

"I was born ugly!" At least, those were some of the first words in Dad's personal handwritten journal and it was the excuse his parents gave for forcing him to live with his grandparents, the Halls. I think no mother gives up her newborn only because he is "ugly." In surmising the various situations that Grandma Verna must have gone through to give her baby up, I don't believe that the baby was moved away due to his looks. I believe he was a product of rape or an affair that happened to Grandma Verna and that is why Grandpa Walter would not be seen with the baby.

Through talk with my cousin Shannon and my own mother, I was told that Grandma Boopsie—as we in the immediate family called her (I'm not sure why)—was a hard-drinking, fast-talking woman who "delighted at a nice-looking man." I think she had an affair in Lehi, Arizona, and that's why they moved after only six months there. But the baby—my father—must have looked just like the other man because my father was handsome through and through and not anything like his parents. Therefore, I think the baby was "ugly"

because he didn't look like either side of the family. So I imagine a conversation between Verna and Walter Hunter might have gone something like this:

"Verna, there are rumors in town that this baby isn't mine. He doesn't look like me or you. Tell me the truth. Are the rumors true?" said Walter.

Hesitantly and quietly, Verna spoke. "Yes, that's true, but I can explain, Walter."

"I know what you told me before, how some man came into the house when we lived in Lehi and took advantage of you. I just don't know if I believe that happened." His voice dropped momentarily to a whisper. "That, that you were…raped," and then at full volume again, "or if you were having relations with another man at the time. I know something happened because that baby looks nothing like me. Tell me the truth or I will smack it out of you!" Walter screamed.

It was rumored that Grandma and Grandpa Hunter had volatile and sometimes physical fights with each other, so it wouldn't be a surprise that Grandpa was shouting and getting physically violent with Verna.

"Walt, we named the baby after you and put you on the birth certificate and everything."

"Well, as far as I am concerned, he is ugly and I won't be seen with him ever," Walter emphatically stated. "Either he goes or I go! I'm not going to be seen around town with another man's baby, whichever way it happened. Do you understand me, Verna? Do you?"

Walter sounded threatening as he grabbed and squeezed Verna's lips together.

Verna broke free and asked, "Well, can we keep him, but never take him out with us?" She was shaking badly and had a hard time dealing with Walter's demands.

"No, we could never do that. We'll have to give him up for adoption. He's not my son to raise, so find him a home or I'll take him from your arms so quickly you won't know what hit you and I will sell him to a couple who want to buy a baby."

He grabbed his hat and left in the cool night air, not returning until late in the night, having had too much liquor. Verna put him to bed and wrung her hands helplessly.

She was so preoccupied with thoughts of where she could find a home for her newborn baby that she didn't get to sleep until very late that night. The thought of giving up her baby was more than she could bear. But being a woman alone, with a two-year-old child already, Elvan, and now with a newborn too, would have made it extremely difficult for her to find another man or to work for a living in the 1920s; she had few options.

The next couple of days, Verna spoke with relatives far and near who might take the child. She sought someone who lived in the state of Texas where she could at least see the child on occasion. After talking to a few close relatives, and giving them the excuse that the child was ugly and Walter didn't want to be seen with him, it appeared that her parents could be persuaded to take the child. She had to talk convincingly about how strongly Walter felt that he would not be seen with the child due to how ugly the baby was and although Verna loved the child, she didn't want to lose Walter.

Grandma and Grandpa Hall would soon take the child in and give him some of the love and care necessary for a family. But, as my dad writes in his journals, they were a "stern, non-demonstrative couple," so it is questionable how much affection they were able to give him. They never thought the baby was ugly, but they rarely praised him or were loving with him. They lived way out on a farm and even Grandma Hall didn't go into town often. "Thus, she was able to maintain the pretense that her daughter was unable to care for the child due to health reasons" (Dad's journals).

My father writes in his handwritten personal journal that he was known as the ugliest baby ever born and until he was five years of age, his parents would not be seen with him. When he was five, the parents, Verna and Walter, were convinced by the grandparents, the Halls, that the child needed an education. Because there was no school near the grandparents' farm, he went to live with his parents for the first time. But he was shipped back to the Halls every holiday and every summer until his early teens, when he was required to work to help support his family of origin.

When our father was five, he moved to his parents' house to start school. His first job was at the corner grocery store where he worked for mere pennies. He made small deliveries of groceries around the neighborhood, swept in front of the store, and put items on the shelves where they belonged. But working at the store with all its goodies was a big temptation. He found a way into the store after hours through the cellar. He broke in and ate all the ice cream, candy, and soda pop he could hold. The second time he did it, he got deathly ill and threw up all night. He never did it again and he wrote in his journals, "I knew it was wrong, but I didn't care. This experience is still vivid in my mind."

Finding his journals two years ago has seriously helped Rebecca and me get a handle on all of the facts of this particular part of his life and with our whole book, really. His journals let us see more clearly the kind of man he was, if any or parts of it are true.

Five was also an important year because it was when he was given his first birthday party with a couple of friends, where his mom served hot chocolate and cookies. His parents "had never even acknowledged my birthday before five. Given that there were three birthdays in October in our family, it was very special to finally have a birthday, let alone a party," our father wrote.

When Dad was also five, he and Elvan, Dad's older brother, were playing at the auto wrecking lot where their father worked as a mechanic. Dad was standing by the side of a car that was precariously balanced when Elvan stood up on the car and tried to push it over onto Dad.

"I pleaded with Elvan to get off of the car, but he wouldn't. Just as I was about to dart away from the car, the accident happened," Dad wrote in his journal.

Elvan yelled back at Dad, "No, Walt, I am going to push this car over onto you. I'll finally beat you and you will be sore and bloody." Elvan continued to rock the unstable car until he was successful and the car landed on Dad, split his lip open, and sprained his arm. A miracle that he wasn't hurt more.

"See, I did win. I'm the conqueror!" Elvan yelled from atop the car. But once he saw Dad's split lip and sprained arm, he knew he went too far.

"Elvan," my father moaned, "go get Dad, my arm hurts really bad!"

Elvan said, "Okay, but I'm telling Dad that you pushed the car over."

"Fine," my father snapped back at him, "just go get Dad!"

Dad also wrote, "It seemed like Elvan was always trying to do things to me." He didn't know why. There are six incidents in Dad's notebook where Elvan tried to deliberately hurt our father.

Many times, Dad's journal gives accounts of events which differ from the way our parents described them to us as children. For instance, our father told us about the time his brother Elvan tossed a match into a gas tank and "…it caused an explosion while I was nearby. There was an explosion, but for some blessed reason, Elvan was not injured, but I was." We understood from both our parents that when Dad was six and his hair was burned off and his head was somewhat burned that he really needed medical attention of some kind. Elvan put a cowboy hat on him and Dad refused to take the hat off until his hair grew back. His parents thought it was so cute that this cowboy hat of Elvan's meant so much to him that he wore it day and night. This is one of the stories, often told at home, which was missing from the journal.

It was known by our mother that Dad was beaten severely by his father, Walter Hunter. He even was beaten when it was Elvan's ideas or doings—when they turned out bad and their father heard about it, Dad would get the beating. With all the abuse in his environment and a propensity of genes gearing toward mental illness, it's a wonder he wasn't a juvenile delinquent by six or seven.

This reminds me of the story Dad told just once to my siblings and me that he took no pride in, but he did smirk about it when he told us. He was about seven when he did this. He went down to the little corner grocery store that he worked at for a couple of years and went in the back and stole the bottles that came through the store at a penny a pop and took them to a different store and turned them in for money. The grocery clerk that he turned them in to said, "Boy, your dad drinks a lot of beer and pop." Well, it had to be timed very carefully because the grocer put the bottles in the back of the store outside only one hour before the recycle truck came to pick up the daily bottles turned in to the grocery store. So Dad took some of the bottles from the back of the store and he and Elvan proceeded to get a few pennies every week from a different store. Not all the details were given, just the highlights, and the smirk came in when he told how he got away with it and "never got caught." That is a direct quote from his mouth and in his journal.

Dad had to take his chances at taking half the bottles that came in every day before the bottle guy showed up around 4:45 p.m., but as close to that time as possible because he knew that the grocery clerk put them out at 4:00 p.m. Dad had to be at the other store by 5:00 because he was expected home by 5:30 to eat dinner with his family. He was saving a small fortune when Elvan, who got half of the money, squealed on Dad and he had to give all his money to his father, received a beating, had to go to both grocery owners and confess his crimes to them and work for free until they were even. He was fired as soon as his debt was paid and told never to come around the store ever again or the grocer would call the police and he would file charges. This story was not put in his journal, probably along with other negative stories that he wasn't too proud of.

According to Dad's journal, Dad was ten years old when he and his siblings—Elvan, twelve, and Wylene, his little sister who was eight—were baptized into the LDS church. However, he was not active in the Mormon faith until his teenage years, when Bishop Mosley came to visit and asked our father to go on a church mission. They'd asked Elvan six months earlier and our dad and Elvan went to the same mission. Our father received his call from church headquarters in November 1940 to the Southern States Mission, and entered the mission home on January 6, 1941. He served on this mission for a little over two years, from age eighteen to twenty, and, he writes in his journal, he had many miracles witnessed by him and others.

I don't have the information or knowledge to know exactly when my father's behavior became what later my many therapists and I would call sociopathic—whether it was during these young adult years or earlier, or not until he crossed the line and molested a child for the first time. I can imagine that being told often that he was ugly and that's why he lived with Grandma and Grandpa Hall and not seeming to be accepted by his parents until his teenage years and all the beatings he received could push someone over the edge mentally. Especially if he had a genetic makeup which could allow even normal environments alone to push his buttons and make him become sociopathic all on its own.

According to our father's journals, his testimony of the church and dedication to the Lord's work came about one month into his mission. He and his preaching companion, now entitled to be called "Elders," were told to visit a man who needed a blessing of health or, more likely, to be eased into the dying process as inspired by the Lord working through the two missionaries. Our father had never given such a blessing and he was anxious and nervous about what was going to occur. From Dad's recordings, I can see how it must have unfolded that night.

"Elder Smith, are you sure we are on the right road?" Dad said as they drove along the dark, unpaved country road.

"Yes, I'm pretty sure," said Elder Smith, Dad's mission companion. "All I can see is by the light of the full moon. There is a small road coming up here on the left that we turn on. President Nelson said we might not see the road sign, but there's one of those orange road cones on the street we have to turn on. There is the turn, I see the cone," Elder Smith said eagerly.

As they made the turn, the street narrowed into a dark, twisted path made for one car only. The drive was now fraught with dangerous tree branches and mud potholes and was barely passable.

"How much further is it?" Dad asked.

"Not much further. In fact, look at all these cars parked here," Elder Smith replied. "It's like a branch church meeting."

They wandered through the cars until they reached the doorway of the home. They knocked and were greeted by Aunt Mabel, who was closest to the door.

"Who might you two be?" said the elderly woman.

Elder Smith spoke up first. "Well, ma'am, we're the Mormon missionaries that the ill man's nephew, Don, sent for, ma'am. We're here to give the sick man a Mormon blessing. What is his name?"

"Rufus," said Mabel.

"Yes. We're here to give Rufus a blessing."

"Well, get to it. I'll get everyone to quiet down. But I don't think he's going to need anything except a coffin and a hole in the dirt for his coffin 'n' him. See, this is a wake and with a wake, you have everyone come say goodbye and take turns digging the hole. What are you going to bless him with?" Mabel said.

"With whatever the Lord wants us to bless him with," Dad said.

"All of you quiet down," said Mabel, "and tell whoever is digging to stop and come inside. These fine young men are here to give Rufus a Mormon blessing. Donny sent for them, didn't you, Donny?" said Mabel.

"Yes, I did and now they be here. Thanks fer comin'," Donny hollered out.

"Elder Hunter, I think it would do you good to give the blessing this time," Elder Smith instructed Dad and gave him a slap on the back for confidence.

Dad was so nervous, his hands were trembling. Eighteen years old and blessing a dying man. So Dad first murmured a quick prayer for God to help him in this current situation and then he closed his eyes, bowed his head, and blessed Rufus that he would be healed, that it was not his time to go, and that he would regain his strength from this terrible disease that had overtaken him.

Dad didn't know the best things to say, but he felt inspired to say, "You're going to get better," to the dying man. He would have been standing there afterward and might have looked like a darn fool, but the man immediately raised his head, requested some water, and then asked why all the neighbors were over. Elder Smith was stunned, Mabel was stunned, the guests were all stunned, and my dad was the most stunned of all. A wonderful experience if it was true! Was it true from a sociopath or maybe he was just narcissistic at this point? We have to remember that he was writing about this and the other experiences in his fifties.

The elders were offered some food. Someone brought out Donny's fiddle and everyone celebrated the good news that Rufus was not going to die, at least not that night. This gave the two elders a golden opportunity to discuss religion with a captive, if not intoxicated, audience of people there for the wake. It was almost morning before they made their way home. Our father wrote, "This is the day I gained my testimony of the Church and I decided to dedicate my life to serving God and his son, Jesus Christ."

This was what my dad's journal read. Was it sociopathy or religion or some combination? I don't know. Maybe Dad was inspired, as he says, mainly from the successful blessing for Rufus.

There were other stories of miraculous events on his first mission. Some were not written in his journals, but delivered in many of his talks at church and discussions around our home. One of the miracles happened to him while he and his mission companion were preaching the gospel to a throng of townspeople, according to his talks in church and in his journals. A man looking for his wife shouldered a shotgun and pointed it at our father's face, yelling for his wife to step out of the crowd and to return home immediately. The wife slowly stepped forward, but the shotgun did not waver. The man told the crowd he should shoot my father because he never "took a likin' to these missionaries going from town to town, preachin' their foolish ideas to men and women who don't need all those fancy notions put into their heads in the first place." Our father's response was to stand his ground and continue preaching, almost daring this man to shoot him. The man stood there for the longest time with his finger on the trigger, and our father continued to bear his testimony to his faithfulness of the gospel and its truth and the glory that would come to anyone who joined the Lord's true church.

The man listened, motionless, until Dad was through talking. Then Dad asked the man, "Well, aren't you going to shoot me?"

The man said, "No, not this time." He motioned to his wife to get into his wagon, and they drove off. A few months later, Dad heard this man and his wife joined the church. Our father took a lot of spiritual pride in that event.

* * *

The U.S. entered World War II and the attack at Pearl Harbor took place while our father was on his first mission. There was a lot of anger toward the elders from that point on as the Southerners felt "these boys should be fightin' instead of out preachin'." Our father had fifteen months left for his mission and tried his best to help the people overcome their feelings about the war and missionaries. But it was hard when their sons were dying in the war to rationalize why missionaries could stay out of the war. Dad's strong testimony and charm helped mend this rift and he continued to baptize individuals and whole families in his areas. At the end of his mission, he baptized the same number of people that his brother, Elvan, baptized in the

Southern States Mission, which were the two top numbers of people baptized ever for that mission area.

According to his journals, our father's first mission was full of miracles, exceptional experiences, and outstanding leadership opportunities. He excelled in every way possible and made a name for himself. Our father even requested that his mission be extended two months so he would have the same or a higher number of baptisms as his brother. Of course, that was not the reason he gave the authorities for lengthening his stay on this mission. He often spoke of the miracles, his experiences, and his outstanding role when giving talks and sermons or teaching classes in the church.

Let me remind you that sociopaths always have the most interesting lives. They have to be the best in order to get what they want. Dad wanted to win the game—the missionary game—and could not have a less tremendous experience nor baptize fewer people than his brother. Dad wanted the glory and the attention for his charm and outstanding performance as a Mormon missionary. As Dr. Ellsworth would say years later to me as I was trying to heal, "It was the right quest, but for the wrong reasons."

While Dad was on his mission, many of his best friends died in the war and he had no time to grieve or even think very much about their deaths. However, sociopaths do not truly grieve. They pretend to grieve with crocodile tears and fake hugs. All of my talk about Dad being a sociopath is backed up by many therapists, including Dr.

Ellsworth, journal articles listed in the back of this book, and Dr. Martha Stout's book, The Sociopath Next Door.

Our father went home and within six weeks, he and Elvan were inducted into the army. They went to boot camp together and after many training classes and exams, our father once again excelled in every course and exam and he chose to be a Radar and Navigator Instructor in Chandler, Arizona. This was a commissioned officer's position and one of high honor and esteem.

Dad writes about two more "miracles" that he experienced while in the military. These were only a few of the many he wrote about. In the first one, his name was somehow left off a roster of men shipping out for the next training in Las Vegas, Nevada. This group "excelled in every way possible" and Dad was anxious to stay with them. However, he needed a furlough to marry our mother. There would be no more furloughs before leaving for the

war, so he was disappointed that he might never get the chance to marry our mother until after the war, if she would wait. He would probably lose her and he was worried. When my father missed his flight to Las Vegas, he asked his commanding officer for a two-week furlough. This was granted and he took the missed flight as "a sign from God that I should marry June. It meant she was the girl for me." He called our mother and they met in Salt Lake City to be married in the Mormon temple.

Just a note about how he met my mother. He was commissioned to an air force base near Los Angeles, California, when my mother moved from her little hometown of Manassa, Colorado, to her married sister's house in Los Angeles to finish high school and go on to take a secretarial course. There was a large Mormon dance called the Gold & Green Ball in Los Angeles in 1944 and he asked her to dance with him. Three months later, during his furlough, they were married in the Salt Lake City Mormon Temple.

The next "miraculous" event happened when he was called out of line to get one more shot while boarding his plane to ship out to his next assignment, which led to his missing that flight also. He was so worried that his commanding officer would be furious that he again missed a flight. But an hour later, the airplane he was supposed to be on blew up in flight, killing all on board. His commanding officer was not angry at him for stepping out of line. In Dad's view, this episode was further evidence that he was special and more worthy of survival than others.

Remember that much of what is written in my father's journals is presented as miraculous. He comments several times on "how special my life is, more than anyone I know." But was this really divine intervention? Was his life spared over and over again? Did he perform miracle after miracle on his missions? We will never know, but it is impossible to ignore the narcissism in his words and his journal reads exactly like what a total sociopath would write.

In 1946, our mother went home to Manassa, Colorado, to have her first baby and be near her family while Dad was in the air force. Dad, on furlough, joined her in Manassa a few weeks later when she felt the baby's birth was close. Wayne W. Hunter, known to the family as Butch from the time he was little, was born on October 20, 1946.

In this period, our father gives two accounts of car accidents he escaped without a scratch, even though the drivers were seriously injured or killed. He boasted that God spared him for more important work. To me, this seems very narcissistic.

Our father was processed out of the air force in Sacramento, California, soon after the war ended and the Japanese surrendered. He met Mother and Butch in Salt Lake City and his civilian life began. He first worked at his father's used car sales lot; after six months, he enrolled at the University of Utah and began selling life insurance part time. The life insurance company soon offered him a top position and a big raise if he would quit school and come to work for them full time. Our father states in his journals that he loved selling and his charm instantly opened doors for him.

His little family was starting to make progress regarding his career and financial well-being when Elder Spencer W. Kimball asked our father to go on another mission in the southern states for eighteen months. He was then made first counselor to mission president Joseph Fielding Smith, who would eventually become Prophet of the Mormon Church. The mission was to assist some of the farmers in the south as well as to develop his leadership roles.

Our mother told us a very different version of these events. She said that since the Korean War was raging, the leadership at Mormon Headquarters could not get the young boys and men before they either enlisted or were drafted into the war. Therefore, younger married men and older widowed men were being called into mission fields to keep the baptismal and convert numbers up and to spread the gospel. Dad claims in his journal, "Since I excelled so much on my first mission to the southern states, I was the obvious choice to go as First Counselor to the President of the Mission." According to our mother, it was more a product of circumstances. We see his journal entry as more evidence that our father was narcissistic to the extreme.

Going on a second mission meant leaving his career, his wife, and his child behind and, at the same time, somehow financially supporting them. My father asked for thirty days to prepare for this transition, but he was given only four days. We believe our grandparents supported my mother and Butch financially during the mission. They returned to live in Manassa again while, according to my dad, he performed many more miracles. He was given a Mormon blessing that he would be a noble and honorable elder and he would "have power over the elements of the earth."

My father began his second mission in Cairo, Georgia, which was afflicted with a severe drought. It was there that he met his seventy-year-old mission companion, Elder Choules, "whom I learned to love and respect…"

Our father and Elder Choules stayed with a convert family, the Butlers. The drought was so bad that farmers' crops were dying and they could do nothing as they watched their livelihood deteriorate along with the crops. The farmers were desperate. Our father and his companion decided to hold a fast; they would abstain from partaking in food or drink until their prayers were answered and it rained. They persuaded the Butlers to fast as well. As they returned to the Butler farm on the third day of their fast, it began to sprinkle. By the time they reached the Butlers' home, it rained fairly well and the ground had turned to mud by the time they walked into the home through the back door. The Butlers prepared a feast for their family and the missionaries. After a grateful prayer, they concluded their fast and ate heartily. After the missionaries talked with the Butlers for a while and my dad and Elder Choules took a short rest, the rain slowed down.

The missionaries decided to travel to a few other farms, hoping to be greeted by happy faces and prayers of gratitude from the other farmers. But at each farm, they discovered no rain fell at all. The disappointment in the farmers' eyes was devastating. They pleaded, prayed, and fasted some more, but could not recreate the miracle. Obviously, my father did not have control of all the elements as he states he was promised! Was his story of the rain even true? To this day, I am unsure whether my father's story about his rain miracle was exaggerated or simply untrue.

Our father tells of other "miracles" he performed on his second mission. His common daily or weekly duties were conducting and arranging meetings, and speaking at meetings and conferences. He worked alongside future prophets of the church and other important leaders and was really making a name for himself, but something was about to change him. It seemed that he was close to the Lord and wanted to dedicate his life to church work. But suddenly, he went very much astray while still doing the Lord's work. He was about to sell his soul to the devil and forever change his destiny.

CHAPTER THREE

The Sociopathic Years

When the Reverend Jim Jones died, along with his 900-plus followers in 1978, I held my firstborn child in my arms and thanked God that I had not been brainwashed into that religion. Jim Jones, from all I read and heard about him, reminded me so much of my father. I spoke to my then husband, Steve, and we again remarked on the physical and personality similarities between the two, except my father had not talked any parishioners into suicide or murdered anyone.

NEW BISHOPRICS

GRANT NINTH, GRANT STAKE

New bishop is Walton W. Hunter, center. His counselors are Clifford S. White, left, and Ralf L. Pollei, right.

This story reminded me so much of my father and the first time he was bishop and how deeply dedicated he was to his congregation who attended the ward he was overseeing. Some of the congregation might have been convinced to drink the poison if Dad told them that God directed them to drink it. When it came time to write this chapter, and to describe my father, I chose to use Jim Jones to give the reader a picture of what he looked like and how he led his people. From this scenario of The Peoples Temple and my research efforts, I came to understand how the final days were for the Jonestown people. The information and Jim and my father's pictures give the readers an idea of the charismatic, handsome, and smooth-talking persons Jim and my father were with their great confidence and leadership qualities.

Mr. Jones and our father had a lot in common. Both were liars, sexual predators, thieves, and con men, and Jones was a murderer. Reverend Jones and Dad were also highly charismatic and very confident and convincing with their congregations who loved and followed them, no matter what.

But church credentials are not sufficient reason to trust someone. In fact, it's especially necessary to check out a religious individual's background in great detail before trusting him, just as you would a stranger with no religious affiliations. That sounds like a very jaded way of thinking, but when your father is Walton W. Hunter and he has committed almost as many sins as Jim Jones has, you must be careful where you leap to next. Trust is what both Jim and Dad thought they had, but no one trusted them in the end.

Our father was an excellent bishop and had many members of the ward convinced that the sun rose and set at his command. He made the right moves for the wrong reasons. His moves were being very personable and charismatic with each and every member of the ward, leading them in a very confident and strong way while using God as his back-up man, saying things like, "God has given me powers that no ordinary man has ever been given," or "God wants you to follow me even when it becomes difficult." The wrong reasons were both men were insatiable for power and control. They were driven by greed and evil thinking. I do think my dad started off with the right moves for the right reasons, if only for a brief time. He had love—a facsimile of love—for people, he wanted his ward to be close, and he wanted to be a worthy servant in the Lord's eyes and for his congregation.

Somewhere in his early life, that changed and he began to molest and rape his daughters. Therefore, very soon after becoming a bishop, he changed and became evil. He didn't care about the consequences; the only thing he wanted was power and control through sexual means. Getting back to the similarities between my dad and Jim Jones, both congregations were willing to follow their leaders to the ends of the earth to show their loyalty to them. The followers in Dad's church ward were as loyal as the Peoples Temple followers, although my father's group would not have given their lives unless church headquarters said to. But they would have done just about anything else to give their loyalty to my father and the church.

Our father gained his power first from his missionary years, then from his military time, and finally as a bishop and a community and business leader. When my dad was released as bishop after ten years of service, the people of his ward would not go to their new bishop, but continued to seek out our father instead.

For example, Brother White came to Dad to relay a message from a group of members of Dad's former congregation. Brother White simply came to Dad regarding a problem they were having with the new bishop, Bishop Coleman. It seemed that the ward members didn't like the new callings they were being given by the new bishop. The callings just didn't match with what they would ever dream of having, whereas Dad had a gift for matching callings (a church volunteer job, e.g., teaching Sunday School) with the right people. I think they just didn't use their faith and cooperation to do the new callings with a smile on their faces.

Dad did try to intervene occasionally with "new" bishops, but it usually blew up in his face, not the members', as it should have. It didn't turn out the way the members hoped it would with their callings and to make a long story short, Bishop Coleman was released from being bishop within six months. The church members went through three bishops over a comparatively short time, but still, some former members of the ward continued to seek out our father. Even after we moved farther away, they still made the drive to come and be counseled. Finally, the church had to realign the ward boundaries, which placed the original members into three different wards. Often, as told by my mother, one would hear the sisters and brothers say, "Walt missed his calling in life, he should have been a paid minister, for he speaks so eloquently and motivates the congregation to obey the word of God so well."

During the time he was bishop, our father's heart grew more selfish and more narcissistic due to his religious successes and his good fortunes as a businessman who owned two car lots in Salt Lake City. Mother told me later in my life that she hated sex. I wonder if Dad's sexual urges had to be satisfied somewhere else. Most men would pick another woman to have an affair, but Dad chose his children, whom he could terrify into silence. Mother got so ill for all nine months of each pregnancy, vomiting even into the delivery room, and yet, she was told to multiply and replenish the world. In other words, have lots of babies, no matter what. Maybe she would only have sex to have a baby. As you will see in Chapter Four, she knew Rebecca was being molested and she didn't care, so maybe she was just glad he had someplace else he could go, rather than having her do "the dirty deed," as she once put it. I wonder if Dad was sexually abused as a child and that was his first example of sex, so he had it in his being to carry out that type of sex and that's what felt normal and familiar to him, or maybe both reasons existed.

In Elizabeth Smart's book, *My Story*, she describes the man who kidnapped and raped her for months. "He is selfish and angry. But he is also very smart, far more intelligent than most want to give him credit for. That is important to remember. This is not a foolish man. Some say that he is brilliant. Indeed this proved to be part of his power, the ability to appear harmless and unassuming, even while he is plotting and demeaning and raging inside." This describes a person who was comparable to our father in many ways. Elizabeth's captor thought he could do no wrong and so did our dad! But Rebecca and I knew very well that our father could do wrong. Both Elizabeth's captor and my father never thought they would be caught. In fact, below is part of Dad's personal handwritten journal entry where he is writing a talk for church and he mentions that one should "never get caught" In fact, he almost didn't get caught until 1989 when I came pouring out with the truth of my rapes and molestations. Here is a sample of his journal where he worries about the truth coming out.

> Tempt you to believe what you do in secret, won't ever get out, Satan will see to it that it does. There are lies preceding any impure act. One, that it is the natural thing to do, second that its not dangerous & third that no one will ever know

After I learned what a sociopath was with Dr. Ellsworth and other therapists I had along the way, I began to do my own reading and research to learn more. I was desperate to try to understand what happened to us, and to make sense of a man with such contradictory impulses, or so it seemed at the time. According to the Harvard psychologist Martha Stout, PhD, author of *The Sociopath Next Door*, about four out of every 100 individuals are sociopaths. Most frequently, sociopaths are diagnosed with extreme narcissism and antisocial behaviors. They often have shady business dealings or conflicts with authority figures. "Sociopaths can cry crocodile tears at will, but they won't be real," Stout writes. I learned that sociopaths cannot love and they cannot bond to people, but they do know when to smile, when to laugh, and when to cry. They act their parts so well that their demeanor very much appears to be real. After reading articles from the Internet and Dr. Stout's book, I feel that there is no special face from which one can recognize a sociopath. They do not look like Hitler, Saddam Hussein, or Ted Bundy; they look like your neighbor next door or like you. Of course, there are also female sociopaths, and they do not look like the Wicked Witch of the West, but like anyone in your neighborhood.

When I read that successful sociopaths play their parts well, like an actor in an Oscar-winning performance, I could see my father up at the pulpit. They can play these roles well—especially if they are successful in their relationships and their careers. A sociopath's marriage, family, job, and religion are his camouflage. Unless he slips up in playing his role—extremes of bad behavior such as molesting one's daughters comes to mind—he will never be caught. Like our father, other sociopaths look for ways to fill their emptiness, whether through sex, power, success, or money. They use fear or other manipulations to keep others quiet about their flaws.

My father needed all four of the above elements to cope with life as he was very empty. He did not have a warm, loving home environment as a newborn, filled with the cooing and cuddling that usually comes from a mother and a father. His dad, Walter, detested him and he was called ugly until his teen years and he was beaten severely by his father. Dad never says anything good in his entire personal journal about his grandfather that took him in, but made special mention of his "loving, kind" Grandma Hall. There were such deficits in his being that he used sex and drugs, lots of prescription drugs for anxiety and what my father called "nervousness." He needed success, both within the church and as a forthright businessman, and he needed lots of sexual attention as well as public notoriety. His goal was to do whatever he wished to do with whomever he wanted to do it with, but to "never get caught." This was evident throughout his journals.

So can you truly love your daughters and sexually abuse them? Can you be a servant of God and commit evil acts? So how can you be evil and be a good bishop? He was smooth. Again, like Jim Jones, he was a born leader with smooth charisma and great speaking abilities. Dad would be asked to speak in every Mormon church ward and at every Chamber of Commerce meeting and at other businesses to motivate staff all over the Salt Lake Valley and outlying areas for years.

I must take you back to 1961, when Dad served longer than most bishops serve in the Mormon faith as bishop. A general length of time for a bishop back in 1961 varied more than it does now. Now it is generally five to seven years. Dad was in for ten years the first time he was bishop and seven the second time. Our father could not handle losing the position of bishop, mostly because he would be losing his powers and influence over this large group of individuals. He would also be losing the rank of bishop and he would be just a ward member with a more insignificant position. The ward members made him a beautiful quilt with every individual's name on it and were to present it to my father and mother the night of the farewell dinner and presentation. So many people came that night that the tables went clear out to the lobbies or foyers. Everyone was looking for our father, but he was nowhere in sight. Mother was wringing her hands, not knowing what to do if he didn't show up.

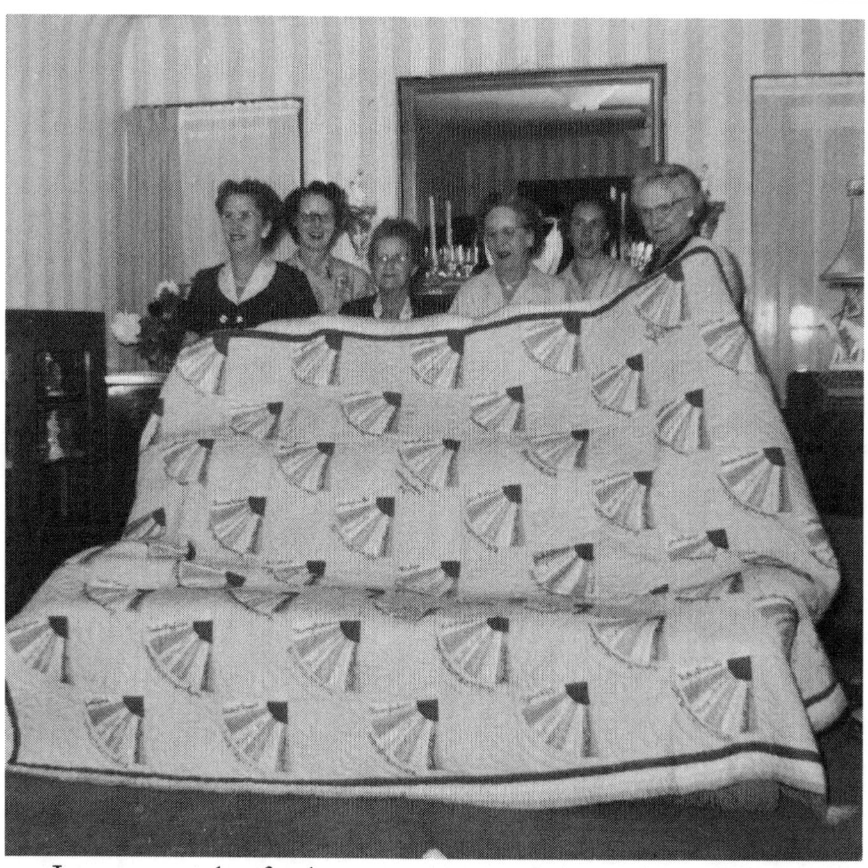

It came to the final presentations of the quilt and some golf clubs—he never played golf—and our whole family was on stage except for Dad. We were lined up like the Von Trapp singers, from my mother to the smallest little one. Mom was behind the curtain, waiting for Dad to join her. Then to the left, we were to come out after a presentation speech was made. First was Wayne (known in our family as Butch), age fifteen, next was Rebecca, age eleven, me, age seven, and Cynthia, age four. Mother was going to make up an excuse that business kept him at the car lot late.

Just then, as the curtain went up, our father came into the alcove and up on stage. This was a momentous moment in time for my family. Something was wrong with Dad and I knew what it was, even at seven years old. He wasn't his normal reserved self; he was louder than usual and he smelled bad and he acted just a little bit different to a child's eye. He was drunk. You could smell it on him, but he still managed to accept the quilt and golf clubs with grace and dignity. We left in a hurry and went home and there was a loud uproar that night between Mom and Dad.

What would Dad do with all his free time now? Rebecca and I are not sure when he started drinking and chasing women, but our father had an employee, Chuck (Charles Van Dam), who obtained a house with money our father gave to him, on Lake Vine Drive in the hills of Salt Lake City. The family moved during the summer of 1964 to a different house also in the hills of Salt Lake City, not far from Lake Vine Drive. The house on Lake Vine Drive was to be Dad's party pad, although Chuck lived there the majority of the time.

Rebecca and I are in possession of a videotape made called *The Godmakers*, by Jeremiah Films, which is an anti-Mormon organization. Several different people who appear to have no vested interest in the film testified to the fact that "the Hunters owned this party pad and every so often Louis," who was one of Dad's mechanics, "would go to South Second Street to pick up prostitutes of every race and gender and Louis would drive them to the Lake Vine Drive house, where Walt and others would drink, smoke, and have sex with the prostitutes or each other."

After Dad was released from being bishop, there were plenty of nights that he didn't come home and we wondered where he was. We were used to him being gone to church meetings when we went to bed, but now, we just did not know where he spent his evening hours. He stopped molesting both Rebecca and me, so we were just glad he was gone.

All of Dad's life, he lived a double life until his retirement, when it was just him and our mother living together. The reason for Jeremiah Films to do *The Godmakers*, a film largely about my father and the Lake Vine house, was to accuse a high-ranking church official of partaking in the wickedness of these parties on many occasions. Jeremiah Films was not interested in our dad; to them, he was just a person who arranged the parties. But we do not believe that any high Mormon Church official was involved. Since my father associated with Chuck Van Dam, who has since died, there is no reason to believe that the church official was involved simply because he was a good friend to my father.

—1964—

I remember one Christmas during this period where my dad came home late on Christmas Eve and gave our mother a silver mink coat. Incredibly, that same evening, he told her he was spending Christmas with his mistress and her children. There was a loud fight, which Rebecca and I heard from our rooms in gruesome detail, and Dad soon slammed the door and left. Mother went out after him, throwing the mink coat out in the snow. Then I heard Rebecca and Mother setting out our toys for Christmas, the toys from Santa. I thought how awful that must be for Rebecca. She was used as Mother's confidante, and Mother told Rebecca how awful Dad was to her and the reasons why she put up with his behavior—most of them co-dependent reasons. This must have been hard on Rebecca. I remember this event as a small eleven-year-old, but although she experienced the whole sad business, Rebecca has no memory of it at all.

An important event happened while living up on Idlewild Circle. Mom found out there was another woman and she went to Bishop Ekins and Dad was almost excommunicated. In 1964, just the tip of the iceberg came out. Bishop Ekins was our new bishop because we lived in a completely different ward as we had moved from Jepson Avenue to Idlewild Circle up on Mt. Olympus in Salt Lake City, where you could see the entire Salt Lake Valley. Being excommunicated might have helped Dad more than the slap on the hand he received at this time. Bishop Ekins allowed Dad to be bad. I'm just not sure if Mom knew how sinful Dad was at the time, nor how much of what she did know she told Bishop Ekins. But again, the truth of how naughty he had been, or was being, came out in little ways in 1964.

In the film *The Godmakers*, Chuck Van Dam also accused our father of some money laundering. Checks for $75,000 or more were cashed. I also remember Mother and Father bemoaning the fact that all of Dad's cars on both car lots were stolen overnight. By whom, I'm not sure, but they mentioned Chuck Van Dam's name as a possible thief. My parents were extremely upset. Shortly after this, we had to move from our large house up on Idlewild Circle by Mt. Olympus to a small condominium in Granger that we rented for about six months. This move was just out of Salt Lake City, completely across town with no hope of seeing our friends from the Mt. Olympus area forty miles away with both parents working at the time. I think we were in hiding because a few months after we moved into the condominium, we loaded up our car with our clothes and a few personal items and left in the middle of the night to move to California, leaving behind important large or bulky personal items such as our scrapbooks, knickknacks, furniture, etc. We took only what would fit inside two automobiles. Our parents didn't tell us why, just that we had to move.

We then lived near our uncle, Millard Brady, in Saratoga, California. Our father's attention was not on Rebecca and me as we were all in survival mode and Dad was too busy hiding from the authorities to bother us. Dad had financed all the cars on the car lots in Salt Lake City with a bank loan. With the cars now gone, he owed a lot of money to the bank and couldn't repay them. When we visited our brother, Wayne, for his wedding in Salt Lake City in 1970, Mom and Dad had to hide out in a dumpy out of the way little motel. During the reception, our father was served one or two summonses, one for the bank's lawsuit for the missing cars and the other, I'm not sure what it was for. It could have been from a different bank.

We went from the height of riches to living in a humble duplex apartment in San Jose, California. Dad was able to get a job as sales manager for used cars, which he found to be unchallenging and he hated working for someone else. Nevertheless, my parents managed to buy a nice house a year later and they installed a swimming pool the year after that. Rebecca and I have many fond memories of pool parties with family and friends.

When I was twelve years old, Mom started working at Lockheed Aerospace as a secretary and all the children were in school. Rebecca graduated from high school in 1968 and started working at I. Magnin, a large upscale department store in San Francisco. Dad eventually opened his own business with a car lot in Newark, California, where he made a good living. He started to plan for retirement and an estate, which would mean a large inheritance for the four children. He was able to buy all his children cars when we turned sixteen.

I remember my first car, a lime-green Chevy Malibu, which all of my friends called “The Green Tomato.” It was about a week before Christmas and Dad drove this car home from the car lot. I admired it and said how cool it was. Well, the neighbor across the street backed into it, smashing in the left side of the car two days before Christmas, so it went to the auto repair shop. On Christmas morning, I opened a little wrapped present from Dad to me. Dad never gave us wrapped gifts. I opened the present excitedly and it was a miniature bright lime-green Malibu toy car and he told me the car that was in the shop was mine when it was finished getting repaired. I was so pleased and surprised that I remember it as one of a very few good moments with my father.

Now that we were teenagers, Dad found other ways to subtly sexually abuse Rebecca and me, but I never saw him do it to my younger sister, Cynthia, who was thirteen years old. He would grab Rebecca and me in a certain way so that he could easily reach our bottoms with one of his arms going around our arms and shoulders and the other hand squeezing our butts and spanking our bottoms until it hurt. We complained and Mom said to him, "Leave the girl (or girls) alone!" or "Walt, stop doing that!" Mom's admonitions would only cause him to do it longer, which drove us to tears, though we tried not to let him know just how upset he made us. Sometimes he even did this in front of our friends or our parents' friends. We struggled mightily, but his grip around us was too tight and we couldn't break free. He thought of it as teasing, but it wasn't teasing. He meant to hurt us. Even though we were teenagers, we still couldn't just yell at him afterward and tell him not to do that anymore. We didn't feel we had that right to tell him in no uncertain terms that we hated it. It was humiliating and painful, both emotionally and physically.

Meanwhile, in the South San Jose 10th Ward of the Mormon Church, Dad held numerous positions, such as Sunday School teacher for the adult class. He was then called for the third time to the High Council, which is a speaking position for former bishops and other leaders. He was also stake Sunday School director, which oversees all of the various wards' Sunday Schools in the stake boundaries (see Appendix A for church definitions).

For all of these callings, he seemed to know ahead of time that he was going to be called and when Mom asked how he knew, he replied, "I just knew." It was the same when the Church authorities called him to be the next bishop of South San Jose 10th Ward in 1970. He also told our mother he would be called to this position and when our mother asked, "How do you know that?" he said again, "I just know." We suspect he had a contact high up in the church and that this was not simply "divine inspiration." I don't believe he could have been so inspired to know each and every calling he was going to have because God told him ahead of time. His personal journal said he was inspired. Was this narcissism or had it been just a hunch? I think he was just lucky or narcissistic about all of these callings. I refuse to believe that this sociopathic pedophile was so inspired by God that he knew of his callings before he was called to them.

Our father also wrote in his personal journals about five more times when Church officials pleaded with him to take high-ranking church positions. He writes that he turned them down for one reason or another, mainly financial. Dad's journals make it seem that he was the most wanted man of the church! There were callings to foreign mission areas for the whole family to Australia, Korea, and to one of the Netherlands missions, he states in his journals. He says he was offered to be stake president if he would buy a home in the current stake president's area, but we couldn't afford to do that. He was offered a bishop's church calling one time, but we had to move to California. What a farce!

Once our father was made bishop again, I began to hate Sundays. Even though I didn't remember my father raping and molesting me at that time, the sight of seeing him up at the podium made me ill, due to all the hypocrisy I saw in his life. To make matters worse, I was a teenager and the bishop's daughter. Everyone watches the bishop's family to see if they are living the gospel and being a good example. I wasn't quite as rosy as a Mormon bishop's daughter should be. I was always at church and attended most of my meetings and I didn't smoke or drink, but I was known to the boys as "fast." I was very sexual and loved to kiss, make out, and fool around. I was doing what my father taught me. I was trying to get love and attention by necking and fooling around with the boys. Still, I never actually had sex until I was a young adult, because sex before marriage was strictly forbidden.

I also started hating Sundays because of my father's behavior during and after church. He was pompous, narcissistic, and abusive. Let me illustrate with the events of a typical Sunday at our dysfunctional home.

—1970—

On a typical Sunday morning around 7:00 a.m., Mom opened my bedroom door. "Time to get up for church, Debs," which was my nickname during my teen years within the family.

"Oh, no, it's Sunday," and I put my covers back over my head as if I could somehow magically make all Sundays go away. "Mom, I think I'm sick and I have tons of homework," I said from under the fort I made out of my comforter. Church meetings were three hours long unless I snuck out for part of the meetings like Sunday School. As you can tell, I hated Sundays, mostly because I was a teenager and I hated all confined places except for church dances, church meetings with boys, and some school classes because they had boys in them and I might like the subject. But Sundays were the worst.

"Deborah, why don't you like Sundays? Do you hate your family? Because it's the only day the whole family gets to be together."

Oh, how I wanted to say, "Yes, I do hate spending time with the whole family." It meant Dad molesting Mom in the family room where the only TV was (for us kids) and Dad complaining about church and all the "brethren and sisters" he saw before, during, and after the church meetings.

"What do you mean by yes? You hate the family?" Mom started to cry.

I must have said yes out loud without the rest of it. I flew out from under the covers and ran to Mom's side. "No, Mom, I meant yes, I want to be with the family today," I said as I gave her a hug. "Of course I want to be with the family, especially you, Mom." I have always had a soft spot for my mother, no matter what she did in her lifetime, although I have good reason to be mean and hateful toward her. It's just him that I hated spending Sundays with. But Mom condoned it and actively participated in abuse. It began to be a main theme for her—condoning and participating in it.

"Okay, now get ready for church and don't upset your poor old mom again," she said, wiping a tear or two from her face.

"But Mom, I have nothing to wear. I wore my blue dress to last night's dance and my yellow dress to school on Friday and just about everything else is in the dirty clothes hamper." This was a stall tactic to see how late I could make her and she might give in about church. Then I could watch that movie we rented without Dad being in the room.

"Deborah, I hate to break it to you that the blue, yellow, green, black, or white dress would be fine, or wear a skirt and a blouse, just not that one black and white skirt," she said. "I really don't know why we bought that. It's too short, but your dad gave in and let you get it with the stipulation that you could not wear it to church."

"Okay, Mom, I'll find something." Mom left my room to gather her music for choir practice. The too-short skirt was exactly what I would wear. Dad let us get miniskirts because he liked our legs. But this business of not letting us wear the short skirts to church was hypocritical and nasty of my father.

"Honey, your dad is speaking in church, so wear something pretty and ladylike," called Mother.

Dad always had his girls come up to the podium or stand where we were sitting, to talk about us and brag about the three of us, but I would try to squirm away. I hated all their eyes on us as if we were naked and doing something very ordinary. It was embarrassing.

"Is Rebecca coming to church, our ward, I mean?" I said.

"Yes, now I have to go. You'll have to bring you and Cynthia to church in your car. Did you hear me?"

"Yes and okay," and the shouting spree between bedrooms was over for the morning. Mother put her music pages under her arm and she was out the door.

This was just as it went every Sunday morning. Dad didn't know about the Sunday morning routine because as bishop, he left for church early for meetings and appointments.

Five minutes later, my sister Rebecca arrived. "Oh, Rebecca, you're here," said Cynthia as Rebecca came through the front door. "Dad is speaking in our ward today," Cynthia added. "You got your hair cut shorter and blonde frosting. I love it." Cynthia was ready for church with her long naturally blonde hair and nice slim figure like the rest of us.

"Yes, I know Dad is speaking," Rebecca replied. "That's why I have graced this house with my presence and will be gracing the church as well. It means we either have to march up to the front of everyone or stand up where we are so that the king can grant us princess-hood once again." She bowed and then curtsied like she didn't know which to do. Cynthia laughed and put her jacket on to go.

"Debs, if you and Cynthia would like me to take you, jump in the car, but we have to go now."

In unison, Cynthia and I both said okay and slammed the front door as we left. Rebecca was now almost twenty years old and living on her own in her own apartment. On the drive to the church, we found out Rebecca was spending her day at the house with us, dinner and a movie. I said that Dad had practiced his talk in front of the mirror yesterday as if he was going to be in a starring role in a play. He sighed where a sigh was called for, he cried on cue—even in front of the mirror—during the telling of Mom's car accident when Butch was small. Butch was now married and living in Salt Lake City, Utah.

"But you should have heard Dad; he cried, sobbed, and then went to dried eyes, sounding chipper and cheerful the next moment. It was odd," I said.

A half-hour later, Dad was giving his speech when, just as we dreaded, he made us come up to the front by the podium. All I remember is after we got up front, he stood us in one line like we were going in front of a firing squad and he put his hands on us to tell what each of our inborn gifts were. First, he went to Cynthia, then to me, and then to Rebecca. At first, he had his hands on Cynthia's shoulders, then on my waist, and last, on Rebecca's hips. I don't remember what our gifts were or what else he said, but I was so embarrassed—especially for Rebecca. He was the king and we four girls, including Mom, were his concubines. It was like an out of body experience. Don McKay was there from another ward. He was the boy I was trying to win over most recently, and I just wanted to die.

Rebecca and I jumped into her car after Sacrament meeting, and told Mom to bring Cynthia home. We just had to get out of there. We didn't stay for the remaining one and a half hours so that all the elderly sisters could tell us how proud we should be to have such a wonderful dad. We went home and ate most of the junk food in Mom and Dad's house.

Before church, Mom put the pot roast with potatoes and carrots in the oven. As it got close to dinner time, I set the table. I loved Mom's pot roast. Cynthia was doing her homework and Rebecca was on the telephone with her boyfriend, Jack. Dad was just arriving home from church and it was time to eat. But first, he had to say hello to Rebecca by grabbing her with one arm in a death grip and spanking her bottom with the other hand. This was Dad's signature hello to Rebecca and me, though not to Cynthia or Mom.

The family had much to say about Dad's speech, but Rebecca was silent, as if trying to hear ants crawl. Of course, I had a thing or two to say, like, "Dad, do you have to bring us up in front of everyone when you talk about us?"

His reply was, of course, "I'm so proud of you, even if you do wear dresses and skirts that are too short, especially for church," and we were off on a discussion of what modesty means.

I thought, Modesty! Modesty! Pretty soon, you will see what modesty meant in our family. I thought of when he ripped Mom's blouse and bra off, we'd see who was appropriate then. Without another word, we finished our dinner and decided to eat dessert in the family room in front of the movie everyone wanted to see: *Love Story* with Ryan O'Neal and Ali MacGraw.

I thought this might send Mom and Dad up to their bedroom to watch something else, but they decided to watch it with us and Cynthia and I grabbed pillows to lie on the floor. Rebecca had seen it in a movie theater so she went back to her apartment.

The movie had no more than just begun when Dad opened Mom's blouse down to her waist. He was lying on the couch with his head on Mom's lap and he was playing with her breasts while she took a bobby pin and dug out all the blackhead pimples on his face. It was incredibly gross, totally inappropriate and endlessly disgusting, and definitely not modest! I still managed to block it out and concentrate on the movie. Children have an amazing ability to block out the most disgusting of behaviors or events that are going on around them. It amazes me now how I—being an extreme extrovert—could stand being in the same room while this went on every Sunday and I said nothing. Father talked all through the movie about people he saw that day.

"Mrs. Smith was in today, complaining, for the second time, that her husband hit her again. So I called him in during today's third meeting and basically told him to knock it off," Dad said. "Why can't these couples get it together so I don't have to intervene?" It was more of a declaration than a question, but definitely a put-down.

"You mean again, this isn't the first time it happened?" whispered Mom.

"No, it's about the second time and I'm tired of her whining. She provokes him anyway. Then there is Sister Jones, who needs help from the Bishop's Storehouse with food again. I need to sit down and find out where her money goes to. I have a feeling she buys those kids of hers too many toys and candy. The kids should be happy with what they have, but it's the second time she asked for help from the Bishop's Storehouse," Dad continued.

"Oh, Walt. Now you need to be patient with these women," Mom said.

"No, I don't. Don't tell me what I should say or do. I had five women in my office today, bitchin' and moanin' and groanin' and no men except for Brother Smith, who barely needed anything," said Dad angrily.

At this point, I got up and turned the television up to drown out his bitchin', moanin', and groanin.' And Mother wondered why I didn't like Sundays?

And that's how Sundays went in our house while Dad was bishop. At some point, I decided to go do homework after the dishes were done. It just finally got to me so I was either on the telephone, talking to a friend or doing homework, or listening to James Taylor playing "You've Got a Friend" for the one millionth time. It was better being cooped up in my bedroom than being downstairs, listening to Dad and watching the peep show inside Mom's blouse and bra.

Again, the defining quality of a sociopath is their lack of conscience. They can lie over and over with neither regret nor guilt. They monitor their body language, their facial expressions, and their words at all times. If they slip and someone notices, it's back to lying again, but even smoother this time. Whether they are climbing the ladder of success within their career, their community, or their church, they do it with all the skill of a master actor.

I will remind you that a sociopath cannot love, but they look like they deeply love their family and friends. Because of the lack of bonding with his parents and others, my father was not able to make any normal attachments with any other individual. His journal shows that he did not have strong emotional feelings about anyone as he wrote mostly about his success in his business endeavors and church powers he gained over and over again. He stopped writing in his journals around 1990. Mother was typing them up and so he ended there, rather than go on to the last five years of his life.

Our father also began molesting our children, his grandchildren, about 1985. As I said earlier, as far as we are concerned, this won him a special place in hell. Each grandchild who was abused has a chapter in this book that will explain the circumstances of their abuse in detail. It needs to be clear that Rebecca's son, Alex, was molested completely out of revenge for Rebecca reconnecting with me and telling me, Mom, and Dad, as well as the rest of the family, that she was also molested. Her circumstances and all the details are in future chapters. This solidified for us that Dad was a pedophile and belonged in jail.

Unfortunately, everyone's sexual abuse was outside the statute of limitations for prosecution criminally, except for Alex's, but he was only six years old and too traumatized and threatened by his grandfather to testify. He had to be older before he would tell, so we never put him through the trauma of a trial or anything.

Our father had many other experiences while being bishop, but none of them have to do with child abuse. We don't know if he molested any other grandchildren. With twenty-one grandchildren, he might have, but so far, just two of the grandchildren have told their story. The memories the two grandchildren have has never been forgotten. We do know that our father had a candy dish in his church office and the children would go in there to get some each Sunday. There may be other victims we don't know about or he might have kept it just to the family. If this book finds more victims, we would like to know, and we will try to help him or her as much as we can.

Dad retired from the car business in approximately 1991 or 1992, and my parents moved first to Southern California, close to Rebecca in Alpine, California, where my father triggered Rebecca's memories about being molested and then molested Alex, Rebecca's son. Having been accused by Rebecca and then about Alex, he, along with my mother, moved again to the Los Angeles area. They were closer to Cynthia and her family as she was The Golden Child and we doubt any of her six children were abused. None of Cynthia's adult children have acted out or had marital problems. Usually, there are signs or symptoms that go along with being sexually abused and Cynthia's children show none of those symptoms.

Dad died in 1995 of congestive heart failure, and my mother told me a few years after his death that he was very scared and restless in the dying process. They had hospice in the home, helping Mother, but he wasn't on morphine or any narcotics of that nature, so he wasn't hallucinating from drugs. My mother told me that, for days before he died, Dad said all he could see were dark figures assembling around him and he was very frightened. In my view, it was a fitting ending for a man who said he knew the gospel was true, yet acted out his sociopathic and pedophiliac behaviors and ruined any chance of a cohesive, loving family. It was a sad way to end the story of Walton W. Hunter's life.

CHAPTER FOUR
Rebecca Hunter

"And so she protects the 'secret' with all of her might. That, in combination with her need to block from her awareness the horror of what she's been through, often results in repression of her entire childhood experience."

E. Sue Blume, *Secret Survivors*

I remember much of my childhood, but my sister Rebecca still has blank spaces—whole years that are missing. As my memories came back, whether in small pieces or an intrusive flood, I remembered more and more what my father did to me. As Rebecca helped me to write this book, more childhood memories returned to her also, but there are still many events, big and small, that she doesn't remember at all. She shared with me what she did remember, and together, we created a way to tell the stories that show what happened in our family. I'm able to put myself inside her story, and tell it through her eyes.

—1960—

The small room was dark. It was the middle of the night, as best as Rebecca could tell. Her baby-blue parakeet was quiet with its cloth over its cage. She always wondered why she got a bigger bed than all the other siblings and why she had a bedroom to herself, rather than sharing a bedroom. Sometimes, the light from the street lamps lit up her room and she was able to see the door opening. It was her father coming in and she knew why. Now that she was a little older, twelve years old, and her father was not molesting her as often, she wondered if he was coming into her room to molest her once again.

"Rebecca, wake up, wake up, baby," Dad said while gently shaking her. "Rebecca, wake up now. It's our secret time together."

Becky moaned and rolled over onto her stomach.

"I want more this time, like the last few times." He began to take off her pajama bottoms. Rebecca grabbed her bottoms and pulled them back up. "I know you are awake, young lady. Take your pajama bottoms and your panties off or Daddy will get angry and you know it hurts you more when I'm angry," her father said, sounding angry and frustrated.

Rebecca just started snoring lightly like she did when she was asleep. After another few minutes of trying to wake up Rebecca and get her to submit to him, he left the room in a huff. As he was leaving, Rebecca overheard him muttering, "I know where I can get cooperation whether she wants to or not," and he almost slammed her bedroom door. With mounting tension, Rebecca overheard her father stop at her doorway, hesitate, and then leave. She felt she was in the clear for the night and soon became drowsy and fell back to sleep. She wondered, if he was not having sex with her or Mother, where would he go now? She thought maybe to Deborah and it worried her.

Rebecca knew Dad was trying to molest or rape her when he came into her room, and being twelve years old, she was confident that she could now fight him off. She decided the last time he raped her that she would kick and scream the next time he tried to mess with her. She just could not stand to be molested or raped one more time. She wondered if Cynthia or Deborah—her younger sisters—were getting the brunt of his anger as she had so many times before. She felt awful for her sisters that he had left angrily, because she knew he would probably take it out on them. She felt guilty about avoiding what

Dad had in mind for the two of them, because she knew her father would probably go to her sisters for sex now. It was very confusing. She began to cry.

Now as an adult, Rebecca remembers being molested as far back as when she was two years old in the bathtub and feels that all of her earliest memories of her father were about their "secret time" together. She feels he even began molesting her as a baby and it continued until she was twelve. As recorded in her baby book, her first word she said was "Daddy." "Mommy" came a few months later. Right after Daddy came a sound Mom could never figure out. Mother spelled it like it sounded, "egret tim," which we think was "secret time," which was pretty good for a fifteen-month-old. Mom wrote, "I never figured out what it meant and soon you stopped saying it. Whatever it was, it sounded cute."

When Rebecca was little, around three to four, Dad tripped her when she walked past him, pushing her down so she would fall, or he pinched her arm and bottom or he pulled her hair. Rebecca learned at an early age to stay away from her father. He was outright mean to her, but not to Wayne or her younger sisters. She often wondered why. We now speculate that it might be because he was the second child to be born into his family of origin, the family which rejected him and called him ugly. Also, his brother, Elvan, was always mean to him. Maybe because he had a miserable childhood as a second child, he found a perverse justification in being mean to his second child, Rebecca.

When Rebecca was only three, she ran up to her father to greet him when he came home from work. He picked her up and blew into her stomach and occasionally, he bit her tummy. She sat on his lap to look at books or they would watch television together. During those times when nobody else was present, his hand was always down her pants. He said, "Doesn't that feel good?" or "You like Daddy to do that, don't you?" As she got older and his fingers would be "tickling" her (as he euphemistically called his fondling of her genitals), Mom overheard him and walked in and said, "What does she like, dear?" or "What's making her laugh?" and Dad would have to make up something to say to Mother.

The threats—as young as she remembers—were almost always the same. "You wouldn't want me to have to hurt you really bad or your mother or your brother and sisters, would you? Because if you tell, I will have to hurt them all and then you might be alive and they would all be dead. What do you think, little Rebecca? Don't make me hurt them all badly!" He also whispered in her ear that he could see her wherever she went and whatever she did. She became certain of it. She believed that her father could see her just like God saw her, all the time, no matter where she was or what she was doing.

One day, while playing at the school yard, Rebecca found a crumpled old Camel cigarette pack with no cigarettes in it. She picked it up and smelled it because she had no idea what cigarettes smelled like. Then she remembered her father's threat: "I will see you wherever you are or whatever you are doing!" and she suddenly dropped the cigarette wrapper. She ran home, crying, because she was terrified that her father and mother saw her handling the pack and didn't see that there wasn't anything in it. When she arrived home, she told her mother about the event with tears running down her cheeks.

Her mother replied, "What are you so upset about, Rebecca? It was just an old empty cigarette wrapper!"

Rebecca walked away from her mother and into her bedroom, shaking her head and wondering why Mother wasn't upset about her playing with a cigarette wrapper. She thought that maybe both her parents couldn't really see everything she did, maybe it was only her father, but she feared that she would get in trouble when her father came home. But when Dad came home for a quick dinner, he didn't say a word either. She was puzzled, but was too afraid of him to ask if he knew about the cigarette pack.

Rebecca walked on glass with her family. She tried not to be seen and tried not to do anything which her mother and father could think of as even remotely "bad." She lived for years in terror, not knowing if Dad was going to try again to molest her or rape her. She just tried to hide and stay out of the way. Most of the time, Dad was at work, in church meetings or at church events, so it wasn't too hard for her to keep away from him. But there were always the mornings and nights when she had to be in her bed and could not hide from him completely.

Rebecca and I often tried to spend the night at friends' homes, but it was difficult. We were too frightened that our girlfriends' fathers would do the same thing to us as Dad did. We thought all daddies molested little girls. So every time we tried to stay at a girlfriend's house overnight, we would wake up the mother around midnight and tell her to please call our mother because we wanted to go home. We would be crying just to get out of there. You would think we would feel safer at a friend's house, but we were too traumatized. Just being away from home where it was familiar was very distressing, and the friend's house was the scary unknown. But we wanted to be normal like our friends. They could always spend the night at a friend's house, but for some reason, we could not. We can't explain it. However, the girls never stayed at our house.

Our parents were always reluctant to take us to doctors. They stated, "We cannot afford it," but there was a time when Rebecca needed an operation and they agreed to it.

"Do I have to have my tonsils out?" Rebecca said, whining the whole time.

"Yes, dear, and remember, we can't stay with you," Mom said. "Dad and I both have to work, but the nurses will take care of you and then we'll pick you up at the end of the day."

"But Mom," Rebecca said, still whining, "can't you stay with me?"

"No, I have to work, you know that!" said Mom forcefully without the least bit of sympathy as she pulled nine-year-old Rebecca away from her and handed her over to the nurse. "Now be good for the nurses and we will collect you at five p.m. I have Popsicles waiting at home for you," said Mom as she hurried to the elevator to get to her job.

Rebecca minded Mother and went to the nurse to put on a hospital nightgown. She was put into a little bed just her size and she went back to sleep as it was early and the operation wouldn't be for hours yet.

After the operation, Rebecca's throat was very sore and she cried as she tried to talk. It hurt so bad that she soon gave up and just lay there listlessly until her father came to get her. The nurse offered her a banana Popsicle, but every time she swallowed, it hurt her throat so she threw it away.

When Dad arrived at the hospital, she was glad to see him for the first time in a long time. He paid the hospital and doctor bill and picked Rebecca up and carried her out to the car. Just as they were getting to the car, Rebecca felt very sick to her stomach and threw up, mostly blood, all over her father. She distinctly remembers thinking, *Now I've got you and there's not a thing you can do about it!* Although she was in pain and felt very sick, she felt like laughing at what happened. Dad wiped his coat off with a handkerchief and put the coat in the trunk. It was snowing and he was in just a shirt and tie. What a mess she caused! She smiled to herself while he was busily cleaning up. Pitifully, it was the only payback she could do then for all the years he molested her.

Our parents found every reason not to take us to the doctor. Sure, they had no insurance and money was tight, but when Rebecca was in the second grade, she coughed and coughed and a doctor in the ward at church came over at no cost to them and diagnosed her with pneumonia. The doctor warned my parents that she must be hospitalized as her life was endangered because it was such a bad case. Instead, they built a humidifier tent over her bed. She did not get antibiotics and was not hospitalized, so the pneumonia became life-threatening.

Rebecca was just old enough to comprehend the concept of death and she thought many times while under that tent that she was going to die. She wondered what would happen to her toys and her favorite dress. She suffered for weeks, coughing up green mucus and not able to breathe. Worse yet, our mother said she was too busy to sit with her and hours went by between Mother's short visits to bring cough syrup or to put mentholatum on her chest. Then they tried the next door neighbor's Indian opium mixture called paregoric. It was made on the Native American Indian reservation where the neighbor grew up and was more likely to have contributed to Rebecca's death than to her cure. Opium was the main ingredient.

It took Rebecca weeks to get over her pneumonia and afterwards, she looked terrible, with dark circles around her eyes and a little skinny frame. She went back to school too soon and fell asleep during lecture time. Recess for her consisted of staying inside with her head on her desk. And our parents never learned from this experience; they continued to avoid doctors and hospitals, even when their children badly needed them.

Once, my fingers were caught in the door of the car at the car lot. There was no going to the doctor. Another time, I was hit hard by a car and had a concussion. When I started throwing up and became delirious, the family gathered by my bed and prayed, but they never sought medical help. Only when Cynthia broke her arm, and the next door neighbor said her paregoric would only help with the pain, were they forced to take her to a hospital to have a cast put on her arm. If they didn't have the money, there was a church fund just to help families with those types of expenses. Yes, they would have to prove they needed it. But then, Dad was bishop and controlled that fund, so who would he have had to prove it to? There were resources. Our parents ignored these events. They were abysmally neglectful parents who dressed up on Sundays.

I wrote this chapter from Rebecca's recollections. When she tried to read it, she lapsed into tears and could not finish. She was so traumatized by the molestations and rapes that it's no wonder she does not remember very much about her abuse.

She does remember one other anecdote from when she was seven years old and our father was molesting her. This time, late one night, he demanded that she touch him intimately and the feeling of it was so intense for him that he was unable to avoid moaning and groaning loudly Hearing the sounds, Mom awoke and walked into Rebecca's bedroom. Rebecca is not sure if Mom saw exactly what Dad was doing to her and what she was doing to him, but she most likely did see because it was a hot summer night and there were no covers over them. As Mom turned around, she heard Dad groan. She said, "You slut!" at Rebecca and she left the bedroom as fast as she entered it. Dad stopped what he was doing and left the room too.

Rebecca thought that surely now her mother would stop him, now that she knew. But nothing was said that Rebecca knew of. Her bedroom was just one door down from her parents' and she would have overheard if Mom raised a fuss or if they were talking or arguing, but everything was silent. Soon, she could hear Dad snoring loudly as he usually did. Of all the things she hated about being molested, she especially feared what her father was doing to her that night and what he made her do to him. But the worst thing that night was her mother did not save her. It was plain as day what Dad was doing with Rebecca and it didn't even faze Mom. Rebecca had once again been abandoned by the mother who was supposed to protect her and stand up for her. It mattered not with Mother because the very next night, Dad was back in Rebecca's bed.

One time, when Rebecca was about ten years old, she was in Mom and Dad's bedroom and saw a suitcase sticking out from under the bed. Mom and Dad had gone to a church meeting, so Rebecca picked up the suitcase and put it on their bed. It wasn't locked and she opened the trunk. She thought maybe it would contain a million dollars or perhaps their clothes were packed for a trip to the South Pacific—she'd just heard of South Pacific from a movie—or maybe it could be boring church records or files.

To her amazement, what she found in the trunk were magazines, lots of magazines, containing pictures of naked or half-naked women. Also books on "How to Enhance Your Sex Life." Rebecca noticed that the books contained all kinds of information to improve your sexual life, but none of it had to do with how to have sex with your little girl. This confirmed her theory that had been rolling around in her mind. Daddies weren't supposed to do things to their little girls sexually. The idea gelled in her mind and she determined that this would be the end of Dad's visits.

Despite her sketchy memories of abuse and trauma, Rebecca remembers some enjoyable things she and her siblings did together during this period of time. We often rode our bikes to the school playground and played on the swings and slides. She loved going to a little grocery store called Natter's Market, where she could buy penny candy and ride her bike home. She ate her candy very slowly and had it for days, whereas I ate mine in one day and then went to her, begging for some of hers. Penny candy is one of my favorite memories as well.

But child abuse was also happening nearby to our neighbors. They were the Cook family that lived next door, Idonna, the mother, Bill, the father, and five children. We played a lot with that family and my mother told me that the children accused their mother and father of sexually, physically, and emotionally abusing them. It's probably not a coincidence that Idonna and our mother were best friends.

Rebecca also remembers great birthday parties and Halloween costumes. Sometimes, Mother was putting the finishing touches on costumes when we were ready to go trick-or-treating around the neighborhood. So there were some happy moments, but for the most part, those good times were overshadowed by the abuse and neglect we suffered at the hands of our parents. Childhood was mostly bad and young Rebecca learned quite early not to count on the good times or to get hopeful because it would usually only be a night or two before her father would come into her bedroom again to ruthlessly molest or rape her.

As an adult, Rebecca started going to a therapist, Greta Wyche, because her husband wanted her to since she hated sex so and because often she would cry out at night when she was asleep, saying, "No, Daddy, no. Not tonight, Daddy. No." David gently woke her as she tossed and turned while saying this and looked so upset. So she went to the counselor that David had been going to.

Greta was a short little gal with some type of credentials from over in Europe, but she was very good and Rebecca's husband approved of her so he talked Rebecca into trusting her. Rebecca found everything Dave said about Greta was true. She had short brown hair and a medium build and was very patient and kind. Her diagnostic skills were great. Rebecca was calling out at night in her sleep, "No, Daddy. No!" more and more and pushed her husband away from her while saying, "No, Daddy. No." She also called him Dad instead of Dave on occasion. He thought therapy could help Rebecca.

She did see the therapist and it wasn't long after that time that Rebecca remembered being abused by her father. She states that it was like a window opened one day and she remembered a lot of the abuse she had suffered at the hands of her father. Yet, a couple of days later, that window mostly closed. The memories were too overwhelming and the majority of her specific memories faded away. But the important thing for me was that she did remember. Rebecca told her oldest daughter about her early childhood abuse and her daughter encouraged her to call me.

Rebecca later went to another therapist and she no longer talked much about the memories because they were just too painful. She coped by having a lot of faith in God and a strong testimony of the Mormon Gospel through all her trials and tribulations. She still believes that there is a God and Heavenly Father who will judge her according to her good works. Rebecca's testimony has just grown stronger with each passing day in the sure knowledge that our mother and our father will suffer in hell one day for the way we suffered here or even more. She is an example showing that you can recover from severe abuse if you pray, go to therapy with a good therapist, and lead a courageous life.

There is a great book called *Core Healing from Sexual Abuse: A Journey of Hope* by Marti Wibbels with a quote that Rebecca particularly likes which says, "When God says we are to come unto him like children, it is because children are born with an amazing ability to trust others, to believe in God. When sexual abuse occurs, the result is a loss of hope, joy, and trust and is a travesty not only against our bodies, but against our souls."

Rebecca does not think about her sexual abuse anymore, she says, but it stole from her some of her zest for life. She loves her seven children and eight grandchildren, she gets some self-confidence and reward from being a nurse, and she loves her Heavenly Father and feels a surety that God will punish both our mother and our father one day. With a master's degree in social work and from work as a county case worker with Child Protective Services and the deluge of both self-help and scholarly books and years of therapy, I agree with E. Sue Blume in *Secret Survivors* that one way the child can cope is to block all emotion about the abuse and about life and live at a lower level of emotions than others do. I am an overly emotional person while Rebecca is a much less emotional person.

Dr. Ellsworth talks about people who do overs and people who do unders. For example, I am overly talkative, overly loud, and overly emotional, or at least I was in the past. It doesn't mean one is bad over the other one. It means that it's good if people can learn to control their overs to a more modest extreme so they are not annoying to others. However, if you like to be overly loud and you don't care what others think of you, then by all means, be overly loud. It's good to have a zest for life.

Rebecca has blocked most emotions away from herself. She finds true happiness with her grandchildren and she loves Christmas, but otherwise, she states, "One learns to stay alive for the good moments. In between the good moments, I am sad for what happened to us. We had a horrendous childhood; one doesn't suddenly say okay now, that's over and now I'm a happy person. A childhood like ours takes the zest for life away." She has happy moments and she and I laugh on a daily basis, but her countenance is often not happy or joyful. That was stolen from her, along with her childhood innocence.

—Rebecca's Remembering—

The song "Yesterday" by the Beatles was playing on the radio as Rebecca drove to the beach on a cloudy, partly sunny day after an intensely stressful week with her kids, her husband, and their business. She was going to the beach to gain some peace and tranquility. The beach on a cloudy or rainy day calmed her so she could go back. Back to the seven children, back to her very difficult husband, and back to a very stressful business.

She walked the beach for several miles before it happened. The window of her past as a child opened and she had to sit down for a while to face what she saw. She saw a scared four-year-old little girl running into her closet to hide from her daddy who just returned from another day at the car lot. The little girl grew frightened as the seconds ticked off the clock. Rebecca saw her dad putting her to bed. Suddenly, his hand went up her nightgown and into her panties, all the while rubbing her leg hard, then her stomach, and finally her vagina. She said, "No, Daddy, no!" and again a little louder, "No, not again! Daddy, no!" Then he became angry for her voice being too loud and he grabbed hard and it hurt. Then the window of memory closed!

Rebecca uncovered her face as she awoke from what had been like a nightmare. Yet she had not slept. She remembered sitting down in the sand, covering her face. But she thought she had to have dreamt this sick scene. Then she remembered that the little girl in a ponytail was herself. Not just any child. No, not any child…it was her, little Rebecca. She started to cry and then scream. She screamed, "No,

Daddy, no, not me, Daddy, no!" People on the beach stared at her, but no one came up to her to see if she was all right.

She stopped screaming as she felt the stares. She was rarely hysterical, but she was caught off guard. She ran to her car, but she forgot where she put it. It began to rain lightly at first, but soon, it seemed like a typhoon. It never rained so hard in San Diego in May! Where was the car? Where? Then she put her hands on her knees and told herself to calm down and think. It was on Pacific Beach Avenue, she remembered. Good. One street over and suddenly, she was at her car. She hurriedly got inside and then she started to cry. Molested by my father! she thought. It can't be so, but that fits in with Debbie's claims of being molested. She tried to conjure up the scene with little Rebecca again, but she couldn't. And to be perfectly frank about it, she didn't need to see that scene again. She dried herself as best as she could with some paper towels, but she still dripped water from her hair.

After twenty minutes, she was very cold and she decided she needed to go home and get into dry clothes and into or under her covers in bed. But what does a mother of seven do when she needs time alone at home and has an uncooperative husband? He would want an explanation and she wasn't ready to share this horrific news with him yet. So she called her good friend, Jackie Hampton, to come and gather the four littlest ones—the other three, teens now, were at a church workshop all day—and take them to her house for a couple of hours. Jackie was a social worker who worked with molested kids, so she would understand, but Rebecca wasn't ready to tell her details. She left it vague. She only told Jackie that she remembered being molested and asked her to leave it at that for now. The covers felt good over Rebecca's head for an hour and a half of sleep, but even that sleeping time was filled with nightmares of being molested.

A week or so later, her husband said, "Why do you cry in your sleep now and mumble, 'No, Daddy, no,' more often? Why do you toss and turn constantly at night?"

Rebecca knew it was time to tell him, but she didn't really want to. She told him about the window of her sexual abuse opening at the beach and then closing soon after. He wasn't surprised by the news. He'd almost guessed from her moans and *no, Daddies* in the night. David said, "Well, I never liked your dad and this is a confirmation of what I expected. I don't want the kids around him."

Rebecca said, "If Mom is there, it will be okay, don't you think?"

David replied, "I don't think it will be all right, but as long as they are never alone with him, maybe. I've got to get to work," and with that, he left.

Rebecca knew her real journey lay ahead of her and it was time to face her newfound secret. She knew nothing would ever be the same again. Rebecca decided to only tell her oldest daughter so she could have a friend there to support her. The other children, especially the older children, gathered clues from the whispering phone calls, her oldest constantly behind closed doors with Rebecca, and their father's extra hugs when he never was a hands-on dad before with words or hugs. It was rare he gave them, but now he hugged them for no real reason. It all added up to something was going on with their mom and dad and it had to do with Grandpa, something bad that no one would talk about.

As Rebecca received counseling, first by Greta Wyche, and then a few years later from Dr. Ellsworth's daughter, Caroline, for a brief time, her vision of being molested by Dad became all too real for her. The processing of newfound incest memories continued. Rebecca felt as if she wanted to fall apart, but she just couldn't because of the small army of children she had to care for at home. She needed to scream in the car by herself or to walk on the beach alone much more often than she was able. She wanted to curl up with a good mystery novel and escape from the intruding thoughts of Dad molesting or raping her. She was depressed and numb all at the same time.

The children's needs were a blessing and a curse. More often than not, she was overwhelmed with making the packed lunches to save a dollar or two and she told the children to buy school lunches. Then she worried about their nutritional needs, but her therapist reassured her that no child, to her best recollection, had gotten some horrible disease or died from school lunches. Eventually, the children all learned to pack their own lunches by themselves and the older ones helped the younger. Soon, the children helped do their own laundry. The older kids chipped in and did the younger two children's laundry too.

Rebecca felt ashamed that she let her appearance go and she didn't curl her hair and put on make-up to drive the kids to school. She found herself driving them to school without shoes, with just bunny-head slippers and pajamas, rather than nice daytime clothes or even sweatpants. It got so bad that she didn't bother to put on her nice robe, but just wore the tattered tie-dye one she made as a project with the young women's program in the church.

That was bad enough, but when, on some days, she stopped driving the children to school and the kids and she slept in until noon, she finally realized she had a serious problem. She was chronically and deeply depressed, even suicidal at times, and it was time for her to check in to the friendly neighborhood psychiatric hospital for some "spa days."

This did not go down well with her husband, Dave, who didn't like the responsibility of the children and the household duties. Rebecca behaved as a completely distraught damsel in distress and it had to stop or she was going to find herself divorced and without custody of the children. That's what she feared. In reality, Dave didn't want the day-to-day responsibility for the children either, so he would have stayed with her almost no matter how neglectful she might have become.

Rebecca had been cutting Mom and Dad out of her life more and more as time went on since her memories of being molested as a child returned. She avoided Mom's telephone calls, she said they were busy with Dave's family when asked over for dinner, and she stopped extending invitations for them to come over for dinner or to stop by to see the children.

One of the last times she was over at Mom's and Dad's house, they made a show of all the new furnishings they had purchased recently. Rebecca went outside by the pool where the children were playing and splashing. Dad came out and sat on the bench by Rebecca and chatted for a moment and then said, with his arm around her shoulder and squeezing it tightly, "You know, all of this and more could be yours, Becky." Rebecca sat motionless until his grip started to hurt her. She broke free and slowly moved away from the bench. She knew she had to confront them both and it had to be soon. Dad was figuring it out for himself that her memories had finally surfaced.

In fact, the very last time Rebecca was over at Mom's and Dad's house was on Easter Sunday, 1992. There were thirteen grandchildren running around and six adults. What a feast was prepared for that dinner table! It was ninety-two degrees so the parents let the children go into the pool to cool off and to get them out of their hair. As everyone was getting ready to leave, Dad called Cynthia, Rebecca, and Mom into his bedroom and stated that something big happened to him while he was bishop the second time in San Jose, California, and he was ready to share it with them now.

Dad now had congestive heart failure and he really put on an act that day of how ill and weak he was. He had not appeared so sick on previous visits. He asked Rebecca to sit next to him near the bed while Cynthia and Mom stood in front of him. He said he saw an apparition before him in one of the pews at church when he was bishop in San Jose. At first, he thought it was Jesus Christ, but it was an angel sent from God who told him that all the wrong behaviors he had committed and all the wrongs he had done against others were now forgiven. He had served the Lord well enough in all his endeavors that he could now be forgiven for any wrongs he did. He took Rebecca's hand halfway through his long, drawn-out speech and he coughed and teared up at all the appropriate places. Mom acted very embarrassed, turning red and almost joking about it, while Cynthia was silent the rest of the day and left in a hurry at the end of dinner. So neither Mom nor Cynthia bought it and he seemed ridiculous even to them. Mom acted very nervous also as he spoke and she literally shook from what seemed to be fear. It was as if the question going on in her mind was, "Can he really pull this off? It's so far-fetched!"

To Rebecca, it was like he was saying, "I just got myself off the hook, so I'm not guilty anyway." Rebecca ripped her hand out of his grip and walked out of the room as quickly as possible.

The men finished getting the little ones dressed and gathered everything for the car when Cynthia and Rebecca stomped down the stairs. Dave said to Rebecca, "What was that all about?"

Rebecca replied, "Dad had a vision. Let's just get out of here, and then I'll tell you more."

Cynthia's kids went up to say goodbye to Grandpa, but Rebecca wouldn't let her children do the same and they all scurried out to the car and drove away. The house was emptied so fast, one would have thought a bomb threat was just called in.

With Caroline as her new therapist, a "spa treatment" under her belt, and Dad closing in on her, it was time to confront her parents with the new memories she uncovered. Rebecca was not a very confrontational person; she would rather have stuck needles in her eyes than have them over for tea and crumpets. But over they came. She simply asked them over to have some homemade pie and as jolly and round as Dad was, he could always eat pie.

Rebecca remembers them coming in and asking where the kids were. It was so quiet. She told them that the kids were at friends' houses except for two-year-old Christopher. Dave, Rebecca, Mom, and Dad all had a piece of pie, either apple or Dad's favorite, rhubarb pie à la mode. After all, Rebecca would only be able to make pie for them this one last time, depending upon Mom's and Dad's reaction to the news of Rebecca knowing Dad molested and raped her. She didn't expect them to take it well.

From that point on, Rebecca doesn't remember too much as she was busy dissociating from the whole business. At one point, while her husband, Dave, was talking, she felt herself floating up by the ceiling. Other times, she moved like a robot, picking up plates and offering soft drinks or milk to her family that had mistreated her so. But she definitely remembers saying something like this:

"Mom, Dad, there have been some changes in my life recently and I wanted to share those changes with you both now."

Mom asked, "You make it sound so serious, dear. Are you and David getting divorced, are you moving, one of you is gay—"

"Mom, just let me talk." Rebecca paused briefly. "I have had some new memories about my childhood. Dad, you molested me when I was little. Mom, you abandoned me when I was little."

Interrupting Rebecca, Mom said, "How did I abandon you, what do you mean, Dad molested you?"

"You abandoned me when you walked into my bedroom and saw Dad in bed with me and I was naked and then you silently left the bedroom. Any other mother would have been appalled and switched the lights on and at least yelled at Dad. But you just kept your head in the sand and did nothing. Worse than nothing, you ignored it for years! And Dad, you are just depraved and sickening. Well, that pretty much does it. Those are the changes in me and I know them to be true."

"Well, we knew something changed with you. You've been distancing more and more from us. We noticed that," Mom said.

"Mom, I would like at least you to go to therapy with me. Will either both of you or Mom, will you go with me?"

Mom looked at Dad like they were facing the guillotine. "Well, we'll think about it and get back to you."

"I think we'll go now. Thanks for the pie," Dad said. And that was the only thing he said. He looked like a kid caught with his hand in the cookie jar, guilty as heck.

Rebecca began taking everyone's pie plates, but didn't offer a second piece. She just wanted them to leave. And they did. With just a whispered goodbye, they drove off in their Cadillac Seville. Rebecca was numb. Numb and exhausted. She really didn't remember what was said or what she did. She forgot to send the rhubarb pie with them so she threw it away. Nobody in their family liked it and it now made her sick that she made him his favorite. She remembered the dissociating that she did and that it was a coping skill that helped her through the confrontation. Eventually, she remembered more about everything that happened in her life over the past six months, but now the future was going to be as difficult as the past.

CHAPTER FIVE

June Brady Hunter

The float was decorated with a blooming cherry blossom tree. Its dainty, pink flowers flourished on the branches and on the bark of the tree were variegated colors of brown and tan. The crew had adorned the float for the twenty-fourth of July parade, the Mormon Pioneer Days in Salt Lake City. Orchids of every color, pink, white, purple, and yellow, embellished the edges of the float. Soft green real grass lay on top for three kimono-wearing girls to sit on the float. Their kimonos were handmade by their mother and were of the most beautiful silk cloth with small and large flowers and a black or white background. The children carried straw umbrellas donated by a dance group in Salt Lake City, painted with cherry blossoms on them as well. They served a dual purpose: to keep the children from getting too hot in the July summer sun and as further decoration, to fit the bill for a perfect Japanese international parade float to celebrate in a Primary Parade of International Pioneers for pioneer days—to rejoice in the day the Mormon pioneers reached the Salt Lake Valley.

Mother and Idonna and the children all had a hand in creating the float for such an extraordinary neighborhood parade. Idonna was our next door neighbor. She and her husband, Bill, and their five children were a large part of our lives. Tom was the child closest in age to me and we played together a lot. Idonna was part Native American and she came with potions and medicines that cured a whole range of ailments. Some were natural cures, like properties of morphine and opium. She had strange ideas on how to handle children, mostly by putting them to sleep. She stood 5' 4" with dark tan skin and long black hair. I was pretty much uninterested in her.

We felt special in our kimonos of red, pink, purple, and green, and our long brown hair was up in a bun with chopsticks sticking out. We wore rouge blush and lipstick red as blood on our cheeks and lips, false eyelashes with black mascara on our eyes, and white powder on our faces to complete the look of Japanese geisha dolls. Our umbrellas helped, but it was a toasty ninety-eight-degree day, so we didn't do the route three times as many other floats did; we just went around the neighborhoods twice. But we won first place in the contest and we left the float out on the street by our house for three weeks. We took tons of pictures so we could remember the occasion and our father even took the morning off to drive the car pulling the float. It's one of the few times I remember him taking any time off of work for a family event. My mother worked hard, creating a special moment in time.

Our mother was a good mother, she was a wicked mother; it just depended on the events of her life. Dr. Ellsworth once told me that the negative things we do to our children outweigh the good things and I would like to add especially if the parents are very wicked. For Mother, the negative behavior that was most cruel was ignoring Dad's sexual abuse with Rebecca and me. Walking in on Dad and Rebecca and then turning around and walking out of the room was unforgiveable. She must not have even mentioned what she saw or discussed the moment with our father as nothing changed, except he got even more brazen in molesting us. Our mother picked up our sheets after we were raped and she didn't even notice the pungent smell or the blood which was clearly visible. She also didn't notice the number of times Dad was missing from the bed at night or early in the morning. Can any mother be so insensitive, so cold, so unfeeling to not save her daughters from such horror? She was.

Then there were the times from when I was seven years old on that she and Idonna would capture me like I was a wild beast to be imprisoned for everyone's safety. Once they had me, they took my legs and dragged me from usually the living room into the bathroom, where they inserted an enema syringe with a red squeeze ball into me and it was attached to an enema bag, usually red also. They loaded me up with a mixture of some kind that made me poop as soon as the syringe came out. I was spanked if the water mixture or poop came out before my bottom hit the toilet and then it would happen. My insides gurgled and growled and I got a horrible stomachache and I pooped for hours until I was wrenched clean. This was done at least on a monthly basis, if not more often. It was violent, it was degrading, it was abusive, and it was something that should never be done to another human being for any reason, given the manner I was given them. I remember I kicked, screamed bloody murder, and no one heard me, no one was around to save me from these savages. This, added to everything else she did that was wicked, sealed my mother's fate in hell. Sometimes I do not know how I survived her attacks. I forgot most of the sexual abuse from my father, but I never forgot my mother's enema attacks on me.

I walked in on Mom and Dad having sex one afternoon and Dad threw a book at me and Mom came out later to check on me and told me that what they were doing was called sex (duh, Mom!) and that it was something you just do with your husband. When I asked if she liked it, she said no, but it is something wives do for their husbands, because they promise to do it when they married. We had no boundaries in that house. I would get up from a bad dream or nightmare and sneak into her side of the bed from time to time and Dad would always have sex with her while I was there. This was another form of sexual abuse since they knew I was in their bed. She wouldn't even try to put me back in my bed or tell Dad no. She was just his little puppet and what he wanted, he got.

One night, a close friend to the family and to me saw our parents out partying at a bar/restaurant. They were in the bar area and Dad had a young blonde sitting on his lap and he was kissing her. Our mother was sitting right next to them and she was drinking her Diet Pepsi (it looked like Diet Pepsi), just trying to ignore him and his lady friend. My friend was shocked and embarrassed for Mother and the situation she was in. I felt bad for Mom, but she needed to show some backbone and walk out and call a taxi, but I know there were lots of women back then who didn't have a dime to their name and the men called all the shots. It's sad to think about.

One reason our mother was such a chameleon and so angry might be because of two major traumas in her life since she married our father. She was very, very sick with her third pregnancy, throwing up almost daily, barely able to get out of bed, let alone cook, clean, watch two small children, and be the bishop's wife. At eight months along, she called Dad at his work and told him, "Honey, you need to come home right away."

Dad said, "Why?"

"Because I'm in labor," Mom answered back.

Dad replied, "You're only eight months along, you can't be in labor."

Mom, raising her voice, said, "Well, I am. So you need to come home and take me to the hospital. Idonna can watch the two children."

Dad hurriedly replied, "I'll be right there, call the doctor and let him know we are on our way!"

They arrived at the hospital thirty minutes later and Mother was whisked away into the delivering room. Mom was bigger with this pregnancy, but the doctor had stated, "It is within normal limits." The doctor didn't realize, or he was neglectful, and didn't tell Mother that she was having twins. Even when Mother asked if it could be twins, he said, "There is just one heartbeat and there is no other evidence that you are going to have twins." Imagine our parents' shock when the first baby was a little boy, but the cord was around his neck and he wasn't breathing. While the nurses were trying to get him to breathe, another little baby boy was born and the other cord was around that baby's neck too and he wasn't breathing either. They immediately sedated our mother and when the twins couldn't be saved, our father told the doctor to dispose of them immediately, which the doctor did.

Our parents could have sued the doctor for not testing for twins. Mother was big, according to another doctor, and he stated there should have been further testing for twins. But our parents decided not to sue the doctor as they were too grief-stricken and the cords could have still been around their necks in any case. Maybe that was why my mother couldn't breastfeed me and couldn't even hold me long enough to feed me my bottles. None of us knows how we would react under those circumstances.

The other reason she suffered so much and became angry was an automobile accident where she hit the rear end of a school bus. She wasn't watching the school bus in front of her closely enough and she rear-ended it quite hard. There were no seatbelts nor any other real safety measures at all for cars in 1950. Her head and body went through the front window of her automobile, shredding her face through the glass. Three-year-old Wayne was with her and had no seat belt on either. He was tossed about in the back seat of the car, along with his toy trucks and cars, but he was unhurt. He was checked out by the paramedics and deemed safe and sound, just scared. Fortunately, a neighbor, Mrs. Clarke, was behind Mom's car and she took him home with her.

Mom was very bloody from all the cuts to her face, which looked like a shattered mirror now with chunks of muscle and flesh open and bleeding profusely. There were small and big chunks of glass all over her face and she was rushed to the hospital.

Dad was contacted by the hospital and told to give them permission to operate with his consent just over the telephone, but Dad said, "No, I have to give her a blessing before she goes into the operating room." They informed him that she was bleeding out and they had her face temporarily bandaged, but he must get there soon. He called his first counselor in the church and Dad asked Jim to meet him down at the hospital to perform a priesthood blessing. They both rushed to the LDS hospital and met at our mother's bedside. My father blessed my mother that she would not only live, but retain her beauty and health as well.

With the bandages soaked with blood once again, the doctors had her wheeled immediately into the operating room and put 300 stitches in her face and neck. The doctors that operated took turns carefully sewing Mom back together. When she healed enough, they took the bandages off and she had healed amazingly better than their predictions said she would, and her eyesight was good too. She wears glasses today and her face healed and she didn't have one scar. It made Mom scared of driving for a while, so Dad had to take a little more time off of work to drive her to appointments and other obligations for a while, but he said he didn't mind doing that.

Some of Mom's and Dad's weird, even shocking, behaviors include the following events. When we went on trips from San Jose, California, to Salt Lake City, Utah, Dad said, "Boy, it's hot across this desert," and had my mom take off her blouse and bra so he could play with her boobs. We three girls were in the back seat and he and Mom were up front, fooling around. I don't know if my sisters were embarrassed, but I sure was. Dad was like an animal and gave no thought to what was appropriate and not appropriate around the children.

Mom was also a martyr, taking the last sliver of cake or none at all and then saying, "It's okay, sacrifice is what all mothers are supposed to do," and then she mumbled under her breath, "Damn children always taking everything," or something of that nature. She mumbled about anything she didn't like or didn't agree with and she is now a demented old woman and still whispers under her breath, complaining about something all the time.

I never needed my father's approval like I did my mother's. Our father took my hand in his when I was sixteen and he said, "I know you're going on a date, dear. But remember, boys only get to touch this and nothing else," pointing to my hand. I must have remembered some things about the abuse because I thought, You dirty old man, how dare you tell me what a boy can and cannot do. This led me to rebel and go further with boys than I would have if he had just not said anything.

I did need my mother's approval, however. She went with us to church events to "get close to her girls," but it just pushed me further away from her. How can you be "friends" and close to your mother when she treated you like she did me with the enemas and not stopping Dad from his abusive ways? I tried to let them be good grandparents to my children and Mom did work hard at it. Working hard was what my mother did best of all.

Our mother was raised on a farm and ranch and she worked at chores from sunup to sundown from when she was little on. After school, she took the cows out to the pasture and her mother warned her if she got into the creek, she would get a whoopin'. She got into the creek almost every time and she always got a whipping. She also had to gather the eggs in the hen house and was spanked if she broke any of them. She was a good egg picker. One more story from her youth is she was the last at the table at mealtimes to get done. She was so slow that the dishes would all be washed and put away before she was done. She knew hard work, but was slower than molasses in getting things done.

One time, we were all in the car to go to church and Dad started the bidding on how many more minutes it would take Mom to get out to the car. Dad took ten minutes; I took nine minutes because I really wanted ten minutes. Rebecca took twelve minutes and cute little Cynthia took one because she didn't want Mom to lose. At fourteen minutes, Dad sent me in to rescue her because we were sure that henchmen took her to the gallows. I found her glazing the pot roast.

I said, "Mom, we all placed bets on what time you would make it to the car and we all lost. Dad says we are now late for church."

She grabbed her things for choir practice and chorister of the songs in Sacrament meeting, but when we arrived, they had one of the other sisters leading the song for the congregation. Mom had tears in her eyes and Dad told us after church to ask Mom if we could help to do anything, and we got up earlier for church.

Mom worked at Lockheed Aerospace in Sunnyvale, California, for twenty years and she worked from 6:00 a.m. until 3:30 p.m. so she could be home with us girls in the afternoon and get dinner made. She worked hard, but if she did, it was to get us more material things. We would rather have gotten fewer things and had her at home. She worked from 1965 on. First, she worked at Aeurbach's Department Store as a secretary and then at Lockheed Aerospace as a secretary and then as an audit coordinator when we moved from Salt Lake City to San Jose, California.

I changed my tune about my parents being good grandparents when the memories of my childhood fully came back and I stopped minimizing events. So they were not allowed a visit from anyone in my little family from the time I remembered the abuse in 1989 and put the puzzle of my childhood together. They hit the top when they committed the crime against Alex.

Our mother never had time to take care of us when we were little, so the neighbors did or we helped each other. Rebecca helped me and Cynthia get dressed when we were little. Wayne took us places or we walked to places like the market or the library alone. As I got older, I helped Cynthia tie her shoes or brush her teeth. I don't even remember Mother teaching us any daily habits that we should do every morning. She used to brag that she could do a load of laundry, cook a pot roast, and prop the bottle for me to drink when I was an infant all at the same time. She said, "Oh, I didn't have time to hold you and feed you your bottle of formula or milk." She always had other things that were more important than touching, holding, caressing, or hugging us. We all grew up to have an attachment disorder because we never bonded with our own mother. She also said, "I didn't have time to breastfeed any of you girls. Anyway, breastfeeding wasn't in anymore." I think she couldn't wait to get a job just so she could stop feeling that twinge of guilt that she may have had. The neighbors in our first house on Jepson Avenue in Salt Lake City took care of us, not our mother.

I am angry for many things she did. There are two things I can't forgive her for. The first is her deep, deep denial of any abuse when you will see how involved she was in the abuse area. I mentioned the abuse in passing language when she lived by me in an assisted living facility a few years ago, and she basically picked up her belongings and called my brother to come move her to Colorado to an assisted living facility by him. There were other circumstances that made that a good decision for everybody. But just the mere mention of the abuse caused her to run. I don't know if it was her guilt, but I think it more appropriately was her level of required denial that keeps her from living by Rebecca and me.

The second reason is what happened with the grandchildren, which you will learn of in future chapters. She very much will be in hell alongside my father for coming attractions, but don't skip ahead. My mother may never be forgiven for some of the sins she committed, mainly because she never repented and said what they were and asked for forgiveness from those she sinned against. Because of that, she, like my father, will never rest in peace.

CHAPTER SIX

Family Systems

"The apes are coming, the apes are coming!" I screamed as I ran as fast as I could. I had this dream for almost three decades. The apes were coming for me and no matter how fast I ran, they ran just a little faster until I knew they would catch up to me. The apes were headed by a fearsome and menacing Father Ape. Right behind him was a snarling smaller ape, the Mother Ape. Then there were three much smaller apes in ascending height from a tiny baby to one the size of a larger child. I was a normal little girl with brown hair and fast-running legs. The apes looked like those you might see in the zoo. Their hair or fur was brown and they ran on their back feet with their arms bent at the elbows to help them run even faster. Kind of like the Tasmanian Devil in the cartoons. Ahead of me was a disgusting, filthy swimming pool, full of sickening brown sludge and floating feces. But I had no choice. I had to jump in the pool to get away.

The apes also dove into the water without hesitation and I was not a fast swimmer so they almost got to me. At the end of the pool, I was able to climb out of the poop and mire and I started running as fast as I could to stay ahead of them. As I ran, I saw that the sludge came off of me. But as the apes emerged from the pool and ran, the sludge of poop did not come off of them. All of it stuck to them, but only a little of it stayed on me.

Soon, I came to a wall and I couldn't find a way around, under, or over it. The apes drew terrifyingly nearer. But just as they were about to grab me, I found strength I did not know I had, and I punched a hole through the wall and jumped through, assuring my safety. The apes couldn't fit through the small hole. But I didn't trust that that was enough, so I still ran far, far away and I built myself a fortress to live in. I hired guards to spot the apes and to warn me if they got close. And they did get close at times, but inside my fortress, I was able to make a potion I could shoot at them. It was a healthy potion, formulated to compel them to be on my side and to get mentally healthy. But they were not affected by my potion. Eventually, unable to get to me and harm me, they went away in futility. Then I could live in peace.

That was my scary dream which I experienced at least weekly, more than weekly at certain times in my life, particularly when I was starting to remember the abuse. I had this dream ever since I could remember and I never knew what it was about until Dr. Ellsworth and I processed it one day during an appointment.

He said, "It looks like the apes are a family, wouldn't you say?" I agreed with him, but why was I involved with an ape family? I still wasn't getting it until he finally blurted out, "Could it be a family you know?"

After a long pause, I said, "Could it be my family? It must be my family. The apes' sizes and shapes coincide with my parents' and the little ape children represent Wayne, Rebecca, and Cynthia."

It took me more than one session to figure it all out. I'm slow! The sludge in the pool was the dysfunction in our family, which was very bad indeed. It came off of me because through all my adult years, I've gone to therapy and found out the truth about our family. I knew the family secrets and knew beyond a shadow of a doubt that if my family remained the way they were, I could not have them in my life. I thank God every day for Rebecca, that she called me that fateful day to tell me she was out of the sludge as well and that she remembered that Dad molested and raped her too. The rest of the apes have not come out of their trance and do not acknowledge how terrible our childhood was, but at least Rebecca and I now know it. As soon as I processed and felt right about the dream, it never came back.

Elder James E. Faust of the Church of Jesus Christ of Latter-day Saints stated in a talk he gave in 1993 that our homes and families are disintegrating in today's society. He further says, "I hasten to acknowledge that there are too many husbands and fathers who are abusive to their wives and children and from whom the wives and children need protection.... As regards to little children, the Lord has promised that 'great things may be required at the hands of their fathers'" (Doctrine & Covenants 83:2, 4-84).

The Mormon faith has started recognizing that there are families beyond repair who may need to be split up for the safety and well-being of the wife and children. Just as in the ape dream, Rebecca and I have had to jump many hurdles to get away from the side of the family not yet enlightened.

John Bradshaw has written several books that were especially popular in the 1990s and early 2000s. Most of his work centers on the individual, but in the book *The Family*, he speaks of multi-generational shame and trauma. He explains that something which happened to our grandmother might still be felt with the current generation. It is carried over if it has not been dealt with in the generation that the trauma or shame occurred in; then new traumas or events occur, bringing more shame to the family, and the shame just continues to build generation after generation. This can be seen in the example given in Chapter Two about the shame surrounding my father being called "ugly" and so he was given to his grandparents to raise. The shame—whatever it was—has been carried out through each and every generation since that event occurred and many other shame experiences that led up to this.

Bradshaw also discusses family roles, family systems, and incest. Every person in the family is given a role. For example, one child might be the Hero of the family, one may be the Scapegoat (which was my role in my family), and there might be a Perfectionist role, an Isolator role, a Rebel role, and so on. My parents' roles were the Addiction role for my father (sex addiction) and the Enabler and Martyr role for my mother.

Often, family members may not be aware of their roles. They just act them out in a trance until something breaks that trance and someone either seeks and gets help or they become aware that their role no longer works for them and they want to change. It is very difficult for the family of origin (the family you were born into) to reframe a person's role because the family might continue to stay in its roles and just ignore the family member who has changed or is trying to change. Occasionally, one family member goes into therapy and this can disrupt everybody's role. Then more family members or the whole family may get help also. This did not happen with our family as shown in the letters described in Chapter One, when my parents had the opportunity to come to therapy with me and to try to heal our family.

As Bradshaw says in his book *The Family*, "Children give up their reality to take care of the needs of the system." In other words, a child may be on his best behavior or deny his own needs, as in the case where the child takes on a junior parent role because the real mother is chronically ill and can't do it. So the child picks up the slack of the family by caring for Mom and the other children. Children often do this when a marriage is not working out and they either act out to take the focus off the marriage and put it on themselves or they become a pleaser, doing chores, babysitting, helping younger children with their homework, etc.

In dysfunctional families, there are boundaries. A boundary is defined as the limit that defines acceptable behavior. For example, in our family, it was all right to go to the bathroom without closing the door. If you did need to close the door and someone needed something in the bathroom, they just came in anyway, and there was no privacy. You were never supposed to lock the bathroom door. We didn't even lock the front door except when we were all gone to work or to school. Toilet privacy is a boundary usually observed in our society and it should have been a boundary in our family—a form of formality—but it was not.

One example of an enmeshed boundary is where everyone in the family is taking care of everyone else's identity needs, at the expense of their own identity needs. For example, my mother could not express her feelings about many things, so I became "attached" to my mother's feelings and expressed them for her by crying, acting out, and misbehaving. Then she was able to express anger because of what I did. This enabled her to express indirectly the anger and grief she felt after losing the twin stillborn boys. Enmeshed boundaries mean that everyone is picking up the slack for each other to keep the system balanced. In a healthy family, the parents would deal with their own issues in a private manner and not let the children know their personal business. In a healthy family, the parents take care of their own needs, and the children's needs. If there is some trouble in the marriage, the parents still take care of their own needs, as well as the children's needs, as difficult as it may be.

"Imagine a mobile like one you might hang over a baby's crib." These were the first words I heard John Bradshaw say on television during a two-day seminar PBS was having about dysfunctional families in January 1987. It lit the fire which has now brought me full circle into my research about dysfunctional families way before dysfunctional meant just about everyone. I was so impressed by his use of a mobile that it has stuck with me for all of these years. Now imagine there is a picture of each family member hanging from a string from the base of the mobile. When one picture is taken off, the entire mobile shifts and is unbalanced. It shifts and everyone has to compensate for that picture—which represents a person—being gone before the mobile can balance itself again. Everyone's role must change accordingly to cover the needs that the lost person used to take care of in the family. Healthy families can do this easily and dysfunctional families have the hardest time with this.

Some boundaries are enmeshed, as ours were, and some are open and flow freely while others are rigid and closed. In some families, there are no boundaries and it makes for a crazy-making family. For example, when I was young, I had no bedroom door on my room. People could wander in and out as they pleased. The boundaries in my family were mostly like that door; not there. There is almost always chronic depression and anger in a family with enmeshed, rigid, or closed boundaries. Individual needs don't get met because they are sacrificed for the sake of maintaining a dysfunctional family system.

Closed boundaries also mean that new people are not accepted easily into the family. When I was fourteen years old, my church had a new program to help Native American children who needed foster care families. Dad was bishop, so to set a good example, he arranged for a fifteen-year-old Native American girl to come live with us. Her name was Rosey. She was very quiet and kept to herself. She hardly ever spoke a word. She also didn't keep her room cleaned up, her teeth brushed, her hair combed, or put on fresh clothes every day. Our mother, Cynthia, and I tried to encourage and support Rosey. She was a very shy person; not like the rest of us in the family. After six months of trying to bring this girl around—to be more like us—nothing changed. Our family system could not cope with this problem and she had to be sent back to the reservation. She was delighted and we were relieved. Had we been a more open system, we might have excused some of the things she did which were not a part of our family norm. Instead, she made us uncomfortable to the point that it was intolerable and she was returned. There is the possibility that my dad sexually abused her and she requested to go home.

When there is sexual abuse or incest within the family system, boundaries are almost nonexistent. Bradshaw quotes Alice Miller regarding incest when she states, "The abused children are alone in their suffering, not only within the family, but also within themselves. They cannot share their pain with anyone. They cannot create a place in their own soul where they could cry their heart out." Incest is the most abusive of all failed boundaries and usually creates the most shame of all the types of abuse. If you are not the one in the family who was sexually abused, you still carry the covert secret of the family system. Finally, Bradshaw says, "Members of dysfunctional families give up their ego boundaries as a way to maintain a family system. Giving up ego boundaries is equivalent to giving up your identity."

What follows are examples of our enmeshed or lacking boundaries and our closed family system. See if any of these were in your own family of origin or are in your current family that you are raising.

"Rebecca, come to dinner, it's time to eat," Mom hollered from the dining room. Everyone chatted a little while and Rebecca didn't come to the dinner table.

So Dad yelled, "Rebecca, come and eat now."

Rebecca was engrossed in a book and oblivious to the requests. Finally, Mom left the table to get her, at which time baby Cynthia fell out of her high chair while everyone's attention was distracted. Rebecca and Mom met at Rebecca's door. Rebecca was just coming to dinner. Mother yelled at her and Dad spanked her hard.

Rebecca said, "What did I do wrong?"

Mom replied, "When you did not come to dinner the first or second time you were called, Cynthia got out of her high chair and fell to the ground. If you had only come on time to the dinner table, we would have all been eating and Cynthia would not have fallen out of her high chair."

Of course, that made no sense to Rebecca, but she took the spanking without tears. She made no attempt to get her parents to explain the logic in their thinking. Rebecca's fear was too intense to be logical in such a crazy-making family. Rebecca still remembers that unfair and unjustified spanking to this day.

In another failing common to dysfunctional families, our mother never taught us any important life skills, such as cooking, sewing, cleaning, fixing things around the house; nothing to prepare her daughters to go to college or get married. Mom did help Rebecca get a dowry of items together for when she would get married. She collected china, made a blanket, picked out wedding colors, and got a wedding planning book. Rebecca, however, had to learn to sew through her home economics class and on her own when Mom sewed beautifully. To this day, Rebecca makes crafts and sews everything in the world. She does knitting, crocheting, sewing, quilting, and needlework. She even made prom dresses and wedding dresses that were beautiful. But all the housekeeping and child-raising skills she learned, she acquired on her own.

I learned to cook on my own and from cooking classes. In my early married days, I decided to try homemade bread, and a double batch at that so I could make cinnamon rolls also. I made the bread dough, but I put too much yeast in it. I thought, Well, that's okay, it will just make more bread and rolls. I punched the dough down again when it rose the first time and I put it in a greased plastic bowl the second time to rise in a warm oven. I left the dough in the oven while I went shopping for some clothes because the dough had to rise for two hours.

I had seen my mother turn the oven to very low and put the dough in the oven to rise, but I had never seen my mother's whole process and I had only watched over the last year I was at home. The difference between my mother's way and mine was that she turned the oven off after five minutes and left the oven door open slightly. I did not know I needed to do that because nobody taught me. When I got home from shopping, I opened the oven door to see that there was dough dripping from the oven racks and a melted Tupperware bowl on the bottom of the oven. How could I have known that Tupperware bowls melt even at 250 degrees? I had to learn a lot the first year of marriage and that included cooking. My mother had not specifically taught us to cook one single thing before I went away to college or before I got married.

Another dysfunctional area of our family concerned racism. Our father was a racist and a bigot. He called black people the "N" word until he died in 1995. He wanted black prostitutes because he could think of them as his slaves and demand that they do exactly what he wanted sexually. He came from the south, as all of our relatives did, but Mother's parents never said an unkind word about any race and they hired many Hispanic people to help them on their farm and treated them kindly. Well, if Dad was a racist, we all had to be racists too or we would have been ridiculed. I deliberately tried to go another way and to love all people of any color or culture, but racist thoughts occasionally still run through my brain and I have to use positive self-talk to get rid of them. Family of origin habits die hard.

As I related in Chapter Five, my mother was very neglectful of us as children. I think if she had gotten close to us, she would have had to stop her neglectful and abusive ways and feelings might have crept in. This was incompatible with the way she viewed her family role. For example, she never read us stories, played games with us, or took us on a picnic. I, in turn, was not as good of a mother as I wish I could have been, but I read books to my children for thirty minutes before naptime every day. We made cookies together and I took them to visit the elderly in our church. We rented a video camera as often as we could afford to (when they first came out) to record special times for our children. I wasn't perfect, but I was better than my mother was. And that is all we can hope for—that each generation tries to do better than the generation before them.

Rebecca's dysfunctional role in the family was to be a surrogate spouse to Mother. What I mean by this is that Mother confided everything to Rebecca. She ranted and raved when Dad left us at Christmas time to be with his girlfriend and her children and Rebecca was the listener and counselor. She helped Mom put out the Santa toys, including her own gifts from Santa. Mother confided again in Rebecca when our brother, Wayne, became troubled in his teenage and young adult years. Rebecca was burdened with problems and secrets whenever something was troubling Mother. Because she could not confide these things to her spouse, Mother shifted that role to her daughter, a heavy load for a little girl. I was a little fortunate in that while I was enmeshed with Mother's feelings, I did not have to be her confidante or counselor.

Cynthia's roles were the Perfectionist and the Golden Child who could do no wrong. She rarely gave Mom and Dad any trouble, she got straight A's, she was a good girl with the boys, and she participated in all of the church activities.

Wayne's roles were the Rebel and the Mascot, defending the family's honor, but acting out in his teen and young adult years.

Dad was the Sex Addict and Pill Addict (he had large bottles of "nerve" pills on his end table by his bed).

Mom was the Enabler, allowing Dad, Wayne, and me to disobey the rules of marriage and family and not saying much about us being in trouble. She was also the Martyr and let us all know it at every opportunity.

I was the Scapegoat because I was the "feeler" in the family and I let everyone know exactly how I was feeling all of the time. I was the first to come out with the family secrets and confront Mom and Dad with them. However, in a dysfunctional family, everybody has to know everybody's business and my news spread almost instantly and was denied just as fast.

Rebecca's role was the Lost Child. She was just a quiet little nuisance occasionally, but most of the time, she was quiet, lonely, and ignored.

The worst boundary broken the most in our family, at least for Rebecca and me, was the right to not share our bodies—the boundary of personal space. It was the right to be in bed and asleep, and not to have our father come into our rooms to do whatever he wanted to do, whenever he wanted to. Another boundary that was broken was the right to be in the presence of our mother and father without having to watch them touching private parts on each other's bodies in the middle of the day in the family room in front of their children.

But maybe the most important right for me was the right to have air to breathe with which to stay alive—to not have my father act as if he was trying to kill me so he could rape me and no one would hear my cries. These were the most basic rights that we didn't get as little children that should be given to all children. I know that other young children have lives even tougher than we did, and I know it is just not right for little children to starve to death or die from lack of water or air. Trust me when I say that I know I had it tough, but other children have it even tougher.

There are many resources out there that can help you learn to have boundaries and maintain them. The first one may be as simple as "I deserve to not be hit by my husband," but then you must do whatever it takes to get you to that goal—whether it is divorce and possibly welfare, or divorce and college to learn a trade, or divorce and protecting your children. You have the right to be safe. Even though that boundary may have several steps to it and may take all the courage and fortitude you can muster, you do have the right to be safe.

Some resources that may help with boundary making, but that may feel awkward at first, include *The Courage to Heal Workbook* by Laura Davis; *The Family* by John Bradshaw; *How I Got This Way* by Dr. Sterling Ellsworth, along with his handouts and articles at www.DrSterlingEllsworth.com; my web site, www.deliverusfromevil.us; www.PsychologyToday.com under "healthy boundaries"; *Things You Should Know about Boundary Setting* at www.skillquestntx.org/adl/SettingBoundariesHandout--2013-07-

17--Optimized.pdf (this is an excellent fifteen-page article all about boundaries); and a multitude of other articles under "healthy family boundaries." *The Courage to Heal Workbook* has an excellent page on setting new rules for yourself and/or for your family, a page on helping you to learn how to say no to family and friends, and ways to nurture yourself and your soul in every way.

I would like to end this chapter by detailing some basic boundaries that I set forth, which have been difficult to enforce at times, and which I still have to remind family and friends of. These are coming from my family I have told you about so far.

1. Start small.

   Setting boundaries takes time, consistency, and patience. It is said that it may take twenty-one days to make or break a new habit. It may take drastic steps to make even the smallest changes at first. Finding causes and the origin of habits helps immensely. This is called "inner child work." One must look into inner child work before anything can make permanent changes. Why can't you say no to your mom or co-worker? Two excellent books for inner child work are Dr. Ellsworth's book mentioned above and Charles Whitfield's *Inner Child Workbook*.

2. Identify and make limits for your physical, emotional, and spiritual well-being.

   Name one item in each category to set a new boundary in and work at it daily. When you feel you have that one down, set another boundary in that category until you feel comfortable. For example, do you want to go back to church (or go to church for the first time), or do you want to get a journal and journal about your feelings, or do you want to start praying to God for things you might need help with?

3. Listen to your feelings.

   If you're feeling trapped in a marriage and no longer wish to be in that marriage, take the necessary steps you need to take to get out of the marriage and be emotionally independent, or go into counseling and see if getting out or working on the marriage is what you'd like to do. That is what I clarified for myself. I got my education so I could be independent and be free from a hurtful marriage. One technique Dr. Ellsworth taught me to do was to finish sentences such as, "I can't say no to my mother because…" Don't take "I don't know" for an answer. Say something and keep doing it until you feel you've gotten some solid answers.

4. Practice self-awareness.

   If you notice yourself not sticking to your boundaries, ask these questions: Have my feelings changed about that boundary or limitation? Is it just easier to stick with my old boundaries? Has something changed with my feelings for that boundary? What new boundary could I set and live with?

5. Give yourself permission.

It will take time for others to see that you have changed. Give yourself permission to say no or to say maybe, but I have to check my other time constraints and see if I can. Saying no to a family member will probably be the toughest. Be strong and write down and practice different ways you could say no to that family member. Be prepared.

6. Do self-care and self-nurturance.

   You probably were not nurtured or cared for as a little child. You must learn to get pedicures, massages, a little box of chocolate or popcorn and a movie with the phone off, a bubble bath, wrapping up in a soft blanket on a stormy night and reading a mystery novel (or whatever you like to read). Learn to treat yourself like you wanted to be when you were a child. Do your inner child work and read John Bradshaw's *Homecoming* book.

7. Get support.

   You wouldn't expect to hand a bicycle to a child and say, "Now go ride it." The child would need support in showing him how to ride it and how to take care of his bike. You need the support, a person or more, to encourage you with your new boundaries. For me, at times, that was just my therapist.

There are many other boundaries that might be more important than my seven that I listed here. Take stock and always listen to your real-self feelings and know that you can always adjust your boundaries, if at first you set them too high. I have a lot of information on my website and blog (www.deliverusfromevil.us) about setting realistic boundaries and goals. I welcome inquiries or further information you may need or have. If you are going through treatment or getting memories about abuse, you must just get through each hour and each day. Boundaries can be made once you've got your footing and begin the healing process.

CHAPTER SEVEN

Disconnection

It had only been two months since I remembered both that my father raped me at the age of nine and the damage my mother took on my mind and body, which I minimized for so long. Dr. Ellsworth had told me at the previous week's visit that we could talk about sending a confrontational letter to my parents about what happened over the past two months and see what their reaction would be. Well, if you know anything, know this: our lot is impulsive. We act or react sooner than later and we always like to do things our way.

So I got a piece of paper and a pencil—I knew I'd be making changes to this lengthy document—and I started out writing Dear Mom and Dad. I could have made it shorter, but I wanted to really stick it to them. When I got to the end of page four, the thought came to me that maybe I didn't know how much contact, if any, I wanted to have with them right now. Maybe I wasn't really ready to state what my boundaries were right now. I went on anyway. I couldn't wait for Dad to know that I knew he raped and molested me and his hand was definitely stuck in the cookie jar, something I hoped he feared all his life. So I planned it out carefully.

I would send them two copies of the letter. I would send them out Federal Express on a Friday. That way, they would each get a copy of the letter on a Saturday if I overnighted them. Mom would be at home, working on the yard or cleaning the house and not at her job.

Dad would be at his mom-and-pop car lot, called Circus Auto Sales, alone on a Saturday. They could read it alone at about 10:30 a.m. and they could have some time to reflect on the letter and call and beg my forgiveness. That's what I hoped for. That's not what happened.

My mind was racing and my hand was shaking, but I couldn't dodge Dad on the telephone any longer. He kept calling and telling me that he wanted me to send all three of my children to him for the summer. They could swim in the pool, he and Mom would take them to Disneyland, Knott's Berry Farm, and other sightseeing places all summer, and that would give me the chance to break up my niece and her boyfriend, who were temporarily living at our house in the same room, the playroom. My father thought they were living "in sin" under my children's noses and he didn't like that. My father said to get rid of them while I still had the good standing of being a good-enough parent or he'd take the children away from me, like Steve had no say in the matter. So, yes, I was still scared of his power and the control he held on me and I needed to "go in for the kill" now while I could catch him off guard, taking back my power and control of the situation.

So I wrote down what I was confronting them with and then set some new boundaries. These boundaries sounded so strict at the time, but reading them today, they sound wimpy and a little wishy-washy to me. My parents were in our lives heavily back then, wanting more and more control over me and my children.

9-4-89 ①

Dad and mom,

This is a difficult letter for me to write. you will both get your own copy of this letter so you can have time alone to contemplate this information by yourself.

You may be thinking we have not spoken because of Dad's call to me several weeks ago. In part this is true. I felt his phone call was just another attempt to control me and my children. What I was doing with Denna and Troy was my business and no one asked for your advice. I felt I was being called an unfit mother and you were going to save my children from me. They are my children and I will raise them how I want and make my own mistakes. you did with me and now its my turn.

I was also not ready to deal with telling you the truth I have known for a while now. I have recovered memories of my childhood I had lost. I always felt my childhood was incomplete but now I have my memories back strong and clear.

There were 2 years in particular I had repressed as a young child. There is a reason I repressed those memories. They hold a truth hard to accept and deal with but I feel the truth has been silent long enough. my favorite scripture is John 8;32. "Ye Shall Know The TRUTH and the TRUTH Shall Set Ye Free." more than anything I want to be free. Free from the pain

2

I have felt for 35 years. Pain so incredible its impossible to explain. I've enclosed my favorite poem. It tells of my pain. It is my pain and I will deal with it as I have been doing. My spirit is strong, stronger than the pain or I would have destroyed myself long ago.

Its time to tell you that I was sexually molested as a child. This is a horrifying thing for a child to live through but even worse are who my abusers were. Mom & Dad, you were my abusers.

Dad, you know you molested me. You can deny it till your death but it won't change what you did to me or what I know. It was not just raping of my little body but of my very soul. What you did was wrong. It was a violation of the most innocent trust bond; that of Dad and daughter. I do not hate you. I hate what you did to me, I despise what you did to me. I do understand that you were physically abused as a child but it does not excuse what you did to me. This sick disease is passed down from one generation to another but it stops with this generation. Our family is healing and we will do whatever it takes to heal. I am beginning to feel an inner peace I have never felt before and I thank the Lord for.

(3)

his help in finding peace. Dad, I know you have a wonderful real spirit but somewhere along the way Satan influenced your life and has ~~had~~ contributed to the negative things you did. I am truly sorry our relationship did not turn out the way it could have but there is always hope for our real spirits to heal.

Mom, you also violated a precious trust between mother and daughter. Whether you want to accept it or not enemas are sexually abusive especially as often and in the manner they were given to me when I was very young. Physchological studies have proven that enemas also severly damage people emotionally. Even if I had not been molested by Dad your enema abuse was horrifying to a scared little girl hiding in the corner of a dark room hoping you and Idonna would not find me once again. I hope you never give anyone an enema again. Also, mom I remember many, many times I would have nightmares and get in bed with you to be comforted but before I could even fall asleep you and Dad would have sex. I would get sick to my stomach but didn't dare move. This was also abusive. I realize you may have had enemas as a child so grew up thinking they were normal. You also may have been sexually molested as a child also. This makes me sad for the little girl you were but as I said this generation is going to heal.

(4)

Mom, I felt you were on a fishing expedition when you were here in June. You told me of a family with incest problems. The story was very similar to our situation. I was not ready to talk about our problems then. I do feel you have known Dad abused me ever since it happened. What I am really angry about is when you saw me go from one shrink to another and into a psychiatric hospital after a suicide attempt why didn't one or both of you have the courage and love to speak up and tell me the truth about my life. Why did I need to wait till now to know things I should have and had the right to know years before. So many, many decisions in my life would have been different had I known the truth and gotten the correct therapy earlier. Neither of you have faced up to the responsibilities you had to me. An ~~Honest~~ HONEST, UNCONDITIONALLY, LOVING relationship without abuse.

You may wonder why after 35 years my memories finally returned. Well, I am finally with some good therapists, and something happened in my life several months ago that triggered the first memory. It was similar to what Dad did when he molested me and memories started flowing. Also my real spirit that my Heavenly Father and Mother sent down here to earth was finally strong enough to handle

(5)

the memories.

Now I would like to speak about the new rules and boundaries in my life. Since we never had any boundaries as kids these new rules may feel different to you. Boundaries are an important, essential, healthy part of life. I don't feel I have the right to decide for my children that they cannot ever see you again. What right I do have is to protect them from being used in unhealthy ways. If you choose to not have a relationship with them or me it will be your choice not mine.

Some things that come to mind and new things may be added or changed as I go through my therapy are:

(1) I do not feel at this time that we should visit you at your home. If you would like to come see us in Portland in the future we would be glad to have you visit. Dad can now write trips off tax wise since he owns the house so visits to us here are fine.

(2). Any communication to my children should be about school, their interests or hobbies or yours, news about family, events, i.e., trips you may have taken or other day-to-day news. Any heavy subjects or ideas such as invitations to visit you must be cleared through me first.

(3) I do appreciate the gifts you sent

to the girls, They were very excited to receive them. I also appreciated you not spending too much. They fit perfect and love them. You are welcome to send gifts appropriate to the occasion or holiday. They have always loved your care packages, mom, of goodies.

(4) Phone calls to the kids are welcome. However, I don't want information pried out of Meredith or the others. They can only be loyal to one set of authority figures and Steve and I are who they should be loyal to. If you want to know information call me. If I can share it I will be glad to. I really don't have any secrets to hide.

(5) another of my new boundaries is about me. I will no longer be the family scapegoat, its time for each family member to take responsibility for their own actions and feelings rather than trying to assign blame and guilt to me. I hereby absolve myself of all guilt. you must handle your own feelings as I am handling mine.

Basically I do not want the kids used as go-betweens for us.

again these boundaries may change as I go through my therapy but for right now this is how I feel about things.

you have given me more monetarily than any parents would and I have always tried to show my appreciation for everything. But money is not love and is not what I needed all those years

Since I knew nothing about being molested when we made the arrangements regarding the house I feel it is appro-priate to reevaluate the situation. Had I known what I know now we would have sold the house out right and never entered into this arrangement. The current arrangement feels very uncomfortable to me. I think it would be a good idea to rethink the entire matter.

I realize that after you receive this letter you would have no part of holding onto our house and returning it to us in your will. I think it would be best if Dad and Steve were to talk about a new plan. I have discussed my wishes and ideas with Steve and he is aware of them. If it is agreeable to Dad, Steve will call him at the lot and they can talk then. Drop us a note and let us know.

Due to a major salary cut in Steve's wages, a change in health insurance and other financial changes in the last couple of weeks; I am deeply concerned about further financial

difficulties.
I know you will think I have completely gone crazy, being overdramatic and am just trying to use you because of my new found memories. Regardless, I am going to take care of me FINALLY!! I will not allow further abuse to occur towards me.

If you wish to share this information with Cindy and Becky that is fine but, I would rather leave them out. This is between you both and me. I can understand why you might wish to confide in them so I would prefer sending them a copy of my original so there will be no misunderstanding about what was said. If I feel this necessary because they have received wrong information I will do so.

I know this letter will change all of our lives. But I feel it is a better, healthier change if we all want it to be. There should not be these kinds of secrets in families. The next move is up to you, Mom and Dad. I hope our family can be honest and face these issues now and heal together.

The kids do miss you and I would like you in their lives but as a healthy grandparent relationship which

(9)

at times they have had. They have had some special memories with you they will never forget.

However you wish to respond to this letter is up to you and I will accept any repercussions or consequences it may bring. My only purpose in writing was to break 30 years of silence and confront being victimized and abused. I feel our family can only be close if at this point honesty is upheld as most important. I also feel we might be able to work through this and might be able to have the kind of relationship we should have had if we each face our problems honestly.

We will await an answer from you so Steve & Dad can discuss the house.

Debbie

You're probably wondering what kind of a reaction I got from them and what the plan was for the house we were currently living in. At first, there was no reaction, but a few years later, I heard from Rebecca that the confrontation letter had them running scared and uniting all my siblings with them. They went to my first counselor and told him "their truth" about the situation and he said I must have had a big break from reality. I will bet you that "their truth" about the situation was all lies, what they wanted him to see, to get the rise out of Dr. Taylor as they did.

The plan for the house was that when we went to take out the financing, Dad put in his name on the loan and when we closed, we would get $50,000 that would be extra cash for my dad which we were to give to him. We are not talking about just any house, we're talking about a 4,500-square-foot mansion on nine acres that was out of this world beautiful. Between the time we were building the house and it closed, my memories returned and Steve talked me into keeping the $50,000 since we would confront Dad about the abuse, he would evict us, and we would have no money to even get an apartment with. I was so out of my mind with flashbacks and nightmares that I just agreed to go along with it to get my husband off my back. I don't know to this day how he got the bank to make the check to Steve and not to Dad.

Rebecca said that's not all that happened. When Steve went down to the Bay Area just after we closed, supposedly on a business trip, he took our toddler with him. He told me, "My mother wants to watch her," and our daughter could fly free. But he really stayed with my parents and blamed everything on me and said he thought I was crazy too—at least in front of them. I found this out years later, after Steve and I divorced. Rebecca thought I knew all along and was shocked to find out that he betrayed me so. He even blamed me for not following through with the plan of giving the money back to Dad; he said that was all my doing. He was a sociopath too! I married a dysfunctional man and went from one dysfunctional setting to another.

The only contact I had in later months was from my mom, asking if she could send Christmas gifts to the kids. Years later, we began speaking to one another on the telephone after my father died. The kids saw her once when we had two of the three in town. Mom was in an assisted living facility and we were all in the same town.

When Rebecca confronted them with her newfound memories, they were almost secretly expecting another accusation and seemed to take it in stride. They didn't call her a "crazy bitch" like they did with me. So my parents did react to my confrontational letter, but behind the scenes where I could not see. We did take the $50,000 and bought another much smaller home by a park. Mom and Dad sold the house and made a $30,000 profit, we heard.

This next letter is from Rebecca to me a week after I confronted Mom and Dad. I wish I kept the letter I wrote prior to her letter, but I did not and I only vaguely remember what I said. I'm sure I was rallying the troops with Cynthia and Rebecca to get them in my corner before I sent the letter to my parents. I was probably already accusing Mom and Dad of abusing me and talking negatively about them. This was Rebecca's answer to my letter, which ended our relationship.

1-25-89

Debbie -

This may seem dramatic but if we can ever have a relationship as sisters things have to change. If you had written the letter as I taped it together I would have been so excited but instead you have to include a continual assault against our family.

You have no right to continue to make accusations and judgements about our family. We have made it clear that we don't want to be involved in your anger and negative attitudes anymore. I can't remember a time when I have seen you or talked to you when it hasn't been about your problems. Why can't we have a relationship based on positive things happening in our lives?

Your letter wasn't even a letter from Debbie to Becky. It was just another way to vent your feelings. If it had been a letter that you had wanted to write to me, Cindy would not have received the same one. I don't want to ever hear judgements or accusations about anyone in our family again.

Why do you have the right to judge the "pain" we're supposed to all be in? The only emotional pain I've had is watching what your actions and dishonesty have done to Mom and Dad. But there has been a very positive thing come out of all this. It has made us aware of how important we are to each other and has brought us closer together. In my case it has lessened the child-parent relationship and brought us together as adult friends.

When I talked to Steve I told him I knew Dad had not molested you and gave him some of the reasons why I felt this way. I have never tried to change your mind or tell you what I think of your "therapy". I have let you do what you have done without trying to tell you what I think. But you are not willing to do the same. Don't include us in your dreams of the ultimate therapy group.

I told Steve I would read some information on abuse but you couldn't just send the information. You have to high-light the statements that would support that Dad and Mom were guilty. Steve's whole letter was trying to convince me this was true. You don't want our help and concern you only want us to agree with your feelings and anger towards Mom and Dad.

When I called you last time you told me to leave you alone. I will not put myself or you in that situation again. If we are ever going to have a relationship it has to be as two adult spirits who were allowed to be sisters here on earth. Please give us a chance to have a relationship

Debbie, I do love you and would welcome us starting to build a friendship based on the positive things in our present lives.

Becky

"I can't believe it," I muttered in my mind. I sat at the kitchen table and finished reading the letter from my sister and went crying up the stairs to the bedroom where my husband lay, reading a book. "Honey, you are not going to believe this, but Rebecca just wrote me a letter that basically says she's done with our relationship if I don't 'knock it off' and stop saying I was abused by Mom and Dad, and start being a part of this family again like I used to be."

"Is that right? Oh, it's okay. Stop crying." Steve gave me a gentle squeeze on my arm as I sat down on the bed, but I was too upset to even notice his supportive gesture.

"She also says I'm not interacting with her like I should. So what else is new? I am the scapegoat in this family if ever there was one.

All they do is blame me for speaking up or blame me for what I said or just plain blame me for everything. She just thinks I am acting out inappropriately and maybe I am, but I've never been abused before." I started to sob for a minute and then remembered how mad I was and continued, "How are you supposed to act when that kind of news is dropped on your head?"

"Let me see the letter, because that's a lot to put on you right now, especially now!" Steve put his hand out to receive the letter, but I held onto it like it was a speech I was giving to my throng of followers.

Further sobbing intermingled with words coming out of my mouth and clenching of my fists made me drop the letter and Steve grabbed it. I was tired of the barrage of letters and phone calls that my family threw at me since they knew something was up. I was not the take-things-slow type of gal. If I had something to say, I said it sooner rather than later or not at all. I had poor impulse control.

"Dr. Ellsworth told you they were not going to take your accusations well. What person would? Deb, you've got to give them more time to get back up on their feet. You told them too soon!"

"I DID NOT! Why should I be suffering while they are not?"

"So you want everybody to suffer if you're suffering!"

"No, just the people that caused my suffering."

"So your whole family?"

"STOP IT!" I said, stomping my foot. "You're trying to make me be logical and sensible when I don't want to be. I told them two months after I remembered most everything, and if I am suffering, and I *am* suffering"—I teared up—"my mother and father should be suffering, too. They did things to me that were mostly buried or that I minimized my whole life. I think that's cause for a little grief."

"Remember what Dr. Ellsworth said," Steve whispered, probably to get me calmed down. "He said that you should pick your responses very carefully right now and not think that other people are making you feel angry or upset. You're in charge of your own emotions. He also said this was likely to happen and it has. Your family is missing you from the mobile. Remember the mobile example Dr. Ellsworth and John Bradshaw speak about? When you made the accusations, it was the same as taking your picture off of the mobile and now it's out of whack. They're trying to balance the mobile with you not on it and that makes them all uncomfortable." He took me in his arms to soothe me, but I resisted some. I didn't think I was ready to be calmed or loved, especially not both at the same time.

I was losing my family. No one believed me and it was hard to change my role. I was sure that Rebecca might understand, but she didn't. She didn't believe that I was molested and raped by Dad and that Mother gave me enemas so violently, and Rebecca didn't support the way I was handling it. Maybe there wasn't a right way to handle something like this. I could have stayed silent, but never let the kids near my parents again. How could I have explained that? I could have handled it calmly, but they still would have taken that badly. I told them the way I wanted to, by sending each of my parents the same letter, but at two different locations. I didn't like their reaction to my letter, but I liked having control for a change. That was new to me.

—Reconnection—

I was upstairs vacuuming my bedroom when the call came in. I could barely hear the telephone ring. The children were at the nearby park, playing and terrorizing neighbors, and Steve had gone to get them. I answered the telephone.

"Hello," I said. There was silence at first. Then as I thought it was a telemarketer, I almost hung up.

"Debbie," I heard on the other side of the telephone. "It's Rebecca."

It had been a year since that nasty, rude letter that Becky wrote about me knocking off the abuse act and rejoining the family. I didn't recognize her voice at first. Then after she spoke a little, I recognized that it was Rebecca. She spoke again.

"Debbie, I remember," Becky said timidly.

I was cold at first, thinking she called me just to chew me out again. But then she said the most wondrous sentence of any sentence I ever heard and I dropped onto my bed.

"Debbie, I remember being molested by Dad also."

I was speechless and didn't know what to say, so I started to cry and I said, "What did you say?"

She replied, "I remember Dad molesting me and I have confronted Mom and Dad with this news."

"OH, BECKY!"

"Don't cry," she said.

"Cry, I'm astounded! And you say you've already confronted Mom and Dad."

"Yes. Mom didn't take it well, but Dad acted like he was half expecting the other shoe to fall. They were speechless, except to say that it never happened and I must be in contact with you and you brainwashed me. Danielle knows that's not true because she is the one who just urged me to call you and tell you about it now. Do you forgive me?" Rebecca said, quiet at the end.

"Yes, I forgive you and you have just given me the most wonderful gift a sister could ever give me. Validation!" I said loudly. "When, how, why, where, I want to know everything."

"Well, I've been going to counseling and it was after one of my sessions that I decided to go to the beach and sit or walk on the shore, when it came to me in flashbacks and I had to pull over because my head was full of these flashbacks of him coming into my room at night and touching me inappropriately. And then the flashbacks went away, but it was so vivid and real that I will remember it always."

"What did Mom and Dad say or do when you confronted them?"

"They both got indignant and said it was all in my head. Mom agreed to go to therapy with me at least once. Dad was mostly quiet and said I was persecuting him like you had."

"Becky, I can't believe it's you, and with news that you were molested also."

"You almost sound happy that I was molested!"

"No, I'm not glad you were molested. I wouldn't wish that even on people I don't like."

"Well, Mom said she was molested when she was little by a brother and it was no big deal."

"No big deal, huh? Did she say if she ever went to counseling? Did she say, Rebecca, who did it to her?"

"No and no. I couldn't get any info out of her, but she said she would go to counseling with me because 'I know it looks bad when two children in the family have declared they were abused by you,'" Rebecca reported.

"Gosh, I just can't believe it," I said and tears came to my eyes once again. It was the most amazing, validating feeling I ever had and it still brings tears to my eyes to this date and always will.

We continued to chat about the children, our rotten husbands—I say that in jest for now—and our houses; we each had moved since we last talked back in 1989 and it was now 1992. We said goodbye, but before I did, I made sure that I could call her anytime and she would call me back. She promised she would call later in the week and tell me what happened in therapy with Mother. She apologized over and over for the way she discarded my claims of abuse and for not being in touch over the years. I explained that all that mattered was that she was here for me now. We talked things out fully and said goodbye.

I lay down on the bed and started to cry in the fetal position. I cried so happily that Rebecca was back in my life and so sorrowfully that she had been out of my life for so long. Steve came in and saw me in the fetal position, so sad one moment and smiling and beaming so blissfully the next, and he said, "Debbie, what is going on?"

"What is going on? Let me tell you about a telephone call I just received!"

I told him the whole story and then he turned toward me with a stunned, shocked look upon his face and he said, "What you've been saying, all the nights I've been up with you and all the hell we've been through, is true. It really happened! It really happened!"

CHAPTER EIGHT

Alexander James

What's that nursery song? Snips and snails and puppy dogs' tails. That's what little boys are made of. I don't know what snips are, but I do know about the other two and that's not all Alex got into! There wasn't a time in his young years that he didn't want to dump, throw, smash, or damage anything in his path. He was all boy. He jumped on the trampoline at eighteen months, he learned to walk on the trampoline before he could on flat ground, he dumped everything imaginable on the trampoline, and then bounced in it. The sprinklers under the trampoline were his favorite. He hated bath time, so sometimes he was washed naked on the trampoline. He generally got his way, even with two brothers and three sisters, because he was so cute and because he had the loudest voice of any of the children. Nobody wanted to hear Alexander cry, no one. He didn't just cry, he immediately went into a raging temper tantrum. When he decided to throw a tantrum, it was the same decibel level as that of rock bands and fireworks.

But when you saw those big brown eyes and the way his lips curled up when he smiled or the way he would share—on occasion—with his siblings, it was heartwarming. The way he sang "It's a Small World After All" and it would come out as "is a smell word afer ul." His brothers taught him by the age of two how to do Michael Jackson dancing to those words. It was just so cute.

He brought home every kind of creature he could fit in his pockets. There were worms, fire ants—everyone thanked him for those—and a dead mouse he held tight in his hand, and I mean real tight, and he said in his cute four-year-old voice, "Can we keep him, Mom?" She got a shoebox and said, "Only while you take a bath." He was scrubbed clean while the mouse was laid to rest up in the woods by his dad. He asked where his "mouth" was and his mom told him she thought he had to go home to take a bath himself. Alex started to cry in the bathtub and even his tears were dirty.

Rebecca was a boy's mom if ever there was one. The boys' dirt, especially Alex's, all day in water and mud and dirt, was okay with her. I had all girls and couldn't even deal with Alex's dirt and I didn't have to deal with him. My girls wore white with pink ribbons and bows in their hair and I would rush the girls into another room before I'd let the plague of dirt be anywhere near them.

I thought at the time Rebecca was neglectful, but I was the one getting so upset over dirt. Laid back and go with the flow Rebecca, while Debbie was being hysterical over in the corner. I made such a big deal over a speck of dirt that my nephews were bringing me worms, bugs, snakes they would throw at my feet as I walked by them, and anything else they could find. Rebecca's landscape around her house was a block of dirt with the house in the middle of all of it. One day, I came back to Rebecca's from doing a little clothes shopping and there were Alex and Bethany, arm in arm, dirty as all get-out.

Rebecca said to me as I got out of the car, "Now before you get angry at Beth, Deb"—grabbing me by my shoulders—"I was left in charge and decided that since Bethany is a bit of a tomboy, she needs to at least touch dirt before she goes home to Portland."

"I let her touch dirt. If she touches under the snow and gets some dirt on her hands, then she's touching dirt."

Rebecca grabbed Bethany by the braids of her hair. "And Beth, what do you have on your hands when you're playing in the snow in the wintertime?"

Bethany said, "Gloves or mittens."

"And Bethany, when do you get to play in dirt at home in Portland, Oregon?" Rebecca asked.

"Never, ever."

"And when do you get to play in the dirt when you are at Aunt Becky's house?"

"When Mom's away and Aunt Becky is in charge of me."

That's when I piped up to argue and my sister said, "Shhhh!" I tried to say another word and Rebecca said, "Shhhh!" We played this little game of Shhhing until we threw both of the little kids into separate bathtubs and waterlogged them both. Alex and Bethany had so much fun. He was five years old and Bethany was almost eight years old and they had a lot of fun that day.

When Rebecca went to therapy with our mother, one of the issues ironed out was whether the children could ever go and see them and go swimming at their house. Mom whittled Rebecca down to where Rebecca said, "Yes, they can go over to your house and go swimming as long as there is never just one of the kids left alone with Dad. Grandpa is never allowed to be with one child alone for any length of time ever. Never, ever!" Mom promised to never let that happen!

So a week later, Mom called and asked if the children could come over and go swimming. Rebecca stalled and she broke down and asked David what he thought. He talked with Mom and she repeated her offer and he was convinced and promised by Dad and Mom that they would never leave any of the children alone with Grandpa Hunter ever and so it was settled. Grandmother Hunter was going to pick them up at noon, on Saturday, then stop and pick up hamburgers for them at McDonald's. They would eat the food at Grandma and Grandpa's and go swimming and then go back home around 5:00 p.m.

Well, that was not what happened that day. What happened, according to Susan, who was ten years old at this time, after swimming, Grandma wanted to take all the kids down to the park. They had been eating Popsicles outside so their swimming suits were dry. They put their clothes on over their suits and then their shoes, only Alex couldn't find his shoes. Everyone had their shoes on and they all looked for Alex's shoes, but they were nowhere to be found.

After a while, Grandma and the kids still couldn't find Alex's shoes. Grandma said, "Well, Alex, we won't be gone very long, so here's a couple of cookies and don't bother Grandpa, he's upstairs sleeping and you stay downstairs and watch cartoons."

Alex agreed and sat down in front of the television. All the kids piled into Grandma's car and she took them to the park. Everything went fine the first ten minutes, but then Grandpa Hunter must have told him to come upstairs or Grandpa went downstairs because for the next hour, something happened to little Alexander that scared him so ferociously that every time he came in contact with an elderly man, Alex would wet himself.

Susan saw something she will never forget. When it was time to go home, everybody started looking for Alex's shoes again. Susan followed Grandma upstairs to Grandma and Grandpa's bedroom and she saw Grandma take Alex's shoes down from her closet shelf. She saw Susan right by her and said she found the shoes in their bedroom, but Susan knows what she saw to this day and will never forget it. Grandma reached up to the shelf high in her closet and took down Alex's sneakers from the closet shelf. Susan stiffened up as Grandma turned and saw her.

Susan said, "Grandma, I just came to tell you that we already looked everywhere downstairs when we looked for them to go the park and couldn't find them."

Grandma said, "I just found them in my bedroom, here on the floor," which Susan knew was a lie.

Susan knew right then she had made a terrible mistake leaving Alex behind and not taking him to the park. She now felt so guilty.

She was the oldest sibling and her mother gave her strict orders that she should never leave one child alone at Grandma's with Grandpa. "Never, ever," her mother said and Grandma had the shoes all the while. Susan knew she would have to explain this event to her mother and it would have to be the truth.

The minute they all hit the door, Alex went up to his mother in a trance and said,

"Mom, do I have to be a grandpa? I don't want to be a grandpa, I don't have to be a grandpa, do I, Mom? I'm not going to be a grandpa, Mom, is that okay, Mom?" He teared up and said it over and over again, faster and more frantic with each breath he took.

Rebecca grabbed Alex gently and said to him, "No, you don't have to be a grandpa, Alex, it's okay, it's okay. Alex, what happened at Grandma and Grandpa's today?"

Alex just kept repeating, "I don't have to be a grandpa, I'm not going to be a grandpa." He either wouldn't say or couldn't say what happened to him. Rebecca scooped him in her arms to soothe him, but couldn't carry him for long because he had grown so much and was now big for his age of six years old. She got as far as the family room couch where his blankie last landed. She tucked him in where he sat and he said, "Mom, don't leave me!" So Rebecca stayed there by him though she wanted to go tell his dad; but first, she wanted to call her friend Jackie, who was an expert in childhood abuse and trauma from her job of working with Children's Hospital in the Child Abuse Screening area as a social worker.

Alex finally fell asleep and she wiggled her arm out from around his body. Then she called Jackie, and they talked about Grandpa getting to him. It seemed like hours, but it was only twenty minutes. They talked about not drilling him on what happened with Grandpa, that it would be better if the experts at Children's Hospital could get him to talk. Jackie said to make him feel safe with Rebecca and to let him know he could tell Rebecca anything and it would be all right. They talked about talking with Susan as to what happened and, if Grandpa did abuse him, whether Rebecca was prepared to put her dad in jail.

Rebecca's mind was racing when she got off the telephone. She told David to put Alex to bed as he was still on the couch, asleep, and he complied. Then she decided she needed to talk to Susan about that day's events. Rebecca knocked on Susan's bedroom door.

Susan said, "Come in."

Rebecca entered the room and said, "Susan, something's wrong with Alex. What went on today at Grandma's and Grandpa's house?"

Susan told her, "Mom, something strange happened."

"What happened, Susan?" Chills ran up Rebecca's spine and she already knew she'd made the wrong decision about letting the kids go over to Grandma and Grandpa's house.

"Well, we couldn't find Alexander's shoes to go with Grandma to the park today, so he had to stay home."

"Susan, I gave you strict instructions not to leave anyone alone at Grandma's, especially today." Rebecca then asked, "Where was Grandpa and, more importantly, where was Alex?"

"Oh, Grandpa was upstairs asleep, so Alex wasn't completely alone. Alex was downstairs in the family room watching cartoons, and when we got back, he was still downstairs, eating the same cookies Grandma left for him and watching TV."

"You are sure he wasn't up in Grandpa's bedroom when you all came home from the park?" Rebecca said.

"No, he was downstairs in front of the same TV when we got back from the park," Susan repeated. "But then I saw Grandma lie."

"What do you mean, Grandma lied?'

"When we were all ready to come home, we started looking for Alex's shoes again and then I followed Grandma up to her bedroom and I saw her take Alexander's shoes down from the shelf up in her closet and then she told me she found his shoes in her bedroom on the floor, but I promise I saw her take them down from the shelf up high in her closet. Now isn't that a lie, Mom?'

"Yes, honey, it sure is," Rebecca said, and then Susan started to cry.

Susan said to her mother, "Mom, I didn't think Grandma would ever lie to me!'

Rebecca hugged Susan and whispered, "Neither did I, baby, neither did I."

The next day, Rebecca called our mother and told her that what she and Dad did to Alex was child abuse. "You are an accomplice to the crime, Mother."

"Just what do you think went on here yesterday and how can you say it was child abuse?" Mom said.

Rebecca said, "You knew where Alex's shoes were all the time, because Susan said she saw you take the shoes off the shelf in your closet. And I gave you strict instructions not to leave any child at home alone with my dad and the first time you have the younger group of children, you leave Alex at your house. How could you do that, Mom?"

"We were only gone forty min—" Mom was interrupted by Rebecca.

"Mom, you were gone an hour, according to Susan. One hour!"

"Well then, Susan can't tell time and she's the one who is lying."

"Mom, as of today, I am severing all ties to you for me and for the children!"

"Oh, Rebecca, don't do that," and Mom started her manipulative crying, but it didn't make Rebecca feel one bit sorry and it was something she wanted to do and probably should have done from the beginning of her memories and her confrontation with them.

"Goodbye, Mother!" and she hung up the telephone on her mom.

Rebecca began to cry softly, not because she would never have the house they promised to leave to her in their will, nor the mother or the dad she longed for so hard. She cried because her children would have no grandparents and because her little six-year-old Alex was probably abused yesterday by Grandpa. If only she had known her mother couldn't be trusted. She would never have guessed that her mother would be an accomplice to child abuse.

It took Rebecca a few weeks to get an appointment with Children's Hospital's Child Abuse Care Center. In the meantime, Alex's behavior got more intense. Whenever he came in contact with a man in his seventies or eighties, he would tell his younger brother, "Ryan, see that grandpa? He's going to die. Don't look at him for very long because then you'll die too. I'm never going to be a grandpa." Ryan was too young to understand Alex, but just the same, Alex was driven to point to all men who were getting old and make his remarks about never wanting to be a grandpa, over and over again.

Alex had a dentist appointment about two weeks after the abuse incident, and although the dentist office was not one of Alex's favorite places to go, he usually remembered the toy from the dentist's toy chest, and lunch at McDonald's usually did the trick to get him to go. Not this time. He wailed, he shook, and he kept crying out, "My mouth hurts," or "I can't go, don't make me go. My mouth will hurt." No matter what Rebecca said, did, or promised, he would not go. He said, "My mouth hurts, it hurts right now."

Rebecca said, "Alex, you aren't at the dentist right now."

"It hurts, it hurts now," and he covered his mouth. They went back and forth with him and the dentist and his mouth hurting, but

Rebecca couldn't understand it. He wouldn't even let any of the kids or Rebecca or David brush his teeth; he wouldn't open his mouth, no matter what any of them said. Rebecca didn't get that part of Alexander's behavior until they had their first appointment at Children's Hospital.

The first appointment consisted of a social worker, Kathleen, and Alex just going in a playroom, where Alex drew a picture of a house, a swimming pool, and Grandpa's face out of the upstairs window where their bedroom was. When the social worker asked him whose house it was, he said, "Grandma's house." When the social worker asked, "Is that the swimming pool you got to go play in?" he said, "It is Grandma's swimming pool," but when she asked, "Who lives there with Grandma?" Alex started getting a panic attack and said his mouth hurt, his mouth hurt. When the social worker asked who was that in the upstairs window, he screamed, "My mouth hurts," and threw up, which ended the session.

* * *

In between sessions, there was more pointing out the old men and talk of dying, and his mouth hurt more whenever Rebecca would try to pry something out of Alex. His behavior at school was deteriorating. He bullied kids around and his grades were slipping. Now they were investigating whether he had a learning disability or if this event with Grandpa had a huge impact upon him or both. It was determined after months of follow-up that both problems existed. He was hugely impacted in first grade by what Grandpa Walt Hunter did to him, and further grades he got illustrated that he couldn't read well. Rebecca was beside herself, trying to raise six other children, keep up with the family business, and do all the laundry, the cooking, and the cleaning, all with a two-year-old running around, mostly naked half the time he was awake. To survive, she began teaching the older children how to do the laundry, the cooking, and the cleaning and also some babysitting.

Soon, it was time for Alexander to go to his next appointment at Children's Hospital. She let Alex stay home from school that day as he thought he was sick and "cannot go, huh, Mom?" when she lovingly but firmly said, "Alexander, you are going to Children's today!" He reverted with his behavior at home by sucking his thumb again and wetting the bed occasionally. Every time an appointment was coming up, he said to his younger brother, Ryan, over and over the Grandpa and the dying business. Alex's small world was closing down and Rebecca stayed up at night, worrying about what was going to turn things around.

At his second appointment, he was repetitious with his words and behaviors and he came into the playroom with one hand around his blankie and a thumb in his mouth. He didn't want to color, he didn't want to play with the boy and girl dolls, so he felt safe with Legos. He started to build a building, but he changed his mind halfway through and changed it into a war ship. It wasn't always about the activity they were doing; it was about how safe he felt. Alex repeated that he was never going to be a grandpa because he was never going to get married and definitely not going to have children because that's how you end up a grandpa. He had it all figured out and was not going to be a grandpa.

Alex got more anxious and irritated the more he was pressured to talk about his grandpa, Grandpa Hunter. He began scratching at the walls, saying, "Where is my mommy? I want to see her. She's going to die. Where is she? My mouth hurts. My mouth hurts! Where is Mommy?" By now, he was in a full-fledged panic attack, crying, hyperventilating, one hand holding his mouth and the other hand on the garbage can. Then he threw up. The door opened and relief came. Rebecca said, "I'm here, I'm here."

Rebecca, Jackie, and Kathleen's supervisor had all been watching behind a colored glass window, and Rebecca was going through hell. Rebecca begged them to let her go to him. Finally, when Alex threw up, she flung the door to her room open and yanked his door open and they were together, at last. Jackie comforted both of them, for she knew what happened to little Alexander was horrific and it was killing Rebecca.

Alex was supposed to be playing in the play area, but he snuck up on his mother and Jackie to scare them and he overheard them discussing Rebecca's abuse, her confrontation with her parents, and her terrible decision in thinking she could trust her mom to obey the only boundary that Rebecca asked them to honor. Grandma had immediately turned around and betrayed Rebecca and served Alex up on a platter for Grandpa to go in for the kill; the killing of his little soul. Alex grabbed Rebecca's leg and they said their goodbyes to Jackie and went to their car to go home.

With Alex overhearing what Jackie and his mother were talking about when he was supposed to be in the play area, he asked his mother, "Mom, if you knew Grandpa was such a bad guy, why did you send me to his house? Mom, how come you sent me, knowing he was so dangerous?"

Rebecca had to pull off the road as she began to cry and said, "Alexander, I made a mistake! I thought I could trust her. I made a mistake," and clutched his little hand.

"You mean Grandma?"

"Yes, Alex. I mean Grandma. I thought she would obey my only rule to not leave any of my children alone with him and she promised me and then she turned around and broke that promise immediately. I'm so sorry, Alex, I'm so very, very sorry!"

"I think Grandpa is a bad guy. I don't ever want to see him again. But can I still go swimming at their house with you?"

"No, Alex, we can't go to their house, any of us, ever again! We'll all go to Water World or the Legos place again. How does that sound?"

"Okay, that sounds good!"

***

The third visit came sooner after the previous appointment than the second one did, so they didn't lose any momentum in Alex's near confession. The goal was to see if Alex could confess to Grandpa's sin in order to prosecute him criminally. Children's Hospital videotapes each session so in case the child says all the right words, they can use it in court to criminally charge the offender.

The social workers at Children's Hospital were prepared to try to start the way they had Alex start before, but when Rebecca arrived, Alex clung to her and did not want her to go away, so they gave in and let Rebecca stay in the session with the social worker and Alexander mainly working together. He decided to draw during this session, so he drew a picture of his dog Sparky and showed his dog off to the social worker, Kathleen. Rebecca inched herself away from the drawing table so that Kathleen and Alex could work together. She thought she might sneak out through the door, but that never happened.

Kathleen was learning just how to help get his ideas, thoughts, and worries out without putting ideas into his head. She said, "What do you like to do, Alex?"

Alex immediately replied, "I like swimming."

Kathleen said, "I like swimming too! Where do you like to go swimming?"

"The beach."

"I like the beach on hot summer days. But I live far away from the beach, so sometimes I'll go swimming in my apartment's swimming pool."

Alex immediately piped up and said, "I love swimming pools too. Maybe I could come to your apartment's swimming pool and we could go swimming with me together." Alex got so excited, his words didn't always come out correctly.

"Well," said Kathleen, "we could do that, but I live a long way away from you and you have lots of brothers and sisters who would want to come also and my swimming pool might not be big enough for everyone. Is there a place close to you that you could go swimming?"

"Oh, there was a place I liked to go swimming, but Mommy says we can't go there anymore," Alex said in a really sad and whispering tone.

Alexander saw his mom what felt like a mile away from him and he ran and sat on her lap with his favorite nice blanket and Theodore, his really nice stuffed bear they bought at the gift shop downstairs after their last appointment here at Children's Hospital. Kathleen summoned Alex back to the table by saying, "You know, Alexander, this might be your last visit here today. Can you come draw me a picture of a swimming pool so I can put it in my office to always remember you by?"

"Only if Mommy comes with me."

Rebecca said, "I'm right behind you, buddy." She made it look like she moved closer, but she didn't move much at all.

"Okay," said Kathleen, "what color water do you want?"

Alexander and Kathleen sat and colored swimming pools. When they were done with their swimming pools, Kathleen said, "I'm going to cut my pool out and put mine by my apartment picture I have in my office. Where are you going to put your swimming pool? It has to go to its home. Where does it belong?"

"At my grandma and grandpa's house."

"I just happen to have that picture of your grandma and grandpa's house. Does your swimming pool belong here, Alex?"

Alex nodded and whimpered a "Yes."

"Here's the house, let's glue that swimming pool right here," and Kathleen was pointing to the back of Grandpa's house. "Then you can go swimming there…"

"No, no, I don't want to give you my swimming pool. I don't want to go back to that house."

"Why not, Alex, why don't you want to go back to that house, Alexander? Alex, let's put that pool in this house," pointing to Grandpa's house, "then you can swim in it."

"Mommy, Mommy, bad things happen there, bad things."

Rebecca said as Alex fell into her arms, "Alex, why can't we put the swimming pool back in Grandma and Grandpa's house?"

"My mouth hurts," Alex began wailing, "my mouth hurts." He held both sides of his mouth in his tiny little hands and fingers and burrowed his head under his mom's arm and then he said, "Because that bad man will hurt your mouth and tell you die die die." He was quiet now and exhausted. Sweat dripped down his brow and the back of his neck and then there was this faint little voice that said, "Can we go home now, Mommy?" It was barely audible as his thumb was in his mouth. He finally looked up at his mother.

She said, "Yes, Alex, we can go home now. Can you tell us who the bad guy is?"

He shook his head and stood up and went to the door with his teddy bear and his mommy's hand and they said goodbye to Kathleen forever. They did not get the words in the right order and he never could say who the bad guy was. He was finished and he would never talk about it again.

Yes, it's true, we had only one way to have Dad put in jail, but it didn't work. Our only hope was Alex, and the little boy had been terrified into silence, almost. We had enough evidence for us and for Kathleen, but we couldn't put that monster in jail.

No wonder it is so difficult to put one of these pedophiles in prison and keep them there; technicalities, the cop looked at them this way or that way. The little child couldn't say, "Judge Jones, Mr. Thomas L. Smith, social security number 555-55-5555. He had me perform oral sex on him at three-oh-six p.m. on Friday, October 24th, 2014, at his home in his garage, while we looked at naked children in various positions. We did this for approximately twenty-five minutes whereupon he then threatened to kill my dear sweet mother and cut off my right arm if I told anyone. That's how strong and brave I am at the ripe old age of five. Now can you please sentence him to prison for six months and let him then live right across from an elementary school or a park where we can start this all over again, but maybe the next time, he'll kill the child. Lucky dog, and then we can put him away for a little bit longer until he gets out and molests, rapes little girls and little boys, and then kills them until he becomes a mass child molester and killer. Oh, please, Judge, please. Oh no, never mind me, I'll just spend my life in and out of therapy, hospitals for suicide attempts, because he told me such wonderful attributes I have and he helped lower my self-esteem so it will be on the floor, unless I'm one of those courageous kids who learns to just expect less out of life and live with depression the rest of my life. Maybe I'll join a monastery and become a priest—oooh, aaah—can I do that? Please, can I, can I do that?"

Alex was lucky, he had a family that loved him, but despite the help they got for him for school, he was diagnosed with a learning and emotional disability. He struggled for another six months or so with Grandpa's abuse, with nightmares, the Grandpa talk, and sucking his thumb. But then it slowly dissipated and life normalized more for him. He has never said that Grandpa abused him or how he was abused. He has struggled in his life. I don't want the reader to think that when he turned seven years old, everything was peachy and the effects of the abuse were gone. They never have been. He has fought for his life to stabilize and it has. He lives far away from home but is happy, likes his job, loves where he lives, and likes life. Whether he has continuing problems, he's not saying, just like when he was six. He keeps those things to himself.

And how did this affect Susan's life and Rebecca's life? Well, Rebecca will never get over what Mom and Dad did to Alexander out of revenge. Revenge has caused her long-term health problems and pity for what Alex has been through. It has also grown a bond between her and Alex that nothing can break, and there is also a strong bond between Susan, Alex, and Rebecca. Only the three of them know what that experience was like. Susan has put the abuse that Alex suffered onto the responsible parties, Grandma and Grandpa Hunter, but it will always be in the forefront of her responsibility in the experience that if only she had insisted that Alexander couldn't go to the park that fateful day, she wouldn't be going either. The day would have turned out completely different. But can you really expect a ten-year-old to be that responsible and stand up to her grandmother? I think that would be child abuse!

CHAPTER NINE

Power

Rebecca went to her stake president about our situation with Dad and the abuse issues. More importantly, she went to tell him about Alex and how our father was still abusing children,

"Hi, Sister Rapp, how are you today?" President Gunnerson said in a cheerful but somber manner. He was a warm and friendly man, but very reserved and quiet in his own way. If there had been a fire in the church building and everyone had to evacuate quickly, you would find President Gunnerson calmly but carefully instructing people in a sober manner to get out quickly.

"Hello, President Gunnerson. I'm fine, how about you?"

"Good. Good." He nodded after shaking Rebecca's hand and sitting back down. "What can I do for you today?" he inquired.

"Well, this is very hard to talk about." And tears came to her eyes. He offered her a Kleenex and encouraged her to go on.

Rebecca said, "My family is not the typical dutiful 'perfect-looking' family as everyone thinks they are."

"Your and David's family?" President Gunnerson said.

"No, I mean my parents, Walton and June Hunter, and me and my sister Deborah and Alex, my six-year-old."

"What do you mean, Sister Rapp?"

"When Deborah and I were young and Alex more recently, we were all three sexually abused by my father. I remember him mostly fondling my private areas, Deborah remembers being molested and raped at the age of nine and Alex last year."

"What happened between your father and Alex?'

"Well, we're not completely sure. Alex's behavior drastically changed after a visit to my parents one day and he was left alone with Grandpa for an hour. He's been up to Children's Hospital where Jackie works. He says he never wants to go back to Grandpa's house and when asked why, he clenches his mouth and says, 'My mouth hurts, my mouth hurts.' He has gone back to wetting the bed, sucking his thumb, and won't allow any of us to brush his teeth. He has never said, 'Grandpa did THIS to me,' but it's pretty obvious to Jackie and me that something terrible has happened in Alex's life."

"Wow. Wow, that's a lot to take in all at once," President Gunnerson said.

A long pause was taken, followed by Rebecca saying, "I don't know if this makes any difference to my father's church standing, but he also had affairs years ago with a number of women that he never got forgiveness from anyone for. I bring this all up to tell you that your daughter, Tracy, often goes to my parents' house and I don't think she should go on her own, even if they insist she bring a friend and come swimming. My children won't be going and I have felt strongly that Tracy should not go either."

"No, she definitely won't be going to their house, but I will be, to discuss all of this over with them. We are probably going to have to hold a Church Disciplinary Hearing regarding your dad. This is really shocking. I don't know what to say except I'm sorry and please let me know if anything changes with Alex's story. You and your sister Deborah will be getting letters if we decide to hold a Court on him, and you let us know if anything else comes up or changes."

While he took it in stride, he was even more silent and quiet than Rebecca had ever seen him. She could tell he was in shock, but anyone that didn't know him would have thought it was no big deal to him. Rebecca thanked him for listening. He said, while walking Rebecca to the car, "Don't worry, Tracy will never go there again. That's for sure! I truly appreciate this information."

Rebecca telephoned me when she returned home and told me about her meeting with the stake president, and now the ball was in his court as to whether or not a Disciplinary Counsel would be held on Dad. I feel the need to explain what a Disciplinary Counsel is like. They are often referred to as courts of love. It is similar to a court regarding repentance and membership in the church. Things such as administering blessings for illnesses, a father's blessing, and the prayer over the bread and water during the main meeting are all things that happen when you have the priesthood powers from the Church of Jesus Christ of Latter-day Saints. Twelve men are in attendance at the court. Men from the stake presidency to bishops to men who are high counselors are called upon to be there. Please refer to Appendix

A for an in-depth definition of these callings. They are different jobs in the church through inspiration and have different levels of the priesthood powers.

They state the charges against the accused; half of the brethren are for the accused through prayer and love and the other half are for the church and standing up for the church standards through prayer and love. They ask the accused if he thinks he is guilty or not guilty and for his reasoning of his beliefs about his guilt or innocence. Then they bring in witnesses testifying on the behalf of the accused or witnesses that testify to the guilt of the accused.

These twelve men make a decision regarding the accuser's guilt or innocence, using a lot of prayer and love in the process. If the person is found guilty, there are a number of options that the stake president can take to help that member of the church repent or not continue in his pathway of sin as a member of the church. Some of the options are innocent of all charges, probation with certain conditions stipulated, or disfellowshipped, which can be like probation, only certain rights and privileges are on hold until you repent and ask for your membership back, usually six months or longer.

The fourth possibility is you will be excommunicated, which takes your membership in the church away until you go through all the steps a non-member of the church would have to pursue and more to repent and come back to have your membership reinstated. You must have the missionary lessons and discuss what you're doing to repent. You must be baptized and confirmed in the church once again. This process can take years. You are stripped of all your priesthood powers, such as giving church blessings (for example, the blessings explained above) or performing all rituals such as going through the temple. Losing the priesthood powers and his church membership would seriously injure my father and his ego.

We did receive letters for a Church Court or a Disciplinary Counsel on my father, and I have included the letter giving the date and time. It was sent to all involved individuals in this case. I know Rebecca and I received a letter and my parents received a letter, and Dr. Ellsworth received a letter regarding his therapy and why he thought I was abused by Dad. I was not privy to who else might have been invited.

My therapist at the time was a very loving, caring woman and we worked together for one year or more. We practiced meditation to Dr. Ellsworth's music tape and I visualized being at complete peace and love, picturing angels of love protecting me, swirling around me, keeping me safe from my parents and any other negative persons or environment that might occur. Little did we know how strong I would need to be and that I would find negative situations when I would need angels to keep my cool.

May 19, 1993

Mrs. Debbie Marsh
13284 SE 119th Court
Clackamas, Oregon 97015

Dear Sister Marsh:

The El Cajon Stake Presidency is considering formal disciplinary action against your father, Walton W. Hunter, as a result of the charge of moral conduct unbecoming a member of the Church.

You are cordially invited to attend the disciplinary council to present your charges and give evidence to your father and the council. If you choose, you may also provide other witnesses to support your charges. However, anyone other than yourself, will need to be cleared by me prior to the date of the council.

The council will convene on Sunday, June 6, 1993, at 9:00 a.m., in the High Council Room of the El Cajon Stake Center, 1270 South Orange Avenue, El Cajon, California. You should be in attendance beginning at 10:00 a.m. Please enter through the door that gives direct access to the Stake Offices on the north side of the building.

If you have any questions or require added instruction, please feel free to contact me at one of the numbers listed below.

Sincerely,

Allan M. Gunnerson
Stake President

Telephone: (619) 444-2620
(619) 582-9601

I was very involved at this time with my brother's wife, Diana Hunter. She was very involved with me and my sexual abuse case against my parents and supported me through the day before the Disciplinary Council. We talked on the phone daily and she really wanted me to "get them excommunicated," as she put it. She and my parents had been at odds ever since she married Wayne. Mom was jealous of her taking my brother away and splitting up the closeness between my mom and Wayne. Because she would not leave her children, one boy and four girls, and work outside the home, my father thought she was trailer trash who was lazy. She called me the day before the Disciplinary Counsel.

She said, "Hey, girl, are you nervous about tomorrow?"

"I am a bit. My therapist, Pat, prepared me pretty well though. Instead of thinking when will this be over, because I hear they're long and boring, I'm going to read about the angels in the Bible and pretend they are all around me," I said.

"Just think of me as one of your angels, onward and upward, giving you peace and serenity. Remember how I tickle my girls' arms and it relaxes them and makes them in an almost hypnotic state? Well, just pretend I am there, doing that to you. Relaxing you more and more," Diana said.

"You're almost putting me to sleep now. I didn't sleep well last night!"

"Well, take some of the bee pollen pills tonight. They can do just about anything. They will relax you so you can sleep and also think about what you will say tomorrow. I wish I could be there with you," Diana said.

"I know. You've been there every step of the way. I can't believe Wayne would not let you come out for me," I said.

"I can't be there with you, but my love and heart will be."

We hung up and I felt so blessed to have a friend and sister-in-law like her in my life.

Rebecca was a nervous wreck and she snapped at me and the kids a couple of times. I could tell she was at the end of her rope because she never snaps. I tried speaking to her about how tense she was and she admitted she was. Two more children came to her with demands or fights and she left things wherever they were and told Susan she was leaving for a couple of hours. We got in the car and went to 7-Eleven for drinks and some candy and headed for the beach. I had flown down from Portland, Oregon, where we got rain almost every day of the year and as soon as we got back into the car, it started raining. Halfway to the beach, it was pouring buckets.

Rebecca remarked, "We never have rain like this. It will be over in a minute or two." Fifteen minutes later, sheets of rain water poured all over the car. "It's because you brought it from Oregon with you."

"Well, are we here? Want to eat candy and sit in the car or turn around and go home?" I said.

"I am not ready to go home yet. Seven big and little monsters to go home to. No, no, please don't make me go back there. I am definitely not ready to go home. Let's commit hari-kari, as they used to say," Rebecca said.

"No, we need to deal with tomorrow and eat our candy in the car," I said.

"What about tomorrow?" Rebecca said.

"I'm quite nervous about facing Dad tomorrow, aren't you?" I said.

"Yes, but what can we do about it? It comes down to what the two of them say and what Cynthia says," Rebecca said.

"No, I think she won't come," I said. "I really don't think she will come."

"I think Wayne might come," Rebecca said.

"But when I talked with Diana today, she didn't say he was coming," I said as I opened another candy bar.

"But what if he is here, would she tell you then?" Rebecca said. "Give me a bite of that one."

"Well, I think she would. If he was coming, I would expect her to tell me. I would be pretty angry if she didn't tell me and she kept it from me. I'd feel so betrayed," I replied. "I know that Dr. Ellsworth wrote a letter with answers to some of the questions they would have in the Disciplinary Council about me and my therapy. He said I did a lot of therapy around my father sexually abusing me, but I might need more," I said.

"Look, it's stopped raining, let's go for a walk on the beach, then we'll go home," Rebecca said.

"Sounds good to me," I said.

Even though it was a bit on the windy side and a little cool, we grabbed our sweaters and walked briskly on the sand that was hit by the water frequently. We continued to talk about our feelings of seeing and facing Dad and mostly how I needed to stay calm and keep my chaotic and rage-filled feelings in check. I must feel that angel that came to me when I was nine years old come to me as strong as when I felt him long ago. Rebecca seemed calmer than I was, but I attributed that to the way she did everything—minimized and shoved down her feelings.

We spent a quiet evening at home, watching a movie and not talking—each in our own world. Rebecca was not much of a talker normally. The movie was unremarkable and I went to bed early. I thought about calling Diana again at home, but it was a little too late for that. I had to take a sleeping pill to get to sleep that night, but walking at the beach that day must have worn me out because I was asleep as soon as my head hit the pillow, so the walk and the pill were both effective.

The next day, Rebecca was up early, ironing dress clothes for her children to wear to church and for herself. I ironed my dress, curled my hair, and got dressed. David would take the children to their ward for church. We were to be at a different church building by 11:30. We got in the car and drove in complete silence. I tried to reach out to Rebecca, but I think she was too busy driving and praying to even hear my questions. I checked my makeup and dress one final time and went inside with Rebecca to the guillotine. Rebecca was in such a trance that she left me in the dust. It gave the appearance that we came separately to the Disciplinary Counsel.

Before I could catch up to Rebecca, a busy little man asked my name. I replied, "Deborah Marsh," and I was whisked off into a separate room from anyone else. I thought this was odd that I needed to be alone in a different room than Rebecca, like we were going to conspire together in a plot against Dad now. The busy little man who put me into my room was now finding rooms for the others who were arriving. There was my mother in her suit that she wore in a picture of her and Dad that she sent me recently and which I tore into shreds and discarded like you would an old shoe. I just got a glimpse of Dad's back in a different shade of blue suit. More people were coming in and I thought I should close the door, but I wanted one more peek. Remember, I was the kid who snuck around to see or hear anything that was going on in the family.

Well, my last look was my worst betrayal and, years later, it still rubs me raw and my heart hurts for what Diana, my sister-in-law, my friend, my guardian angel, supposedly did to me. I could somehow forgive my mom for what she did to me when I was a child, but I will never forgive Diana for betraying me so much. Walking in was Wayne, my brother, and arm in arm with him was Diana, his wife.

I shut the door immediately so they could not see me. This really threw me for a loop and I started having my first real panic attack. I couldn't breathe, my heart was beating fast, I was getting dizzy, and I was getting warm all over. I'd never had a panic attack before. I found my way to a padded chair and tried to take in a couple of long, deep breaths. I really tried to let my body relax and I opened the window. I began to relax, my heart stopped pounding, I wasn't dizzy any longer, and I started feeling cool air coming through the open window. This didn't happen for a while. It took time to get myself calmed down and out of my attack; now I was just crying.

What was Diana doing here? How did she talk to me at noon yesterday, wishing me good luck and to say she would be praying for me, and then turn around and be there by 11:30 a.m. on Sunday for and on behalf of them? How did I know she was there for them? Mom took her other arm and squeezed her hand tight. My mind couldn't wrap around a betrayal of this magnitude. I saw her go with Mom and Dad into their one room together. I must have heard my angel or angels calling me and saying, "She is insignificant compared to the work you have to do here today." So magically, it was gone. The heartache, the fury, the pit in my stomach, just gone, and I concentrated now more than ever on Dad and the task before me.

I was brought into a different room where the main body of the court was held, and Rebecca was there, Mom and Dad were there, but Wayne and Diana were not there; they were tucked away, I guess in Mom and Dad's room or a room of their own. There was no little sister, Cynthia, either. I think she decided to miss the party this time. Of course, I can't blame her; what a long, fun party this was going to be. There were many men already in the room when I walked in. All in white shirts, dark ties, and suits. Sitting formally and somber. I sat down in a chair. Numb. My eyes met everyone's, but no one's. I couldn't look at my parents in the eyes yet, so it was a good thing that President Gunnerson was sitting where he was. I could focus on him and his words. He welcomed everyone here and spoke about this court.

President Gunnerson said, "This is a circle of love. A court of love in that if the accused individual, Walton Wahn Hunter, is innocent, hopefully, there could be no hard feelings and we all will have done our jobs well. However, if he is guilty, there can be love also, to help the guilty party repent and come back into the church through hard work and sheer determination because he feels love from the church leadership and church members and he desires to be a member of The Church of Jesus Christ of Latter-day Saints." He went on to say, "Our words today should be kind and respectful to one another and although there may be anger in our tone, we can pray and keep it to a minimum." I felt five years old and I needed a booster seat to see everyone in the room and my thumb to comfort me. Obviously, I didn't do either of these, but I felt my every breath was scrutinized.

After we had prayer and instructions, we were escorted back to the separate rooms, alone, that we were in before, and we had to wait until it became each one's time to go into the big room and make our allegations.

It seemed like we each waited an interminable amount of time in our rooms alone—except Mom and Dad, who were either in their separate room being supported by Wayne and Diana or in the main meeting room with all the brethren—but it was only a few hours. I imagined angels with beautiful white flowing dresses and robes that glistened circling around me. I said, "Give me strength, dear Lord.

Help me be not frightened, but calm and serene in thy eyes so I may go and do the things we were meant to do on our life's journey. Please, dear Lord." I reached out and touched the angel right next to me. Even though they were not physically there, I knew they could feel me and see and comfort me.

Then the hall monitor man led me into the main church court room where everyone was, to give my accusation while sitting directly opposite of my father so we had to look each other in the eyes while we spoke. I sat straight up, as tall as a 5'2" woman can be. My hands were on the table, interlocked with each other and as tight as they could be. Both feet were tippy-toed as the chair was too high for me. My hands were where all the nervous energy was and they stayed interlocked and clenched the whole time. I had to give the charges of rape to my father and address him straight in the face as asked by the stake president, President Gunnerson. I think it was the singularly bravest situation I have ever been in and I handled it considerably well, given the fact that I was dissociating tremendously from being so nervous and saying the actual words of molest and rape to my father's face. It was the amount of emotional energy and physical restraint as casting a spell on a baby, only this baby was not innocent; he was as guilty as Satan would have been to Jesus.

The stake president let my father have his say first and then I was to respond to what he said. Guess what he said: "She's crazy!" Just what he told me he would say if I ever told anyone about our secret times together. He elaborated, of course, by saying I was a liar, I never told the truth; even when I was little, they caught me telling lies. "She is absolutely crazy, she's been hospitalized several times and attempted suicide a dozen times or more." He enumerated on my craziness, listing all the times I did odd or crazy things in great detail. He and Mother must have stayed up late at night several times to remember the things I did because of my turmoil or depression and then exaggerated by ten times what actually happened in my life, and then some total lies were sprinkled in for good measure.

Then it was my turn to speak. I was overwhelmed by his enormous list of what accusations he blamed me for, and I was just faced with a history of many things I did that were unstable. At first, I was speechless, but then the few words I had to say seemed perfect for the situation. I said, "Many of the things he said today are true, but the reason they are true is because he raped me when I was a child." And as I said it, I looked straight into his eyes so he would know I wasn't afraid anymore, but I was very nervous. I still thought of Dad as a great wizard who could twirl around the room, draped in black robes with a wicked look on his face and a golden staff in both hands, waving it around and saying, "I look at you men and my daughter down there, accusing me of horrendous acts. Of course I did these malicious acts for I am all about evil. I praise Satan in his glorious abominations unto man that me and his followers get what they want and deserve. Satan is the way and God knows this." He would then be lifted up with his staff high above him and electricity and booming thunder would occur and then he would say some warning and angry words in another language and all of our heads would fall off and we would become death incarnate. But now I wasn't that nervous. I blew it way out of proportion. Then Dad was able to refute what I said. Of course, what could he say? He scoffed at what I said and denied all charges. I don't remember the exact quote or words he said, but he did refute it.

Then the brethren in the room were able to ask questions. All I remember is one man asked what Dr. Ellsworth's therapy was about or what was it like? I explained it as simply as I could: "Dr. Ellsworth believes there is a positive self in each of us and there is often a negative self also. When we are born, we are all positive, but as we grow up, our parents or other people throughout our childhood help us develop a negative self that can be small or large. They help create this negative self by putting us down, yelling at us; other kids in our lives may call us names or bully us and it can have a number of instances or situations. The goal in therapy is to become as real or positive as we can be and learn from others and our own mistakes." Then another man asked me, "What do you think your mother will say about your dad's affairs with other women?"

"She will definitely deny these affairs. Mother lives in complete denial," I said.

I thought that these were a group of strangers I would never see again, but Rebecca knew most of the men because they lived in her ward or area. How much more difficult would it be for Rebecca when she had to face and answer questions from this multitude of men who were her neighbors? I also wondered what lies Dad would make up and accuse Rebecca of when she came in this room.

They led me back to the same room. I was proud of myself. I stayed calm, didn't go ballistic when he listed all I did because I was crazy. I answered soft-spoken, given that I often speak louder than the normal person does, and I gave simple answers to the charges and the questions they asked. I was very proud and I immediately imagined angels singing in a heavenly choir for me. It was the Halleluiah Chorus they were singing, which was very appropriate.

Then there was more waiting. I was just about done waiting, so I opened the door and there was the hall monitor and I asked if I could go to the bathroom. He escorted me to the bathroom and I came out and he was gone. So I walked into the foyer or lobby to see what time it was and realized we had been here five hours. I walked quickly back to my room, but as I passed, I saw Rebecca in the same seat I was in when I made my accusation, so I realized it was her turn to make whatever accusations she was going to say.

It's odd that Rebecca and I had all the time in the world to discuss the events of that day the past couple of days I'd been with her, but we didn't talk at all about what we were going to say and what our "stories" would be. Jackie told Rebecca that we should go to the beach or play games. Rebecca loves to read the scriptures; that's why we went to the beach in the pouring rain on Saturday and brought the scriptures with us. So we in no way prepared for the Disciplinary

Council and we're glad. Hopefully, it didn't sound rehearsed or prepared.

Rebecca told me after the Disciplinary Council that Dad told the men that Rebecca was divorced from her first husband and that she had a long-standing affair with another man after her marriage. Our father was trying to paint her into the "loose" woman theory. He didn't lie with Rebecca, but she was still nervous, just combating those charges.

So I was crazy and she was a slut. Is that any way for a "loving" father to act toward his daughters? He was not human, he was a sociopath. A loving father would have come to therapy in Oregon, a loving father would not have accused us of being crazy and loose, a loving father would have said, "Where is the misunderstanding, sweetheart? I didn't do the things you say I did." He would have been more loving, more hurt, and more genuine. If he really loved us, he would not have attacked us like he did, at least with me. But remember what Dr. Stout said: sociopaths do not love, they act like they do. So he had been shakable. If he was playing such a good part to act like he loved his daughters, then you would think he would act that part and let the brethren know how much he loved us. Hurt, yes; demonic toward his daughters was not good in brethren's eyes!

About an hour after I came back from the bathroom, the sweet hall monitor came with Rebecca to say we could go home now. We had been there for six hours with no scriptures (dumb on our part), no church book or magazine to read, nothing but my purse to clean out. I did have a garbage pail in the room, so my purse was clean and organized. I had a wiping cloth so even the inside of my purse was clean.

We walked quickly out of the building when our part was over and drove back to Rebecca's home, nervously giggling like school girls who just got the meanest teacher in big trouble with the principal and board members finally, after all these long suffering years. It was good to talk about what went on inside the Church Court and how that was the bravest thing we ever did in our whole lives. (Even till the date this book was published, it's the bravest thing we ever did.) To face a monster and twelve men's serious faces, judging and examining our facial expressions, our body language, and our words was dreadful. I very much felt like I was being judged, not Dad.

Rebecca and I were not able to talk much when we got home because there were seven hungry mouths to feed, plus three hungry adults. Rebecca fixed dinner and we all ate. I could have used a little more talking time, which soothes me, but Rebecca likes to go inward and not talk so I called my husband, Steve, and told him all about it. All the details of how long it took and that Rebecca and I had not expected my dad to be so confrontational and attacking as he was. Just when I was about to hang up the phone, there was a knock at their front door. I looked at the clock and it was 9:00 p.m. I thought that was strange, because anyone that knows Rebecca's family knows to come to the back door. The front door has tall weeds and grass and you can't even see the walkway to the front door.

I walked into Rebecca's living room and she was speaking with President Gunnerson at the doorway. I spoke up and said hello to him. Rebecca asked him to come in and sit down, which he did, and when he spoke, he spoke very softly, probably so the children didn't overhear the news he had to tell us.

He said, "Sisters, we just dismissed from the Disciplinary Council and I'm on my way home, but I told the other brethren that I would stop by and let you two know what happened…what our decision was regarding your father."

Rebecca said, "Wow, you went this late, you must be very tired."

President Gunnerson said, "We had a lot of praying to do," and a gentle smile came across his face. "Well, we excommunicated him."

Rebecca asked, "How did Mom and Dad take the news?"

"Your father was very stoic and your mother just kind of fell apart."

I said, "Well, that's too bad."

President Gunnerson said, "Well, I better get off to my family. I'm sorry you sisters had to be there most of the day."

"That's okay," Rebecca and I said in unison.

"Thanks for coming by so late," Rebecca said.

And we closed the door and it was all over. The one event we were so scared to do all of our lives was over. We had climbed the mountain, looked the dragon squarely in the face, and slayed him dead. Well, maybe not dead, but seriously wounded. We weren't out to kill my father, but we did want him excommunicated. We just wanted the hypocrisy to stop. If he wanted to go on looking the part of an upstanding citizen and church member, we would always remember the truth; he was a child molester. We couldn't stop him from doing things he shouldn't be doing; that was up to him.

So seeing Dad's church powers go away was as good as it was going to get. As President Gunnerson said, "It was better that Walt die not a member of this church and have an opportunity to go to heaven, ready to repent and ask for forgiveness unto the Lord, than it is to die a member of the Church of Jesus Christ of Latter-day Saints and be full of sin." Church power was of utmost importance to my father; the next was money.

CHAPTER TEN
Bethany Michelle

"Now Raggedy Ann and Andy, it is your tea time, so come with me and I'll show you to your chairs," four-year-old Bethany said, dressed in her finest dress-up dress and my high heels. "Samantha, the tea is for you, but you go in last, so the rest of the dolls can clap for you, okay?" Little Bethany seated the dolls in their places around the little chairs and table purchased just for tea parties with young preschool friends or dressed-up dollies. Her eight-year-old sister had used it with her friends and dolls when she was younger and her eighteen-month-old younger sister would soon do as well. In fact, she was beginning to bring the dolls and Little People collection she had in her toy chest and talked mostly gibberish to them with the little tea set she got for Christmas recently.

"Now here she is, Miss Samantha dolly," Beth sang to the Miss America song she must have heard me singing or on the TV recently. "Now, Miss Samantha, you will sit next to Barbie and Ken while I show tiny baby doll where we get diapers changed." She ran down the hallway with her infant baby doll to change something and I could hear her voice fade the farther away she got, "I'll be right back." And about two minutes later, her voice grew louder as she came back into the crowd of dolls. "I'm back. Now, tiny baby, you are all set…you need to have a bottle? No, this is a tea party, you'll just have to learn to drink from a cup and not spill! Mom, I need some tea," Beth said.

"Will lemonade do?" I said.

Whispering, she said, "Okay, but don't tell the dolls it's not real tea. Samantha might throw a fit. Mom, this is supposed to be a real tea party," Beth said in such a dramatic way that even I, the mother of this bunch, believed her.

I looked at her, so cute with pigtails. She was so proud that she had gotten dressed up, fixed her hair, put on my high heels, and put my blush on her nose and cheeks. She looked more like a clown than a tea party organizer. The high heels were too large and she threw them off halfway through the party and exclaimed, "Mom, I really need some high heels my size, okay, Mom?"

"Okay," I answered back to this precious little girl.

"Can we go now? Huh, Mom, now?" she said, jumping like a ballerina doing a pirouette, but not really.

"We can't go now, you have a party going on. I think it's time for cookies," I said excitedly, hoping to get her mind off of going right there and then for shoes.

We went into the kitchen together and got some animal cracker cookies and Beth put one on each tiny tea set plate, completely covering the plate. A little later Beth finished her tea party, which ended abruptly due to Samantha getting snotty to the other dolls and then throwing a temper tantrum which led to the time-out chair, and then the doll was naughty and again went in the time-out chair, leading to Samantha going straight to bed for the night at two o'clock in the afternoon, blinds drawn, lights out. The rest of the dolls tipped halfway out of their chairs, their faces in the food or the cup. It was a sad scene. A sad, sad scene. She had been so cute for her party to go so wrong. I was busy getting dinner started and what I should have done was sat her down and processed why the party went so badly, but being a busy mom, I didn't.

Beth was the cutest little girl. Anyone would be lucky to have her for their child. She had fair skin, big round blue eyes, a pixie nose, and pinned back ears. Her fingers were so delicate and her strawberry-blonde hair so shiny and thick. She looked best with bangs cut just to her eyebrows and then you could do a French braid or a ponytail. Doing her hair up away from her face showed her features off best. The teenage babysitters we had always fixed her hair cute, even when we weren't going anywhere special. She always had rosy pink cheeks and in the winter time, when she went skiing with her dad, she came home with red chapped cheeks and red lips that needed healing ointment.

She took ballet lessons from four years old and up and was a soldier in *The Nutcracker*. When the mice came in to ruin things, she was one of the many soldiers that battled them to keep the nutcracker safe from harm. She loved ballet and the teachers—who were very strict—often whispered to one another and pointed to her and then would tell me her arm work was delightful and very good. Her legs, on the other hand, had a mind of their own. The patella, or kneecap, would dislocate and go to the side of her leg and she would fall to the ground. When she was nine years old, we had her undergo knee surgery to correct the dislocation of her patella.

However, back in 1991, the technology just wasn't good enough to give us an answer as to whether this very painful operation, where the surgeon—recommended by the ballet company—would tighten the ligaments around the patella so it probably wouldn't go out any longer, would work. He had to take into consideration the growth she would have between now and when she would be full grown.

His reputation and strengths as a medical doctor and surgeon came highly recommended, as best we could check up on. So we went with the surgery as she pleaded with us to do it, so she could continue with ballet and have good, strong legs to help her get up on her toes for next year when she would start wearing toe shoes. We even flew her favorite cousin out to help her through the recovery as it was an intense operation and recovery process. She had the operation and it just about killed her to recover from such a profound surgery. Looking back now, I know our thoughts were too geared toward her becoming a prima ballerina.

However, after a couple of regular hard classes, her knee tried to go out and it hurt very badly, even more than it used to, because it was so tight. She just screamed now when it tried to go out because it hurt so much more. We felt terrible for putting our sweet Beth through such a traumatic experience and for what? To be a dancer really shouldn't have been that important for an eight-year-old, but it was to her and it was mostly important to us, her parents. We had the right intentions for the wrong choice in front of us. Nothing was worth what little Bethany had to go through.

We, as parents, had a lot of wrong values when raising our children, so we made a lot of mistakes. We adopted our parents' values that should have been really discussed and examined before we had children. Steve and I didn't know what we were doing or if what we were doing in our life was harmful to our three precious girls. But like any young couple, we were very materialistic and wanted bigger and better everything. We didn't budget well and we didn't discuss decisions, we just jumped into decisions with the wrong values and for the wrong reasons. We forgot everything Dr. Ellsworth taught us.

We were building a very large home in Boring, Oregon, on nine acres of land with a three-car garage and a gorgeous deck to watch the morning sun rise over the grand Mt. Hood where the family went skiing each year. There was even a nice playhouse Steve built for the girls. Steve was doing the plumbing and electrical work, watching the workers doing other work each day; basically acting as his own general contractor and somehow keeping his workers in his electrical shop doing their jobs to support us. They say one can do anything when they're young, but this house took it out on us and our children.

Steve had to stay in Boring, Oregon, living with neighbors, while the house was finished. Now looking back, it was a gargantuan mistake that caused pain and impaired relationships. It was a gorgeous house on nine beautiful acres that the Lord created. The pine trees and fir trees were all clumped into one spot on our and our neighbor's land. The fields were mostly gold ragweed that we were all allergic to, and the sun rose over Mt. Hood and set over two green hills.

The Christmas Tree Train was just over those two small hills and you could hear the small train's whistle when it was climbing those two hills in front of our house. Every year, we would go on the Christmas Train to get any kind of tree they had, and there were lots of different kinds. It was the perfect spot for a family's house to be built. We sacrificed many things getting that house built, but the most important thing we sacrificed was our daughter Bethany. We didn't know that we were sacrificing our little six-year-old Bethany until 1993.

The girls and I went to live with my parents in San Jose, California, exactly 1,000 miles from our driveway to their driveway. Our original house was rented and now we had the new house we were building only halfway done, but the paint, flooring, marble around the fireplaces, and wallpaper were picked out, so my presence was no longer needed.

About sixty miles before we arrived at Grandma and Grandpa's house, Beth threw up. We stopped at a gas station in Concord, California, and cleaned up Beth and the car as best we could until we got to our destination. Beth claimed to have another headache, but at six years old, she just said, "My head hurts so bad, Mom." I told her to lie down and we would be to Grandma and Grandpa's very soon and she could go to sleep in a nice clean bed. She fell asleep and slept until we arrived in the driveway of my mom and dad's house. As we got out of the car, I hurried her along so I could get her in bed. We did the usual hellos and kisses, except I wasn't convinced that she had a headache; I thought it was the flu she picked up at school. I thought what six-year-old gets migraine headaches which began at four years old, the last time we went to Grandpa and Grandma Hunter's home; last Christmas a little over a year ago in 1986.

We all said goodnight about fifteen minutes later and were just all going to sleep when Beth threw up again everywhere. Normally, my mother would have cleaned it up, but she couldn't bear to do it any longer and it wasn't her child, so I got the duty. Around 11:30 p.m., we all tried to get some sleep, but I made my older daughter sleep with Beth so she could come get me if Beth got sick and threw up again. We all slept well until Lindsey—the youngest of the bunch—arose at 6:30 a.m.

Beth felt better the next morning, so I blamed her illness on driving or motion sickness. We had driven straight through to San Jose—a lovely thirteen hours—stopping only to change diapers, go to the bathroom, eat a quick snack, and get gasoline. I was just glad it wasn't the flu that we could all come down with.

The kids played dress-up with Grandma's trunk. She had gathered vintage clothes and jewelry over the past few years for the granddaughters to play with. The girls loved it and they played all day, stopping for a quick bite of lunch, which they made into a tea party. At dinnertime, they cried when I told them we were having Chinese food and that they needed to take baths and showers right after dinner. They put back all the lovely clothes Grandma Hunter had for them. They were careful to fold them and not to smash them down in the trunk and I helped them put the box away for another day. We were going to be at Grandma's for two to three months and there would be plenty of time for them to play dress-up again, but now we would have school lessons in the morning and homework and then they could play the rest of the day.

That's how most of our days went, except for days that we went to the science hands-on museum or to the zoo, where we would ride the zoo trains. Weekends, my father was home and could help my oldest daughter with her math homework. I could help, but if she was stuck, she wanted her grandpa to help her. They seemed to have a very special bond between them. In fact, I thought from all appearances, he held her in the highest regard.

It was now the end of March and the house still had a little way to go before it would be enough along that we could drive home and move in. Beth continued to have flu-like symptoms at least once a week, but each time she had these symptoms, they would just vanish when the girls were having fun, especially swimming in Grandpa's pool. After pool time and bath time, the girls would be naked, but wrapped in a towel, and sent upstairs to get warm with Grandma's electric blanket and with Grandpa. I thought nothing of it until I remembered my abuse two years later in 1989 and said, "Oh my God! What have I done?" I quickly asked the girls if they remembered Grandma or Grandpa Hunter ever touched them inappropriately.

They all said no. Zoe, at barely four, said, "What does inprolitaet mean?" I told her about good touches and bad touches. None of the girls said that they could remember Grandma or Grandpa touching them inappropriately except when Grandma gave them a bath. I told them that was all right, but they should learn how to clean private areas on their own.

I now thought of all the headaches Beth had every time we went to Grandma and Grandpa's house and how violently ill she became. I can put all the puzzle pieces together now, looking back at it, but she also got really sick at home as well. I took Bethany to the doctor when she was seven years old and he told me they were migraine headaches. She was probably getting them both at Grandma and Grandpa's house and at home. She needed the room darkened, she liked soft lullaby music playing in the background, children's aspirin or Motrin, a bowl by the bed for throwing up in, and covers pulled over her head. Beth had to get just the right hours of uninterrupted sleep or a migraine would come on. She learned to choose which slumber parties to skip and which ones were worth getting a migraine.

Migraines and her bad knees began ruling her life. She couldn't do certain activities or most activities in P.E. at school. Even school dances—when she got older—would jumble her legs up and she'd be on the floor. She couldn't keep up with her friends when they ran for games, scavenger hunts, running from one house to another house, anything that would involve less sleep, more stress, and use of her legs.

—1993—

I had just arrived home in Oregon from San Diego from the Church of Jesus Christ of Latter-day Saints Church Court regarding my father's standing in the church and our allegations of rape and molestation. I got out of the car and Bethany came jogging up to me and said, "Mommy, Mommy, are you home? I'm so glad to see you." Beth just went on hugging me until we got into the house, which was less common these days now that she was almost twelve years old.

Once I was in the house and started unpacking my clothes, Beth came in and asked me, "Mom, did they—the men at the Church Court—believe you and Aunt Becky?"

"About what?" I asked her.

"You know, about Grandpa doing those things to you when you were a little girl?" Bethany asked.

"Yes. They did, they did believe us!" And I gave her a kiss on the cheek.

"Did the men really believe you, Mom?"

"Yes, Beth, they really did!"

"Okay," Beth said as she walked out of the room.

A few minutes later, I was going into the kitchen to make dinner as Bethany came walking out of her room, and we met in the hallway.

"Mom, I have something to tell you and I hope you'll believe me," Beth said.

"What is it, Beth? You've been acting differently than you usually do all afternoon. Now what is it?"

"Grandpa touched me in places he shouldn't have touched me!" Bethany said, closing her eyes the whole time.

"WHAT?" I yelled, wanting to cover my ears. I did not want to hear these words. It was like a dagger into my heart. No, it can't be true! NO, NO, NO! Honestly, I was thinking more about my pain and plotting my father's death than about Beth and the courage it took her to finally tell me. A million thoughts went through my mind all at once to the point that I knew it was my turn to respond to her. "Beth, come into my bedroom with me." And I shut my door and took her two hands into mine and said, "What did he do to you?"

"He just touched me, Mom, with the bad touches they taught us in school."

"Did he just touch you in your vagina or did he do more than touching?"

"What more is there than touching?"

"You know, Beth, did he have sex with his penis inside of you?"

"Ooh, no, Mom, he just touched around the front part of my bottom. Now that's all," and Beth slipped out of the room faster than she entered it. What in the world was I to do with this information? I was in a tailspin, that's for sure. I had no idea where Steve was, as he had drifted off to 7-Eleven or the nearest gas station. I know, I'll call Rebecca. She'll know what to do or at least help me process all of this.

"Hello, Becky, you are not going to believe what Bethany just told me…" And I began to cry.

I cried on and off for months about Beth and it triggered my own issues with my own incest experiences. When I wasn't crying, I was thinking about how I could get a gun and if I did that, I think it would have satisfied me, but I couldn't get a gun. I was a marked woman, having tried to kill myself earlier in my life before I remembered the abuse. Once you've gone to the "loony bin," you can no longer get a gun easily and I was too naïve to know the illegal or unethical ways to get a gun. And besides, my father was not worth going to jail over and my children didn't deserve to be motherless. I was in a bind and needed to do something with my ugly anger feelings.

I couldn't kill him, but I could try to sue him. He was rich and Rebecca and I would see no inheritance, so we decided to sue him and we started looking for a lawyer that we could trust to do the job right. Meanwhile, I started to immediately calm down. I was in a power struggle until the Church Court and here I was, right back into my anger. I was also very depressed, which I had been most of my life. I just kept thinking, How he could do this to Bethany? My precious ballerina—although no longer in ballet classes due to her knee disability, she would always be my prima ballerina. He stole her innocence, confused her sexuality, and robbed her of any nice, fun-loving grandfather she could have had. Her other grandfather, Steve's dad, didn't care for children, but at least he didn't molest them.

My thoughts still race whenever I think of her being sexually abused and the other stressors in her life that she has had to unfairly deal with. In writing this chapter, I have had to stay as focused as I can be as my mind still wants to dissociate from the atrocities she had to endure, but the same is true about all the lives he ruined or tried to ruin.

Then there is the matter of how he picked his victims. My father tended to pick the children he had the most control over and who had the vulnerabilities he could pick on. For example, Beth was immature and prone to temper tantrums, so he picked on her because he could frighten her into silence. She also had a weaker personality and at four and five years old, he could pick on her and gain control. Alex had some school and life learning disabilities and also a difficult personality, and Grandpa knew he could scare him into complete obedience. These two children were weaker than other grandchildren who had more sure-footed personalities and were more confident.

Whatever the reasons, he picked family, as far as we know, to molest and rape them into submission and remain quiet for a long time. If only I had recovered my memories two years earlier, I could have saved the grandchildren and if only Bethany had been able to tell me about the abuse two years earlier, we could have had him arrested for molesting small children. There are a million what-ifs that didn't work out. We would like to know if he molested any other children. After all, he did have a candy dish in his church office both times he was bishop.

When Alex came forward, he was too traumatized to tell our attorney what Grandpa did to him, let alone say it in a courtroom. So since Grandpa couldn't be prosecuted criminally, our civil lawsuit went to a settlement. In the end, we were just glad to have it over with.

I am very proud of Bethany. She went to college and graduated with an accounting degree. She is in the process of getting her CPA license and she has an excellent job and career ahead of her.

I love Bethany with all my heart. I have not always done right by her and I've made many mistakes. My hope for Bethany is that she can one day forgive me for the mistakes I made and that she finds her footing in her life. I often think of that little girl in dress-up clothes, serving her dolls tea—or lemonade—and cookies with my high heels on and my wedding dress hat covering half of her face. She is my prima ballerina and always will be. She is one of the many, many blessings I have been given. My other two children are among those blessings as well. May your child never be sexually abused and have to endure the lifelong issues and nightmares that come up as an adult.

There is a song by Celine Dion called "The Prayer" that I wish to dedicate to my daughter. It talks about guidance from above and having faith and the light from above to guide us to a place where we'll be safe. Like the song, having a place that is safe is all an abused child wants and desires.

CHAPTER ELEVEN

Retribution

The Church Court partly validated our charges of sexual abuse against our father, and he was excommunicated. However, Rebecca and I felt that we needed to do more, especially because Bethany came forward after the Church Court completed its deliberations. But, except for Alex, all the abusive acts took place too long ago to prosecute, according to the very restrictive statutes of limitations for criminal charges. In any case, poor Alex was so traumatized that he would not have been able to give sufficiently specific details for a criminal trial. Then we learned that civil law had less stringent requirements, including longer periods before statutes of limitations came into play.

Rebecca also learned that Mom and Dad planned to rewrite their will. Rebecca was the executor of their will, but now it would be changed. They would make our other siblings the sole beneficiaries and the executors. At one time, Dad bragged that he and Mom had accumulated a million dollars—a considerable sum. Considering all of this, Rebecca and I felt strongly that we should have our share of Mom and Dad's money, if nothing else, for all the suffering we sustained and to compensate us for all the costs of hospitalizations and psychiatric care we paid for out of our modest earnings. We also thought by doing this that it was another way of getting our power back and to help us feel more in control of our abuse and with Dad.

After many telephone calls back and forth and discussion about our ethical and moral rights about trying to get our inheritance—which would never happen now—it was decided that we would sue our parents in civil court. I flew down to San Diego to find a personal injury lawyer and to go with Rebecca to see him. We also decided that I should bring Bethany in case the attorney wanted to question her about her experiences with Grandpa and the abuse she suffered in his hands.

We basically picked the best and biggest ad in the yellow pages for a personal injury lawyer, Ray Vecchio, because Rebecca couldn't find any recommendations in her small circle of friends. We made an appointment with Mr. Vecchio and saw him two days later in his office by the courthouse. We hired him, gave him filing costs, and he filed a lawsuit. However, before he filed the lawsuit, he wanted to see Bethany and Alexander, so we made another appointment to come back in two days with the children.

Bethany was twelve years old and very strong and clear about what we were doing and why we were doing it, given the least information she was told. She was also very clear about what Grandpa did to her, but this suing them for money ended up giving Bethany a taste of entitlement and later in her life, this entitlement issue arose often.

Alex was now eight years old and we were hoping he might be able to actually tell. We really hoped he would say or draw a picture of what Grandpa did to him. He had not brought up the abuse issue with his mom for a while now. Rebecca prepared him, saying, "There is a nice man that wants to talk to Beth and you about Grandpa. Grandpa touched Bethany in her private area and she is going to tell him what Grandpa did to her. It would be good if you told Mr. Vecchio something Grandpa did with you or draw a picture of it." Alex was clingy to his mom the next two days and started sucking his thumb occasionally, but he agreed to go with Bethany to see this man. When the two days passed and we were at Mr. Vecchio's office, he called the children in to tell what happened to them. Sweet little Bethany put her hand out for Alex to take and they walked in together, hand in hand.

The door opened and Mr. Vecchio and the kids came out and he asked the kids to wait in the waiting room for a minute. He brought us back into his office and reported that Bethany remembered being molested at four years old and again at six years old by her grandfather. Alexander, on the other hand, sat and scribbled on the paper I gave him. He said it was a picture of him, but it was mainly just scribbles. Mr. Vecchio asked Alex leading questions that he wouldn't be able to ask in court and Alex just said, "I don't want to be a grandpa ever." Mr. Vecchio said there was no way he could question Alexander in court. Bethany acted almost rehearsed and I immediately piped up and said, "I haven't even talked with her about it ever since she told me. She is telling you what she knows and she communicates very well for her age."

The lawsuit was filed in March of 1994. The plaintiffs were Rebecca, me, Bethany, and Alex, and the filing took place in San

Diego Superior Court. After reviewing the facts of our case, Mr. Vecchio agreed to a contingency fee arrangement. The pretrial documents are public record and anyone wishing to read these can do so. You just drive to the massive Superior Court building in downtown San Diego, walk deep into the basement past airport-type security, and then you ask one of the helpful clerks for case number 674635. You will get a reel of dusty microfilm—as of 2014, this case had not yet been digitized into zeros and ones to be preserved forever inside a computer.

The documents are extensive, repetitive, and written in dry legalese. But there is no mistaking what they make clear—all the horrible things that I, Rebecca, Bethany, and Alex separately and independently told our attorney that our parents or grandparents did to us. To spare the reader all the "whereases" and "therefores," I summarized the contents of the suit below.

Our attorney, Raymond Vecchio, presented to the court at least sixteen "causes of action"—each a separate and distinct, detailed set of events of specific abuse and the evidence for these. I describe these here as they are alleged in the suit. All of us told the truth. And this is only about what we clearly remembered. I am sure there was much more that our minds are still repressing.

The papers say that for five years, our father, "by means of threats of violence and the use of physical force…forced Deborah to submit to sexual intercourse, and touching and fondling of sexual organs" to satisfy his own brutal desires. The papers point out that I could not have "reasonably discovered" the memories until 1989 because I required extensive therapy before I was able to muster the strength to remember. My recollections make up the "First Cause of Action."

Next, the lawyer turned his attention to Rebecca's remembrances. Again, he wrote, by means of physical force, threats of violence, and intimidation, our father forced Rebecca to submit to "oral copulation, and touching and fondling of sexual organs" to satisfy his base desires.

The Third Cause of Action is about Bethany. It charges that in October of 1986, with threats of violence and actual use of physical force, our father, her grandfather, touched and fondled her sexual organs when she was only four years old. The charges continue with reference to January of 1988 when the same thing happened again. She was then six years old.

The next cause of action states that in August 1992, our father forced his grandson Alex to submit to oral copulation and fondling. He was six years old.

Several of the charges document what our mother did. They say that between 1957 and 1962, she forced me to submit to "penetration of [my] anal opening with a foreign object...by means of force...menace and fear of...bodily injury." I had been three to eight years old. Our mother is also charged with "intentionally providing...Alex to our father..." so he could be abused. The legal documents also charge both of our parents with assault and battery, referring to their repeated threats of physical violence and actual severe corporal punishments.

The lawyer continued with these additional charges:

- intentional infliction of emotional distress;
- malicious aggression for the purpose of humiliation, causing mental anguish and physical distress;
- causing injury to physical and emotional health, injury to the psyche and the nervous system, causing the development of severe depression and suicidal tendencies, headaches, chronic bladder infections, body aches and palpitations.

In the pretrial papers, the indignities and injuries suffered by my sister, my child Bethany, her child Alex, and me are detailed meticulously by the lawyer. And it is all a public record.

The last of the complaints were from my husband Steve and Rebecca's husband David. These dealt with the long-term effects of childhood sexual abuse on diminishing our ability to "provide love, affection, companionship, comfort and sexual relations." The lawyers termed this a "loss of consortium." The legal terms do not begin to describe the anguish and distress caused by changes in sexual functioning, which were the direct result of what Dad and Mom did to us as children.

Among the many supporting documents was the testimony of Dr. James Madero, Alex's psychologist. He attested that Alex was telling the truth.

The defense was conducted by Kevin E. Monson, a Mormon attorney. Ironically, my hard copy of the rebuttal by our parents did not print well and some of it is hard to read. I do not have the energy to return to the courthouse for a fresher copy. But the portions I can read are outrageous enough! They tell that the opposing lawyer asked for a summary judgment against us because, he said, there were "no triable issues." So I suppose, in his legal opinion, forced oral copulation and the violent rape of little girls and boys are not "triable" issues. I found it strange to see the extremes to which legal defense attorneys can push language and argument in order to defend their obviously guilty clients.

Their main defense was that everyone charging abuse lied or misinterpreted well-meant parental actions. That would include all four of us, recounting our stories independently, and the psychologists, some of whom knew us for more than a decade, and who testified without exception to the overwhelming probability that the charges were entirely real.

The other line of defense was equally reprehensible. It relied on the convoluted and complicated statute of limitations which at the time required that "...within three years of the date, the plaintiff discovers or reasonably should have discovered that psychological injury or illness occurring after the age of majority was caused by the sexual abuse." But this defense is absurd and wildly unfair. Much of the injury and subsequent illness occurred before the age of majority for each of the victims. And the very nature of the consequences of child sexual abuse is that the victims suppress the memories as deeply as the mind is able, so that they can remain as sane and functional as possible. They asked Rebecca to bring in Alexander for a deposition so both attorneys could question him. Rebecca was allowed in the same room with him, but could not utter a single word.

Alex was being questioned because they thought they could trick him and get him to recant his story about the abuse. Rebecca was quite nervous about what Alex would say or do. He was only eight years old and not smart enough to catch on to their more tricky questions. Rebecca and Alex drove to Mr. Vecchio's office and were escorted to his office. At first, Alex stopped and said, "I don't want to go in there."

So Rebecca turned to him and said, "You know what, Alex, you don't have to if you really can't do it. Mommy understands. But if you could be just a little bit brave and go in there, Mommy will be with you the whole time, I will be even a little more proud of you."

Alexander said, "I'll do it, Mom, just for you and for me. Can you hold my hand the whole time we're in there?"

Rebecca said, "I don't know. Let's go ask Mr. Vecchio if that would be okay." Rebecca stepped back into Mr. Vecchio's office and said, "Mr. Vecchio, is it okay if I sit by Alex and hold his hand?"

Mr. Vecchio said, "Well, yes, that would be okay, but your hands would have to be up on the table."

Rebecca said, "Why? What difference would it make?"

Mr. Vecchio said, "Well…you could be doing sign language down below the table or one squeeze means one thing and two squeezes—"

Rebecca said, "That's absurd! Don't be ridiculous."

"Oh, it's been done! Hands on table or no hand-holding, or maybe you would like a chair away from Alex!" Mr. Vecchio said.

"Thank you. We'll hold hands up on the table," and Rebecca walked briskly out of his office.

Rebecca informed Alex that they could hold hands, but it would have to be up on the table. Alex seemed to be okay with that and they walked into Mr. Vecchio's office and sat where he pointed to. He was gruff and distant this morning, like he'd rather be anywhere else but there. Pretty soon, the telephone conference had all three of the people on the telephone: Mr. Vecchio, Mr. Monson, and Alex. Rebecca could not hear the questions and felt quite cut off from the whole ordeal. She heard things from Alex like, "I don't want to talk about that," "Bad things happen at that house," or "I can't talk about it, it makes my mouth hurt." He ended up with his head burrowed in his mother's lap. That's when Rebecca raised her hand and said, "That's enough."

They asked Rebecca a few questions about what happened right after Alex arrived home from his grandparents that day. She knew to not answer too long; make the attorney have to ask another question if they want more information. Just keep her answers short. My husband, at the same time, was going to law school and gave her that information, along with other recommendations as well.

After two or three questions for Rebecca, they were through. The attorneys would speak with each other later and decide what was best for the case. Alex unburied his head from his mom's lap and was sucking his thumb. Mr. Vecchio could see the remarkable change Alex went through each time he had to go back to the days he was abused. There was a clear change in personality and habits. He immediately went back to five-year-old or even four-year-old behavior, insecure and scared. Mr. Vecchio said goodbye and that he would be in touch with me and Bethany as well, but that call never happened.

After all the lengthy paperwork, claims, charges, and rebuttals, a trial date was finally set for July 14, 1995. But the trial never took place. My father, ill with congestive heart failure, died in January. Nobody from the family told us of his passing. Our brother-in-law finally called Rebecca to let Rebecca know that Dad passed and to not ask for a settlement at that particular time as Mom's CDs had not matured, but would be ready to take funds from in two months. Rebecca telephoned me and informed me that Dad died and Kevin asked if we could wait two or three months for the settlement. I, of course, said that was fine and Rebecca relayed the "yes" answer to our attorney and to Kevin. And so, we waited. There was no other communication from my parents or my siblings now or in the future. They just don't deal with me or Rebecca.

We think both attorneys got cold feet and lost their enthusiasm for the conflict. Our parents' attorney must have believed that the four of us, each with his or her own independent story, would have been very sympathetic and believable. If the case went against them, our parents would have been branded publicly as child abusers and would have sustained a very large jury award, perhaps greater than their entire holdings, which we later discovered to only be $250,000. Dad once again either lied or hid the money quite well.

On the other hand, our attorney was lukewarm about the case from the start. While he believed our story, he tried to dissuade us from proceeding further by telling us that a jury would view our aging parents as a couple of little old harmless people. How could we drag these little old people through a trial with claims from so long ago?

Mr. Vecchio told us it was time to settle. I don't know if he was aware of my father's death. The exact amount of the settlement escapes me and it doesn't matter much. What I remember is that after the lawyer took his percentage, and the rest of it was split between my family and Rebecca's, we had about enough to remodel a kitchen and pay off some old bills.

We agreed for practical reasons. Mainly, we had no desire to drag the children through vicious cross-examinations and no taste for having to repeat the sordid details of the abuse in a public forum. Our father led us to believe he had lots of money, but we were pretty sure his real "fortune" was very modest. Mr. Vecchio did not want to risk a long trial for the meager returns a contingency agreement would bring him. In the end, everyone agreed to bring the case to a close. We made our point. Nobody would pay out a significant portion of their total funds if they felt they were innocent. So the case was settled out of court on June 16, 1995. Mom, using Dad's estate, paid the settlement amount.

In our case, justice was slow, fragmented, and insufficient. But what we got out of it was a lot better than none.

Because we did not know of our father's death at seventy-five, we did not attend the funeral. Rebecca and I remained estranged from our mother until we moved her to San Diego in 2012. To some extent, we were estranged from our siblings for many years. We are still estranged from our siblings to this day because of other reasons. I do love my mother. However, I feel she will owe me till the day she dies. Being that much older, almost ninety, it might not be too much longer that her mind will remember anything, or that she will even be alive, but I must never put myself in the position of being in charge of her. I do love my mother; don't all daughters love their mothers?

CHAPTER TWELVE

Hypocrisy...Spiritual Bankruptcy

When I first started to have body memories and then head memories, there came again the message striking me that said, "You are bad!" It came back just like the nightmarish memories of the first rape! They went hand in hand together. If I thought about the rape, then I thought how bad I was. It was drilled into my brain and I couldn't get rid of it until Dr. Ellsworth taught me to go back to when that thought first entered my life and to rescue the little girl.

I screamed at my dad to go away and I got a taxi for him to leave in and then I envisioned him getting on a plane and going far, far away to a remote island where airplanes drop off bad people, bad thoughts, and bad things, but never take any of those things back; it was a one-way flight. There were pedophilic men and women, horrendous ideas, and items used to molest or rape little girls or little boys. At the time, I wasn't dreaming of little boys, but their molesting acts, thoughts, and things would also be at this island as well.

This is called doing inner child work. Dr. Sterling Ellsworth's book, *How I Got This Way and What I Can Do About It,* and Dr. Lucia Capacchione's book, *Recovery of Your Inner Child,* are the two best books on inner child work. That thought that I am bad tries swimming off the island and the thoughts return a little during depressive moments, but those are far and few now.

I was damaged far more spiritually than physically or emotionally. My idea of God was more of a hellfire and damnation God than it was of a kind and gentle God. When I was a child, there was a large painted picture hanging in the main chapel meeting area of Jesus Christ with little children on his lap and standing near him, a well for water, and small animals. I looked at that same picture every Sunday for Sacrament meeting, which was ninety minutes long.

I had a totally different viewpoint of Jesus Christ than I did of God. The only connection I had with God was when my parents taught me about Satan and how God had two sons, Jesus Christ, who was good, kind, and gentle and Satan, who was not so good, kind, and gentle. Both were to come up with a way they would rule the people of this universe. Jesus said he would let humans have their free agency, yet also have the humans suffer the consequences of their decisions. Satan said that he would force the people to choose the right way to behave and think. God chose Jesus' plan because it allowed the people to choose the way they behaved and thought, and yet, they would suffer the consequences. Satan caused a riot up in heaven and was cast out. I realize I simplified the story, but that is basically what happened. Therefore, I see God as an angry, unkind father. I know in my head he is not, but getting it into my heart is something entirely different.

In doing my research into how adults who were sexually abused as children experienced spirituality, I found that they had a great deal of difficulty. One particular article told the story of a little girl named

Rose who was dropped off by her father to mass and catechism lessons at her Catholic church every week. Rose was eleven and was being sexually abused by her father. Rose learned that if she was a good girl and continued to go to church every week and learned her catechism lessons, she could pray and God would answer her prayers. She prayed that God would stop her daddy from raping her. Nothing happened; she continued to be molested and raped by her father. She prayed harder and worked harder at being a good girl, but as she continued to pray and try harder, her father just continued to molest and rape her. Rose gave up praying. Pretty soon, she stopped going to mass and to catechism lessons altogether and said, "There is no God or I know he would have stopped my father from hurting me." As Rose grew up, she was thrown out of her home since she would no longer let her father rape her. Do you think she had a near-death experience like I did and suddenly had a complete turn-around about her faith, the Catholic Church, and prayer? It is unlikely she went back to her church unless she had a spiritual experience like I did with my dear angel when my father was raping me and smothering me. But I had an angel and I still have doubts about God and the religion I grew up in.

It is so traumatic for me to go to a Mormon Sacrament meeting that I shake and cry at the mere thought of it. I loved the Mormon hymns while growing up, but to sing one now gives me great pain. Like the hymn "Love at Home" or "I am a Child of God," or even "Mother Dear, I Love You." I have never sung the song "I am a Child of God" without big tears rolling down my face. Even when I was a Primary teacher, I would cry through the part that says, "Has given me an earthly home with parents kind and dear." My parents saw to it that I would never step through the Mormon doors of a chapel again. But I have nothing but the highest regard for that faith. It teaches of a loving Jesus and a loving God. I just never got the lessons about the loving God.

When a child is raised in a religious family or where there is a God talked about, the first representation of a God is the mother and/or the father. If the parents are loving and kind and do not abuse the child, he or she would think of a God that is that way and probably not have the torment that an abused child has. If the parents are abusive, angry, and manipulative, they will think of a God that is demanding, unkind, and angry. That will be their first impression of God. That doesn't mean it can't change. However, it is unlikely to change if the parents abuse them as small children.

Vicki Polin talks about when allegations of child molestation are brought to the attention of community leaders, teachers, parents, or relatives and the details are discussed, it often brings out negative outcomes for the victim and it follows them throughout their life, particularly as the child gets older. Rose's mother might have used words like, "Well, what did you do to bring Dad to do such a thing as that?" Or "You know nobody is going to marry you now, you're spoiled goods." Or even perhaps worse, "You're just making that up and I don't want to talk about it anymore."

Religious communities are especially judgmental. There are stories of abused children's families having to move to another part of town or another town entirely as a result of community pressure. Not only does the survivor struggle with their trust and belief in God and their community, so does the survivor's family. The more our different communities, leaders, and teachers are educated on issues relating to child sexual abuse, the easier it will be to heal the oozing wounds. Vicki Polin, in her book *How Survivors of Childhood Sexual Abuse Experience God*, says, "Our communities need to do some major wound care, some individuals may require 'spiritual surgery,' while others just need a topical ointment. But together as communities…we can come together and heal the wounds."

Anne Pritt makes a strong case for survivors of child sexual abuse when she states that "a basic defense children use against sexual abuse is to shut down their feelings." But this also cuts off other feelings, i.e., positive feelings, as well. Therefore, any loving feelings from God and Jesus or other spiritual events or beings are not able to be felt also. She talks about the innocence of children by quoting a former prophet of the Church of Jesus Christ of Latter-day Saints: "The terrible vicious practice of sexual abuse…is beyond understanding…. It is destructive in the lives of children. It is reprehensible and worthy of the most severe condemnation…. Shame on any man or woman who would sexually abuse a child. In doing so, the abuser not only does the most serious kind of injury. He or she also stands condemned before the Lord."

Anne states in her speech that the Mormon gospel "teaches that when bad things happen to people, this does not make them bad. No one can destroy another's possibility for eternity. We are judged only for our own desires, intentions, and actions, not for the actions of others against us." From my dialogue in the beginning of this chapter, it was branded into my brain and the very seed of my being that my dad would not be raping me unless God told him to. In some way, I was condemned to be the worst being of all beings. I was bad. I took the rage and the anger from my abuse and built it up over the years into such an angst against mankind that I destroyed my own family. They will have little to do with me now that they are grown and I miss them dearly. I have repented of my terrible rage because time does heal most wounds, but also I am in a relationship now that seeks peace and stability. He does not cheat against me, raise a hand against me; he respects, honors, and cherishes me and my temper is much better than ever before.

I now know it was not I who committed the deadly sexual abuse sins. My father did. Remember, and this is of great importance, that when my father was near death, he reported seeing dark, evil spirits. It hopefully will not be me that goes to hell, it will be my mother and father who will go there but I know that is up to God. They not only tried to kill my spirit, but they tried to blame it all on the victim. I, in turn, took the whole matter out on my family and now pay the price of not having them or my grandchildren in my life. It is like people say—it's how you respond to a situation that you are held accountable for.

I had it so ingrained in me at even eight years old that I was bad that when it was time for me to get baptized into the Mormon Church, I became frightened. I was afraid that God would send a lightning bolt down to earth to strike me as I arose from the water. My brother had just reached a certain level of the priesthood that gave him the right to baptize individuals into the Church of Jesus Christ of Latter-day Saints—I think he was sixteen years old—so my parents decided this would be a good experience for both of us. My mother got me ready to enter into the baptismal font by putting all the white clothing on me and sending me forth to meet my brother in the font, which is like a large Jacuzzi without all the bubbles. I was just sure the booming voice of God would say, "How dare you try to baptize this evil one. Present her to me." Something would happen to give me and all my sins away.

Sometimes a little dabble of hair would not be immersed completely and a leader over all baptisms would nod and that could mean yes, she or he was immersed completely and the baptismal prayer said correctly so everything was fine and finished. Or it could mean no, do it again, something went wrong. Some of the hair had not immersed or part of the prayer had not been said correctly. Either way, the one getting baptized got dunked again. We fixed my long brown hair into braids so the hair was under control. We did anything we could to make it go off without a hitch. Except for one thing; I was a sinner. It was too late, nothing could be done about it now.

The time came. Everyone was in their correct position. The audience, consisting of family and friends of our family and of other families that had someone also getting baptized that same day, was poised. In less than thirty seconds, the world would know of my shame. The prayer ended, I was dunked, lifted up out of the water, and…nothing. No lightning bolt, no booming voice, no gasping audience. Wayne did his part right and excelled in his priesthood duties. Everything went into slow motion for me once I looked, heard, and saw that none of my dooming predictions happened. I put my hand in a saluting position, wiped the water off my face with the other hand, and touched my eyebrow and said, "Whew, nothing happened." It was subtle, but I said it and the audience wondered why I saluted them. They all laughed and thought of my comment as silly. It was a daunting experience for me; to everyone else, I was just another baptism.

On the way into the shower area to rinse and get dried off, I thought, I got away with it again. Meaning I was still bad, but I didn't get caught this time either. From a child's perspective, I was as guilty as my dad was for the molestation we equally participated in. That's how twisted my mind was before he raped me. After he raped me, my mind went completely haywire and I felt it was then all my fault and he was merely following God's order.

This feeling and those thoughts have been with me to some degree or another since that first rape. If there were further rapes, I simply don't remember them, but he did continue to come into my room at night now and then. What I do blame my father for now as an adult is blocking my connection to God. I had the large picture in the church of Jesus and the little children to come unto him inscription. I often thought deeply about this painting and saw how open and loving Jesus was to the small children and animals. I am sad about all the missed years I lost a connection with God and I wish it could be that easy to let God into my life and make up for lost years. I work at it every day.

When Rebecca was eight years old, she too was baptized into the Mormon faith, and then the church offers a further ordinance that accompanies the actual baptism and that is called a confirmation. Baptism is to wash away any sins you may have had and confirmation is where you actually are confirmed through another prayer or blessing to become a member of the Church of Jesus Christ of Latter-day Saints. It is an honor to become a member of this great religion and to be known as a Mormon.

It came time to confirm Rebecca in Sacrament meeting, which they used to do as part of the main meeting in front of two to three hundred people, usually all members of the Mormon faith. A chair is brought up near or by the podium and three to five men surround the child and all their hands are put on the child's head and the prayer is said. It is usually a father giving his son or daughter the confirmation blessing. There were only three men participating in Rebecca's confirmation and Dad went behind her and the other two brethren went on either side. The entire congregation could see her now. With all hands on deck, Rebecca started giggling as the prayer started and giggled out loud for everyone to hear as the prayer and then the blessing part went on. When Dad heard her giggling, he pretended to sneeze and whispered, "Stop that," in her ear. Rebecca continued to giggle, only louder. By the time the blessing portion ended, she was almost roaring with laughter. She shook the men's hands to say thank you and when she got home, Mother sternly asked her, "Why in the world did you laugh through the entire confirmation today at church?"

Becky replied, "Well, I thought of a funny joke Dad told me."

Mom said, "What was the joke?"

"Oh, Mom, you wouldn't understand it and now I don't remember all of it."

"Yes, I would, now tell me it."

"Mom, I told you I don't remember it now."

"Go to your room, you embarrassed us," Mom said, still mumbling something under her breath.

"Okay. I'll gladly go," said Rebecca as she skipped to her room.

Being so joyful to go to her room bothered Mother terribly because Rebecca was so disrespectful of her. But Cynthia started crying and Mother went to attend to her. When Dad returned home to eat a quick bite before going back to the church for more meetings and appointments, he asked Mother, "Did you ask Rebecca why she roared with laughter all the way through her confirmation?"

"Yes, and she said she thought about a joke you told her that made her laugh so hard," Mother said.

"I didn't tell her any joke!" Dad replied. "What joke?"

"She said that she didn't remember it now and besides, she said I wouldn't understand it. Is that true? No matter what I said, she wasn't going to tell me even the part she did remember," Mother said.

"Well, she will tell me. It was so embarrassing. Where is she?"

"I sent her to her room," Mom said.

Rebecca heard her dad's footsteps coming toward her room and she quickly put her book inside of the scriptures so he would be less mad at her. He opened the door to her room, but closed it right away so he could speak to her privately. He said to her, "What prompted you to laugh all the way through your confirmation, young lady? I can't believe how embarrassing it was for your mother and me. The entire congregation heard you. I never told you any joke," Father lectured her. "Just what was so funny, young lady?"

Rebecca spurted out, "You were."

"I was. What kind of an answer is 'I was'? Why was I so funny?" Dad asked.

"You, baptizing and confirming me, you who molests and does other stuff to me, you use your priesthood 'powers' to baptize and confirm me. Now do you see what's so funny about that?" Rebecca replied.

Dad just turned and walked away, slamming the door on his way out. Rebecca scrambled to her bedroom door to see if she could hear anything. She did hear something; Mom and Dad were talking about her laughter and she distinctly heard Dad at the front door, kissing Mom goodbye. He said, "Just leave her alone about it now. Leave her in her bedroom without dinner and she'll learn she can't do that to us ever again. I don't think it was a joke. I guess she just got the giggles. I don't know. Kids!"

When it was time for dinner, Mother told Rebecca to get ready for bed and to change into her pajamas or a nightgown. Rebecca wondered if Dad would be in later that night and decided on pajamas so it was more difficult to get to her. It was an emotional weekend and with school tomorrow, she decided to get into bed before Mother even came in and was asleep with a smile on her face when Mom came to check on her.

What should have been an endearing, spiritual experience was nothing more than hypocrisy to Rebecca. But she was getting used to double standards in her home. Dad preached about the gospel to his congregation and then lived a completely phony life at home. It was called crazy-making at its finest. Our mother and father were hypocrites and it would only get worse as the years moved on.

Children who were sexually abused as children can and usually do struggle as adults with drug addiction, criminal behavior, alcoholism, prostitution, psychological disorders, and suicide. Some choose abusive partners, some choose chemically dependent partners or partners with psychological problems or a partner with intimacy issues. For these women, the child abuse of their past contaminated nearly every aspect of their lives and shattered every ounce of their identity.

Jan Coates, author of *Set Free: Stories of God's Healing Powers for Abuse Survivors*, has also written an article that talks about finding God for those people who have been abused as children. In this article, she states that as an abused survivor who reached the lowest point of her life, she cried out to God for help. He answered her prayers with love, mercy, and grace. "I'm living proof that it doesn't matter who we were yesterday, or what we did—it matters that God wants to do something with our lives today."

In a study of seventy-five women, Terese A. Hall wrote an article called "Spiritual Effects of Childhood Sexual Abuse in Adult Christian Women" and set out to find the long-term spiritual functioning in adult survivors who had been sexually abused as children. She used an instrument or test called the Religious Status Inventory (RSI), which asked questions about their spiritual lives now that they were adult survivors. They used three groups of women to compare spiritual qualities to one another. The first group (1) of thirty-three women were sexually abused as children and were in therapy. The second group (2) of twenty women were not sexually abused as children, but were in therapy. The third group (3) of twenty-two women had not been abused sexually and were not in therapy.

The abused group (1) showed significantly lower spiritual functioning (going to church and identifying with a religious community, praying, and trust in a higher power, etc.). The other two groups, (2) and (3), were significantly similar to one another, but both were at a higher level of spiritual functioning than the abused group. "It appears that sexual abuse adversely impacts spiritual functioning in three broad areas: a sense of being loved and accepted by God, a sense of community with others, and trust in God's plan and purpose for the future." The study also showed that most of the abused participants felt some degree of depression. They had little to no hope for the future when it came to spiritual matters. It is studies like these that help us reach out and treat survivors with mercy and love and help them find spiritual growth in whichever way they wish to grow.

Our family did have the sense of community until we were uprooted from Salt Lake City. We didn't feel that sense when we made a move a few months after we moved to San Raphael, California, and then to Campbell, California, for about one year and then when we first arrived in San Jose, where we started going back to church. I don't know if we went to church during the year we were in Campbell. Dad had to work at the Chrysler dealership most Sundays, so he was not able to go with us to church in Campbell.

Maybe we either didn't go to church or we were only involved minimally, but I don't remember having a church community when I was twelve or thirteen years old. We returned to a great sense of community when my dad was called to become bishop of the San Jose 10th Ward. I went to Girl's Camp my first year there. I was in a stake musical production. There were Saturday night dances, Wednesday night Mutual meetings with the boys, and early morning Seminary classes with the boys. There was almost too much of a good thing because our grades suffered, at least mine did sometimes, but boy, was it fun. I found my testimony of a higher power through that group. But there were other things lurking around my spirituality that were not fulfilling.

The next religious group I tried to identify with was my husband and my Mormon church group in Boring, Oregon. I enjoyed my callings to be Mia Maids Leader (the teacher for the fourteen- and fifteen-year-old girls), Primary teacher (mostly varying ages of young children), and Nursery leader (babysitter of children eighteen months to three years old) while the rest of the congregation was in various meetings, i.e., Sunday School and individualized meetings. There is no experience more sacred and special than when a four-year-old comes running up to you at church and says, "You're my teacher and I love you." Then when the parent trying to catch the four-year-old says how wonderful you are and how little Johnny thanks God every night in his prayers for his Sunday School teacher or Primary teacher; it is a joy to behold!

I no longer agree with many of the principles taught by the Mormon Church. I would love to join a similar church where I believe in the majority of the principles taught. I feel very out of touch, not having one church I believe in wholeheartedly, and I will keep searching until I find that special church and am able to find God in it and a real sense of community as well. I believe in serving one another and feel that is what we are put on this earth to do. I believe strongly in some of the Buddhist principles, but their sense of community leaves something to be desired. I guess you must pick your battles carefully and choose the church that is closest to your heart and principles.

I think the Mormon Church is a fine church and community for families. Most wards do not have much of a single-adults program, however. My mother's last ward in Huntington Beach, California, had a great singles program, but most of the other wards I have been in have not.

There is a song that I'd like to close this chapter with. I sang this song almost every Sunday and it always had me in tears. The words go like this:

> *I am a child of God, and he has sent me here,*
> *Has given me an earthly home with parents kind and dear.*
> *Lead me, guide me, walk beside me, help me find the way,*
> *Teach me all that I must do, to live with Him one day.*

CHAPTER THIRTEEN

Survival

A friend of a friend emailed me a poem called "Pull the Covers Over My Head: A Depression Poem" by Amie Merz. (I had previously found Amie's name on a superbe website called Healthyplaces.com). This poem describes exactly how depression feels! At least for me. I've been depressed my whole life until recently, but my depression still comes back from time to time. I'll never get over the first time I tried to commit suicide. I was thirty years old and in my assigned room at Holladay Park Hospital, which was a little psychiatric facility in Portland, Oregon, and I was so scared.

"Hi, my name is Julie. What's your name?" my new roommate said to me.

"Debbie," I replied.

"What you in here for?" Julie said.

"What do you mean?" I asked.

"Ya know, like depression, anxiety attacks, wild, crazy behaviors," Julie asked inquisitively.

"Those would be the ones," I admitted as I thumbed through a magazine on my twin bed. I didn't want to admit yet that I tried to kill myself with a handful of Paxil and Xanax due to depression, anxiety, and crazy behaviors.

"You married or alone like me?"

"I'm married with two children. Here, I have a picture in my purse." I grabbed my brown purse and pulled out my wallet. I showed her the picture and she said, "What do you have to be depressed about with that gorgeous husband and darling two children?"

"I don't know, except my husband and I don't get along very well, we fight a lot. I just lay on the couch and watch television and cry till I'm numb."

"I have to confess to you. I saw your chart when the nurse was away from the desk. Why did ya try to kill yourself with all you've got going for ya."

"I don't know that either. I just don't want to be here anymore."

"It's not that bad, is it?" Julie got up to turn on the light because it was beginning to get dark. I preferred the darkness, but it was her room first.

"Yes, it is that bad and I don't appreciate you looking at my chart. What are you in here for, by the way?"

"I have a haunted house and can't stay there because one of the spirits is trying to kill me!"

The nurse came to the door and said the doctor wanted to see me now. I said a hesitant goodbye to Julie and asked the nurse if I could get a new roommate because my roommate was a little bit crazy and the nurse replied, "Who isn't in here, honey."

What I didn't know at the young age of thirty was that I had been molested and raped by my father and my mother wasn't far behind him. Dr. Ellsworth explained, after I remembered, that my outward behaviors of depression, anxiety, and acting out were symptoms of my abuse that had not come forward into conscious thought yet, the real reason for my long-term depression. In other words, I was acting out, but the reason was I had not remembered being abused yet. I discovered that you can have terrible depression or anxiety attacks and not know the exact nature of your depression. Through time and counseling, the reasons will most likely appear. Depression and anxiety run in my family, but so does dysfunction. It took me years to know exactly what I was so depressed about. Depression is one symptom of post-traumatic stress disorder (PTSD).

PTSD is a condition that develops after experiencing or being exposed to an event that physically harms or threatens to physically harm someone. This harm, or threat of harm, may be directed toward the sufferer or another individual. According to Natasha Tracy, signs of post-traumatic stress disorder include:

- Self-destructive behavior such as substance abuse or overeating.
- Feeling emotionally numb
- Difficulty in maintaining close relationships
- Guilt or shame
- Hearing or seeing things that aren't there
- Serving in the military in a war zone or having been abused as a child

People with PTSD are at greater risk for:

- Anxiety or panic disorder
- Agoraphobia
- Obsessive-compulsive disorder
- Social phobia, social anxiety disorder
- Specific phobias, e.g., fear of heights
- Major depressive disorder
- Somatization disorder (physical symptoms with no medical origin)
- Suicide
- Dissociation

The signs and symptoms of PTSD may come and go, but those who seek professional treatment by a PTSD therapist may heal twice as fast as an individual who does not seek treatment. I have had PTSD several times in my life. Even now, some of the symptoms are rearing their ugly heads from writing this book about my abuse. My anxiety has increased significantly and my emotions are overreactive. I was told by another therapist not to dwell or go over my childhood abuse any further. I had years of treatment regarding my abuse and was at peace with it, but a couple of years later, I thought my story might be helpful to others and my story wouldn't bother me anymore. But I can barely finish this book due to the high level of anxiety it brought up. Writing this book is a good example of how PTSD can ruffle my feathers still.

The level to which one gets PTSD depends on the age one is abused, the combination of traumas (emotional abuse and sexual abuse), the frequency and duration of the abuse, the relationship between the perpetrator and the child, and the child's resiliency factor. The resiliency factor often determines how affected the child is by the abuse and what the long-term consequences are going to be. It determines why some children have severe long-term effects of child abuse and why other children come out of the experience unscathed. Positive attachment to the abuser, a child's self-esteem, their intelligence, the inhibition or uninhibited amount of emotions the child has, humor, and a child's independence all may contribute to a child's resiliency.

This is a lot of information, but it helps uncover how my sister was affected by her abuse and why I cry at every hangnail. My emotional regulation was worse than my sister's; her intelligence is higher. She learned from the beginning of her life to be as independent as she could be while I was clingy and co-dependent. We are as different as night and day, yet similar in many ways also.

One long-term consequence of the abuse and neglect we received as children was that Rebecca and I sucked our thumbs until we were married. I was the most stubborn as I did it at school until sixth grade. My teachers told my parents that I would stop once I was in first grade and the kids started making fun of me. But they all got used to it and my thumb went in my mouth often until third grade. I had Mrs. Billings in third grade and she had no problem embarrassing me by saying in the middle of reading or doing an assignment, "Deborah Hunter, take that thumb out of your mouth, would you please." It was worse in sixth grade, when the boys started to taunt and tease me wickedly about my thumb right at the beginning of the school year. I started liking boys, so I stopped sucking my thumb at school and was careful to do it with just my siblings, not with my parents in the room. When I met my husband and we started having sex, I was able to quit completely. This was a long-term consequence of abuse, but more importantly, neglect. Because my mother would not hold me very often and my need to be cuddled was so high when I was a baby or even a toddler, I resorted to thumb-sucking to help me with my insecurities.

When I got depressed, I would not eat and when I was getting my memories about the sexual abuse back, I did not eat to the point that I got down to ninety pounds at 5'2". Our neighbor was a doctor and friends with my husband. He noticed how thin I was getting and remarked about this to Steve. He asked me to come in to see him and I did. This was the first time I was put on antidepressants. They made me hungrier, but they made me sleepier too. I slept more, but did not gain much weight. I just stopped losing weight. I think I could have easily gone into a spiral and become anorexic.

In many of my groups on sexual abuse, the group leader would have great quips or sayings that I still remember today. For instance, "The only way out of the pain is through the pain." And "Depression—it's all in your head and in your heart." I learned that the last saying is almost correct. It is almost exclusively in your head. It's an easy explanation. A chemical imbalance in the brain is what causes the brain to go into depression. This chemical imbalance may have happened as a child, trying to cope with the unthinkable horrific child abuse you were experiencing. There are more physiological ways that can put someone into a depression. They are:

- Faulty brain wiring—There is a very involved explanation. Suffice it to say the frontal lobe of the brain, the cognitive processes (thinking part of the brain) are lower in depressed individuals. The emotional part of the brain impedes the ability to suppress negative emotional states. In other words,it becomes very difficult to break negative thought patterns. This varies among individuals.
- Brain atrophy—An article by Therese J. Borchard on the website PsychCentral states that parts of the brain lose volume, namely the hippocampus and the limbic system. "The more severe the depression, the greater the loss of brain volume." No new brain cells can grow. For this reason, Dr. Peter Kramer believes that depression is the "most devastating disease known to mankind."
- Hormonal imbalances—The formal definition is too difficult to understand, but if thefight-or-flight responses are called upon too often in one's life—like with trauma victims—this can contribute to depression.
- Genetics—There are many variations that can increase a person's likelihood of getting depression. Many of my aunts and uncles and cousins have experienced both depression and

anxiety, so it was very likely that I would get these illnesses also. Many of my family members were also molested as children and this too seems to run in families.

- Brain inflammation—In his bestseller, *Grain Brain*, neurologist David Perlmutter, M.D., explains that the basis of all degenerative conditions—including depression, anxiety, and the bipolar disorder—is inflammation. The most prominent stimulator of inflammation is our diet. Finally, something we can control. It seems the main culprits in our diet are gluten products and sugar. Many studies have been conducted using twins and the same results come out to be diet, gluten, and sugar.

The long-term effects of our sexual abuse left Rebecca and me wanting a relationship where we could be emotionally close to a man, preferably one that we could marry. However, every man we dated or were with has been emotionally distant or emotionally unavailable, just like our father. But each relationship felt familiar and comfortable. Since we did not get our emotional needs met by our father, we were, in essence, trying to marry our dad—without the child abuse—thinking this time, we would get our emotional needs met. We were not successful. We met our ex-husbands through the Mormon Church and we dreamed of building a family and a pleasant home with a beautiful spirit about it.

The problem is after a few months or a year or two, we all four began to get our needs met through dysfunctional ways and slowly over the years, we got tired and drew upon our easy dysfunctional childhood coping skills that we learned from our parents.

I wanted more affection and sex in our marriage, so I started bitching about it and trying to be the boss. My husband wanted less sex because of the bitching and more control, so he started flirting with other women and having affairs. My sister wanted more babies. She was getting her emotional and affectionate needs met with the children and she began distancing herself from her husband, both emotionally and sexually. Her husband wanted fewer children and more sex. When he didn't get it, he went looking for much more control in his life and affairs with other women also. We all did the perfect behaviors to drive each other apart. This can happen to women that just have emotionally unavailable fathers, but those of us who have also been abused are more impulsive and vulnerable.

There are no definitive signs that a child has been sexually abused or molested if a doctor does not see bruising or other signs that only an M.D. would be able to see. So one looks for behaviors that are there that indicate the child has probably been abused. In me, the behaviors were sucking my thumb, not speaking until I was three years old, and going back to wetting my bed. These are classic symptoms that the young child has been traumatized in some manner. My sister learned to speak at the normal age—twelve or eighteen months—with momma or dada, but it was what came with it, soon after, that was striking. Our mother tells the story of baby Rebecca saying, "No, dada," with the emphasis on the word "No," and shaking her finger in a no, no manner.

I had many acting out naughty behaviors like chewing my mother's wedding ring to pieces while it was on her dresser one morning. I asked her how she knew it was me as I have no memory of doing that and she said, "I just know… It was just in your nature to do something like that." I know a three-year-old child doesn't even have all of her teeth yet, let alone the strength to chew through gold.

I was always the scapegoat in the family. Someone in our family would have a problem, I would get the blame, and it would become history. There's a story about me leaving the back door open on a cold, blizzardy winter day and letting dozens of mice into the house. I was four years old and it was truth, as far as my family was concerned. The next winter came and we were all in the family room, watching television on the first cold winter snowstorm night, and we saw dozens of mice coming into the house through the fireplace bricks. We could hardly believe our eyes. The family admitted that it probably was not me leaving the back door open. It was the mice coming by the droves from between the bricks. We all slept in Mom and Dad's bedroom that night. So I was blamed for everything in our family.

There is an article put out by the U.S. Department of Veterans Affairs & the PTSD: National Center for PTSD entitled "Child Sexual Abuse." It is so well written; probably a committee worked together and wrote it. I would love to print it all out for you, but there are rules about that, so I will paraphrase some of the less well-known statements it makes.

Some child sexual abuse survivors may show symptoms of PTSD; they may act in a nervous, upset manner. Some may have long-lasting bad dreams. Besides the ape dream in Chapter Six, I had another dream that I was speaking in front of a group of church people and they looked at me in disgust and like they didn't understand me; like I was speaking in a foreign tongue that was dirty and nasty. Pretty soon, in ran the men in white jackets, including anyone who wore a white uniform like nurses, doctors, dog catchers, in the olden days. They were all there to take me away to the insane asylum where crazy people live. These people first put me in a straitjacket and a mask like a gag so I couldn't get away and no one would understand what I was saying because of the mask over my mouth. They took me away in the paddy truck. I had this and the ape dream until I remembered my father abused me and then both dreams stopped. The dreams have never come back, not once.

The child who is sexually abused might learn that the only way to get attention or love is to give something sexual or to give up their self-respect. Some children believe the abuse is their fault somehow. I had the hardest time trying to get into my head and my heart that the abuse was not my fault. I was sure I was bad through and through because my dad might have also planted that seed along with, "You like it, don't you." These thoughts would make me want to hurt myself, through either cutting or pounding on some part of my body.

I still have to say to myself about other things, "I did not cause this problem. It is not my fault."

Almost every childhood victim describes the sexual abuse as negative. Most children know it's wrong and the children who do not know it's wrong are either young or are mentally delayed. I knew from four or five that it was wrong when Daddy touched my genitals. The scene at the car lot was wrong when my dad did what he did. I always knew what he did with his inappropriate touches was wrong and I would get very angry with him. But we are taught that we can't be angry with our parents when we are young or we would dissociate or get in trouble so most of us chose to dissociate.

I haven't mentioned much about dissociation, but it is the one coping mechanism Rebecca did to escape the years and years of horrible sexual abuse she was put through by my father. She does not remember much of her childhood, nor does she want to remember. Recently, there was a serious life-threatening medical issue with one of her children and Rebecca began to dissociate. I would tell her something like directions to the medical doctor's offices and she would write them down and then not only did she not remember the directions, but she would forget the piece of paper and she would call again and again. She couldn't remember the directions and she called me at every turn. Later, I found the piece of paper and the directions were written all wrong. She was dissociating from one thing and thinking about something else, like her child.

"Dissociative disorders are characterized by alterations in perception; a sense of detachment from one's own self…, from the world…, or from memories" ("Adults Surviving Child Abuse," www.asca.org.au/about.aspx). In other words, this is an altered state of consciousness. The more severe or lengthy the abuse, the more the child will use dissociation to escape the horrendous pain of the trauma. Survivors use this disorder into adulthood, continuing to use it as a way of avoiding difficulties in their lives. It's so automatic that they don't realize they're using it. Recovery of dissociation is learning to stay present during traumatic or daily problems. Severe use of dissociation called dissociation amnesia occurs when the person is unable to remember personal information for a lengthy time period called blackouts. A person can, in severe cases, form new identities. These new identities are called multiple personalities or Dissociative Identity Disorder.

Anxiety is the last disorder I will focus on. I am more vulnerable to it than I am to all the others. Dr. Ellsworth has often told me: "anxiety and panic attacks are a feeling of apprehension associated with symptoms of tension. It is different from fear as fear is a response to perceived danger. When fear occurs inappropriately, anxiety can escalate and a panic attack can occur." If you experienced childhood abuse of any kind, you are more likely to experience frequent or generalized anxiety. If it continues to escalate, it could result in a panic attack. Panic attacks develop quite rapidly and must have four or more intense symptoms. They are:

- sweating
- trembling
- feeling of choking or trouble breathing
- chest pain or discomfort
- nausea or abdominal distress
- feeling dizzy or fainting
- feeling of being separate from one's body
- fear of losing control or "going crazy"
- fear of dying
- numbness or tingling
- chills or hot flashes
- heart palpitations or rapid heartbeat

There are seven major types of anxiety or nervousness:

- Generalized anxiety disorder—excessive worry about everyday problems
- Panic disorder—intense anxiety
- Agoraphobia—fearful of leaving home
- Social phobia—intense fear in interpersonal situations
- Specific phobias—such as fear of heights, of elevators, giving blood
- Obsessive-compulsive behaviors—repetitive thoughts and behaviors
- PTSD—when a person experiences a terrifying ordeal (vets, child abuse)

The most severe my anxiety gets is dealing with my mother. I have very conflicted feelings about her. She is a chameleon who becomes very loving to the person she is with, even though she has talked about not liking that person. Right now, she is living with my brother, Wayne, in her hometown and with her daughter-in-law, whom my mother had talked about disliking and distrusting for the past twenty-five years or more. Now that Mom lives with her, she says nothing negative about her, but raves about her, even when on the phone and no one is home with her. She is a chameleon!

I came back into my mother's life when I was going through my divorce in 2001. I did not have many girlfriends at the time and the ones I had were tired of hearing that my husband was once again cheating on me and yet I wouldn't leave him. I always said I would when I got my master's degree and had a good job and as soon as I did, I did leave him. Well, I needed a friend and my mom was a six on listening skills with ten being great.

I started having panic attacks during the divorce proceedings and so I would call my mom and she would listen and give appropriate feedback. And for the first time, she was actually on my side! My mom was validating me appropriately! Now there's something new. At one point after the divorce, I stopped functioning. I went into a deep depression about my life and leaving my marriage of twenty-eight years and leaving my youngest daughter behind to live with her father in the house and schools she grew up in, losing the house so she could stay in it, the whole icky process. I couldn't go to work; I couldn't even get up out of bed.

My mother asked if I wanted to come to California and live with her while recuperating from my divorce and until I found a job. I decided after three months of fighting with my mother about the childhood sexual abuse—she still didn't believe that it happened—to take a nanny job in San Diego, California, where Rebecca lived. It paid well, plus room and board and had two darling little girls. It was easy enough and boy, was I in line for a big surprise. Chasing after two preschoolers, doing some housework, doing cooking and dishes plum tuckered me out. I had weekends off and I would go to my mom's home to sleep for two days. That's all I did was sleep.

When I retired from hospice work as a social worker, I started going up every weekend to help my mother as she was getting elderly. We would go to the grocery store, the pharmacy, the doctor's office on Fridays or Mondays, Target, and to her mobile home office. Then Sundays, she wanted to show me off to all her friends at the Mormon church and, on Sunday or Monday, I would go home for four or five days. I no longer brought up the childhood sexual abuse as it would upset her greatly and I would be soothing her. I kept this up until one day, she fell and broke her pelvis and did other internal damage. She had to have extensive surgery. Wayne was not able to come as I believe he was in the hospital himself. After she was done recuperating from surgery, she went to a nursing home close by my sister's house in Orange County.

Wayne and Cynthia were not speaking to me at that time and I dreaded running into them in the nursing home. Of course, they blamed me for coming out and saying Mom and Dad abused me. I was the scapegoat in the family and everything that caused any ripples was my fault. Cynthia visited a couple of days a week and I drove up to Orange County twice a week from San Diego and stayed with her all day. I did the weekend trips to Mom's house out of obligation and love, but mostly because I was the only one that was available and willing. After three months, Mom got out of the nursing home and went home to finish her recuperation. We all knew Mom could no longer live alone. I suggested in-home help because she fell too often. Hiring a retired Mormon lady to live with her would be ideal, or a college student with a relief worker on weekends or me. But I was wearing thin and began to resent Mom, even though I still loved her, even after all the childhood abuse and the ignoring of the problems through the past few years. But I wasn't going to allow them to put Mom away in some dive of a nursing home so it wasn't a problem to them.

Wayne flew into town and we all met, including my love, Pierre, to back me up. Neither of them, Wayne and Cynthia, spoke about my voice counting, but it didn't because of the sexual abuse allegations and the Church Court and the civil lawsuit. Rebecca was out of the picture and I never expected her to lift a finger to help Mom because of what Mom did to Alex. For some reason, she was off the hook by Cynthia and Wayne.

Cynthia was ready with the solution she and Wayne wanted. Mom would go to Alamosa, Colorado, one town over from where she was born, and live in an assisted living center and Wayne, whose house had been up for sale for a while, would sell his house and move to Manassa, the town she was born in. He would take care of her needs from there, about thirty minutes away.

Mom did not go easily and Cynthia, with power of attorney, packed up her house and sold it, which was a huge job and I commend her for doing that. I went with Mom to the assisted living center and introduced myself and Mom to everyone in the place. I stayed for a week and got her totally settled with everything she needed. She clung to me constantly, holding my hand, my arm, or a piece of my clothing. I had feelings of leaving my kindergartener behind in class the first day of school. I truly had feelings of love for my mom and, at that point, I felt that we made a pact somewhere before we came to earth that I would be her friend, no matter what. We had been through a lot of turmoil, but somewhere, somehow, we loved each other at that moment.

She did not stay at the assisted living facility for very long. I called once or twice a week to see how she was adjusting and she begged me to come and take her back to California. I explained that she could not go back to her home and would have to live at an assisted living situation by me. She pleaded with me, "Butch is never able to visit for one reason or another and it's going to start snowing soon and then I'll be stuck here all winter alone. Please come get me."

It was hard for me to ignore that for very long. So I and a good friend, Karin, drove in a rented minivan to Alamosa, Colorado, spent one night there, and moved my mom's things into the car and drove home with Mom. We only had Mom's permission to take her out of the assisted living facility, not my siblings'. I am not sure they even knew beforehand that we were doing so. But as bold as I dare be, I took my mom out of the facility and we took a road trip together to California. There was a massive snowstorm three days later.

I arranged for an assisted living situation fifteen minutes from my home to take her immediately. My fiancé bought her everything we could not put in the minivan. A bedroom set, a brand new TV, a small refrigerator; we arranged to move a number of things she had at her home in Huntington Beach, California, and basics like milk, cereal, Pepsi, and other favorites. She met two ladies that she liked real well and she ate meals with them, played cards with them, and went to activities with them. She seemed to be fitting in to the routine and we came and got her every two or three days. In the beginning, that seemed fine, but in the long term, she wore us down. Even Rebecca broke down and she mostly started taking some snacks and supplies to her and staying and visiting and helping her around the room. Rebecca even did some activities with us. She opened the door to not forgetting what she did to her child, but rather putting it to the side so Mom could be part of this new family. Rebecca had very mixed emotions about helping Mom, the woman who had set up her son to be horrendously abused. Rebecca became vulnerable once again to Mom's ability to hurt her if Mom chose to.

Things went well for a few months and then my left leg began to swell and was very painful. I've always had loose ligaments around my knees, so they could dislocate if I got off balance or just dislocate whenever they wanted to. But Mom became more demanding and more depressed about everything and it became harder and harder to get her to go down for lunch and then she started saying her stomach was upset and could she have some soup sent up to her room for dinner. I was able to get her off of a couple of her tranquilizers by getting something milder and then taking her off all of them. I think it was the tranquilizers that were contributing to her falling all the time. Then I got more physically impaired in my legs, Rebecca got tired of trying to get Mom out of bed, and Pierre was tired of taking things to her that she left at our house.

At this time, I was addicted to shopping, and having been made her power of attorney, I became, I'm ashamed to say, one of those wretched people that took money from their mother's bank account to shop. Down deep, I felt she owed me more than I received and I shopped with her money. She found this out and called Wayne and begged him to come and get her. At the same time I was taking her money, I told her that she couldn't come to Thanksgiving because Bethany wanted to come—Mom had just moved back by me and she had no one else—but Bethany just couldn't be in the room with Grandma. Mom became anxious and said, "Well, if you're going to start up with the abuse thing again, I'm not coming for Christmas either, so then you can have Bethany all the time. Take me home." I tried to explain that I wanted them both, but Bethany was very hurt by the sexual abuse and as I tried to talk faster to try and reason with her, she put her hands over her ears and said over and over, "Just take me home," like a child would. This and my thievery pushed her over the edge and she called Wayne to be brought back to Colorado immediately to live with him and Diana.

Pierre came to my rescue and put the money back into her account and we let Wayne know that we did that and that she was welcome to take everything we purchased for her back to Colorado with her. Before Mom left, however, she had Rebecca bring her something from the store and she went to find her wallet afterwards and couldn't find it. She called up Rebecca and called her a thief and said that Rebecca took her wallet. Mom said she looked everywhere and Rebecca was the last in the room so she must have taken it. That was it. Rebecca was hurt beyond repair. She tried to understand that Mom was becoming more and more forgetful, even more demented, but Rebecca was devastated. Once again, Mom hurt Rebecca when Rebecca thought she was protected from being hurt by Mom. I apologized to Mom for taking her money and Pierre explained we counted the money I took from the receipts I kept—I always planned to pay her back, but it got out of hand. No excuses. I told her I did it and I would never shop for frivolous items again ever. The damage was done. I'm proud to say I have never shopped except for necessities again.

Wayne arrived three days after Christmas and packed her up with everything and took her away to Colorado. This was a lot of old family business and the sexual abuse was intertwined among it. If I wasn't abused or if Mom even tried to believe me, I wouldn't have taken her money and become resentful of her. If Rebecca and Alex had not been sexually abused, Rebecca wouldn't have been so hurt by Mom calling her a thief. Oh, what a tangled web we weave! And the missing wallet? It was in Mom's purse. The purse was in the bathtub!

In an article by S.W. St. Clair, he writes about the social stigma AIDS had on society as a whole. I simply took his premise and changed it to childhood sexual abuse to relate to what we deal with in our society every day.

Imagine a society afflicted by a disease which attacks twenty-five percent of its daughters and one in six of its sons. Imagine also that this plague, while not immediately fatal, lurked in the minds and bodies of these young children for decades, making them up to sixteen times more likely to experience its disastrous long-term effects. Finally, imagine the nature of these effects of life-threatening starvation, suicide, persistent nightmares, drug and alcohol abuse, and a whole host of intractable psychiatric disorders requiring costly life-long treatment.

Does any of that sound familiar? This is what living with sexual abuse feels like to me. And what if the medicine and treatments for this plague didn't work and you had to cope however you could, sometimes with alcohol or drugs? Wouldn't a society be responsible to combat such a nasty social disease?

Prevention of child sexual abuse is not easy. It is done in the dark of night and since no one suspects Dad or Uncle Bob or the helpful neighbor of doing the molesting in the home, he can get away with murder. Soul murder! There are programs in the schools that you could volunteer with or start a program yourself. It's teaching the parents, the children, and the teachers the signs to see if a child is being abused. Reading them children's books about their private bodies and taking care of uncomfortable feelings with adults and who to tell if they have been touched; children as young as three need to know this. The school staff needs to be aware of what to do if the child is telling them or showing signs of being touched inappropriately. The most important people to look for symptoms of abuse and to believe the child if he or she does come forward is crucial. Wouldn't it have been nice to have someone believe us and prosecute the person who did this when we came forward? Let's hope this is changing for our children in today's world.

CHAPTER FOURTEEN

Coping Skills

There is a story about a lion cub who was born among a herd of sheep. His lion mother was killed, so the herd of sheep took him in and brainwashed him into thinking he was a sheep. Did they tell him this maliciously to trick him? No, they were ignorant. They knew how to be sheep and that's all they knew. Although they did not mean to hurt him, he grew up thinking he must be a sheep. The skills he learned were garbage and did not help him cope with his difficult life. Being a lamb was not his true identity. As he grew, he heard a tiny voice and had a feeling he was not a sheep. This tiny voice told him to "eat the sheep." He did not listen to this inkling in his head. Eating the sheep went against everything he was taught. Then there was another tiny voice that said, "Don't eat the sheep; they are your brothers and family. They raised and taught you. They love you."

The two conflicting voices and instinct were his real internal Self and his environmental external Self. Since his external Self (what he was taught) did not match his internal Self (what his instinct told him), the lion cub became very anxious. In fact, he became quite neurotic because he believed he was a sheep, but the voice telling him to "eat the sheep" kept driving him crazy. He was trying to believe the lie.

When the lion went out into the world, away from the herd, what would happen? Would he be nervous? Of course he would be. It's quite silly though! The lion had all the coping skills to deal with the world he would meet. Out in the world, away from the herd, was where he belonged, but he was brainwashed with lies. The lion was very worried because he knew lambs couldn't survive living with a lion. If he covered himself up to look more like a lamb, he thought he would gain confidence and overcome his fear.

Perhaps he could roar loudly—like a lion with a bad temper—or talk too much. An even better cover-up would be to put on a real lion skin to fool everyone into thinking he was powerful—like a person who had a superiority complex. But who would he really be fooling? How ridiculous, a real lion wearing a lion skin! He believed the lie about his true identity and tried to fool everyone with cover-ups.

This is how we were taught—to be lambs when we were really lions. The long road lies ahead and Dr. Ellsworth and I took months and months before I was committed to finding out who I truly was and reteaching the lion how to be a lion without eating any lambs. It was hard finding out for myself, with Dr. Ellsworth's help, what lions eat, what lions do, and where lions sleep. It was well worth the difficult path. I just now need to keep honoring myself as a proud, beautiful lion (human spirit) by treating myself well, nurturing my inner lion—the lion raised as a sheep—and nurturing her the way she was not nurtured as a Supreme Being. No, I'm not getting cocky. We are all supreme beings at different levels of knowing that and treating ourselves as this Supreme Being, the lion. Reading Dr. Ellsworth's book has shown me that I am a lion too.

This story from Dr. Sterling Ellsworth's book, *How I Got This Way and What to Do About It,* points out how we have all been taught bad information by our parents, friends, other family members, anyone who wants us to think we are less than what we are—kings and queens. Many people live their life like a lion brainwashed by constantly being dragged down with lies. People are constantly putting you down and making you believe that your opinions and feelings don't matter. In other words, that you are unlovable and incapable. Dr. Ellsworth knows that all human beings are capable and lovable and may need to learn who they truly are and grow in capable, lovable ways.

Sometimes the struggle to remove the brainwashing and to live our true identities is too difficult and it just seems easier to live one's life as a lamb. And some children stay lambs their whole lives and don't challenge the lies. Their cover-ups are smoking, drinking, drugs, and overeating. They have forgotten that they are noble kings and queens. People who remember they are royalty are going to want to be treated royally and nobly. Dr. Ellsworth's goal for all of his patients is for us to find our True Self (or Positive Self) and become less and less like our Negative (or False) Self.

Dr. Ellsworth has been my therapist and mentor for nearly thirty years, on and off. I've seen counselors since I was twenty years old, some male therapists and some female therapists. Dr. E, as I sometimes call him, was the first therapist to take my lion coat, lift up a paw, and say, "I know you are under there, little Debbie, please come out." I did start coming out slowly. I didn't trust him, even though he claimed to not be the same old therapist I had been going to over the years. He started talking about my positive and negative selves and how our thoughts lead us to our words—both spoken and unspoken—which lead to our actions which lead to our behavior. We worked for hours on my internal thoughts, which were mostly negative, and how we could make that a positive thought and how it led more and more into positive behavior. I also learned about Love Supplies.

Love Supplies are ways of expressing positive love that everyone needs in their lives. Often, we do not get our love bucket full during

HUMAN LOVE SUPPLIES AND THEIR SUBSTITUTES

BY STERLING G. ELLSWORTH, Ph D

from "How I got This Way and What to do About it,"

	REAL SELF — GIVES AND GROWS *GENUINE LOVE SUPPLIES* (mostly giving)	NEGATIVE, FALSE, SURVIVAL, SELF *LOVE SUBSTITUTES* (mostly taking)	
	1. **Empathy** Listening, understanding, say back their feelings in your own words, or "uh huh," "I see." Put yourself in their place - see through their eyes, honor feelings. (Don't steal turns).	1N. Fake or inaccurate empathy, agreeing or stealing turns, interrupting, nonlistening defensiveness, comebacks, "what ifs," and "yeah buts." Dishonor feelings, looking for. evidence against what is said, argues.	
	2. **Verbal affection** Praise internals, reassurance, appreciation, encouragement, "I love you", questions to show interest and concerns and any body language showing "I like you", genuine courtesy.	2N. Praise performance and appearance only, pleasing flattery or criticism, faultfinding, corrections, disagree, rebels, argue, tease, yell, scream "word rape," silent treatment, closed up, I'm sorry.	
	3. **Physical affection** Non-sexual touching that gives, not takes: hugs, pats, holding rocking, cuddling, snuggling, hand holding, skin contact, nursing infants.	3N. Touch to get and to take, duty hugs, sexual touching or cold distant, reserved, no physical affection. Overuse of food, sex, drugs, violence.	
	4. **Trust** Space, try it alone, "I trust you to try it again," "I trust you to learn from your mistakes." It's ok to be alone, to be on your own, to learn your own adequacy. I know you are a good person and capable.	4N. Over trust, neglect, distrust, suspicion, overprotect. No space or aloneness allowed. Constant concern and surveillance, space becomes escape and withdrawal, apathy, passive rebellion.	
	5. **Explaining** Timely advice and guidance, teach, instruct, solutions, answers, questions, and finishing sentences to gain insight. (usually best only when asked for).	5N. Put-downs, sarcasm hostile belittling, advice, boast, questions that complain, embarrass, humiliate, superiority lectures, one-up, correct-all, or silence, neglect, shy, no guidance, don't know," you are stupid to ask."	
	6. **Assertiveness** Strict kindly discipline, setting limits, rules and consequences, firmness and clarity, loyal adherence to personal standards and values, openness, not in charge of other's feelings.	6N. Hostile assertiveness, meanness, domineering, rude, harsh, threatening or nonassertive, pleaser, doormat, weak, permissive, inconsistent, ambivalent, neglectful.	

our childhood. If you were sexually abused, all of our love supplies were forced out of us by perpetrators and people that only had fake love or love substitutes to give us. Below is a chart of positive love supplies and false or love substitutes.

My favorite love supply is empathy (1) and physical affection (3). If I could be in someone's arms and have them listening to me with an occasional "Tell me more," I'd be the happiest woman in the world. Oh, wait, I do have that now. For many of you, trust would be in your top two. It would be my third love supply. I thought these to be very strange when I heard of love supplies.

The neat thing as a couple or as a family is to put everyone's name on the refrigerator and then put their top three love supplies up next to their names and then when someone is sick or grumpy or down, everyone can see their top three love supplies and do one of them for that person. Let's say Dad is grumpy. Mom could arrange a nice quiet dinner for the two of them—feed the kids early—and watch a rough and tumble adventure movie with a backrub afterwards. Twelve-year-old Petey could say I love you to Dad and the twin girls could make him a sweet card. That ought to take care of his love supplies (1), (2), and (3). Love supply numbers leave it more up to the individual to come up with a number 2 love supply to give from your heart. My ex-husband wouldn't pick the top three for himself. It was just another sign toward our divorce. It's another way to communicate and a reason to stay in your positive or Real Self.

Most therapists won't touch their patients these days, but one of the things I loved about Dr. E was a hand on my shoulder, saying, "You can do it," as I left or a side-by-side hug when I arrived. He knew when to be serious, which was most of the time for me. He knew when to tell me the truth, e.g., "I've seen a lot of your negative the past few appointments. Is your positive still in there somewhere?" He does appointments by telephone if you don't live near him. Thank goodness for me because he is near Eugene, Oregon, and I'm in San Diego, California.

He got me the most frustrated with "finishing sentences." He started out with "Tell me about your feelings today."

"I am very depressed and sad."

"Let's do some finishing sentences to figure out your sadness. I'm sad because…"

"Because I was sexually abused by my parents and I'm sad about that."

"And what else are you depressed and sad about?"

"Well, I'm not happy about the fender-bender I was in last week. We have a thousand-dollar deductible so that's killing us now."

"You sound more frustrated and maybe angry about that than sad and depressed. Is that true or am I wrong?"

"No, you're right!"

"So let's do this again. I am sad and depressed because…"

"Because Steve went skiing last weekend and he's going back up there next weekend both days. I'm glad he's got inexpensive skiing forty-five minutes from our door, but does he have to go both days two weekends in a row?"

"I don't think you're there yet. One more time. I'm sad and depressed about…"

I sobbed. "Steve has all these interests and friends and I don't have any friends and I certainly don't want to go anywhere. I almost came here in my pajamas. No one likes me." And I cried for three or four minutes. "No more questions, Dr. E."

"What love supplies do you need right now, Debbie?"

"I think number one for right now."

"What's that one, Debbie?"

"That's a kick in the butt and told to get out of bed and clean the house. Bathe the kids, curl their hair, wash the windows and wash all of our clothes, and cook a five-star dinner! I did all those things yesterday; today, I just want the day off."

"A kick in the pants is not a love supply, Deborah," says Dr. Ellsworth. "Now a day off nurturing and taking care of yourself, that is one of the best love supplies—self-care."

I promised Dr. Ellsworth that I wouldn't die dumb. That means I have read his book a couple of times, tried all his basic points and exercises, and am in my real Self more than I am in my negative Self. I'm not perfect, but I am trying. The main crux of Dr. Ellsworth's work is about inner child work.

Charles Whitfield, who wrote the book *Inner Child Work*, also wrote the introduction to Lucia Capacchione's book, *Recovery of Your Inner Child*. He quoted Alice Miller, a renowned instigator and pioneer of inner child work, stating, "'Only when I make room for the voice of the child within me do I feel myself to be genuine and creative.'" Each of us has an inner child, just like the lion that was abused and mistreated as well as brainwashed to believe the sheep's lies. Inner child work is to relearn through drawing with our left hand and right hand what the inner child wants to know now and what she needs. It's a way to nurture the inner child in each of us and she will speak back as she wishes. It's also a way to reteach the lion how to be a lion and through childlike, not childish, ways, reach the damaged child in each of us. One does not make or push the inner child to draw or write a certain way or to put a time limit on it, but my inner child wanted to draw and write her feelings out as soon as possible. The only zinger was Dr. E told me I had to do it with my non-dominant hand. For me, that meant I had to draw with my left hand.

My first drawing I made with my left hand was very telling of what my family life was as a child. Dr. Ellsworth told me to just draw my family, so I drew a picture of my mother ironing sheets with an old-fashioned roller iron and three or four baskets of sheets she had to do and I put her behind prison doors with bars all around her. Then I put my little sister pulling at Mom's skirt and offering a book to Mom. Cynthia wanted Mom to read the book, but Mom had no time for that. Then I drew Dad coming home, swinging the key ring around in front of himself and combing his hair so that every strand was in place. In other words, he was a very cool cat. He drove a very fancy car which was quite elaborate. Finally, I drew myself on my pink bicycle, pedaling away from home and going to the grade school where I would be safe with my second grade teacher, Mrs. Wintergreen, and have some fun playing tetherball.

Dr. E was the one to see all the symbolism I drew. Me going away from the house to someone I felt totally safe with. Mrs. Wintergreen always walked past me during assignments or tests and put her hand on my back gently and said, "We don't hurry and we don't worry." She was obviously talking to my inner child. My mother did nothing but work and work hard, neglecting us children by ignoring my little sister wanting a book read to her. My father speaks for himself. Dressing suave and debonair and full of himself. Running away from home, that's what I wanted, but I was never quite able to go to a friend's house overnight. But my picture shows me breaking those handcuffs that kept me tied to them. This is what doing inner child work is.

Writing with your left hand (or non-dominant hand) is very interesting too. Once I was frustrated with my husband and I went upstairs to do finishing sentences myself and I took my journal in my left hand and she wrote in great big letters: STOP. That's all my inner child had to say was Stop. I think she meant stop the fighting, stop the cleaning, stop the children from fighting over the television station, just stop all the noise and demands put on me.

I finished sentences and decided that my husband and I were both in our negatives and I would talk to him about that and negotiate our differences. The kids resolved the TV thing and I did enough cleaning for the day so I could take all the children for an ice cream cone to treat the children and my own inner child. I didn't always do this the appropriate and healthy way and still don't at times. For instance, I haven't had the time lately to goof off and play with my inner child due to the book, my medical problem, and other responsibilities. As soon as I get the book out to an agent or a publisher, I plan to play and read and do all kinds of things, if she can just hold on a little longer.

Recovery of Your Inner Child has similar instructions and I agree with Ms. Capacchione that inner child work should be done with a counselor or therapist to help you interpret them with you. But what if you don't have a therapist? How does one go about finding the type of therapist that will either do inner work with you or help interpret inner work for you?

In an article by Elvira G. Aletta, Ph.D., off of the PsychCentral website, she gives ten ways to find a therapist. First, she says to forget the yellow pages. They are expensive to advertise in, yet, on the other hand, a therapist doing well might want and have the resources to advertise in them.

1. Ask a professional that you already trust, e.g., your accountant, a lawyer, a dentist, a physician. You do not have to state why you're needing that referral.
2. Ask friends or family members.
3. Get a referral from a therapist; they refer each other all the time.

4. Use resources at work like the Employee Assistance Program.
5. Schools and universities, e.g., your child's school, nurse, or social worker.
6. Customer service at your insurance company.
7. On the Internet, there are two sites that have a referral system. The first site is PsychCentral and it also has articles that will help you as well. The next site is HealthyPlace and there are also articles. The article also recommended WebMD and Psychology Today.
8. After you have a few names, Google them to see if they have a website or a blog.
9. Don't limit yourself. In other words, find a good therapist and don't limit yourself to how far away he is or if she's only a social worker.
10. Look at little mailers or neighborhood community newspapers.

She warns: Don't use Craigslist!

I would recommend getting three or four names and seeing if you could have ten minutes of their time to speak to them. Have some questions for them like:

- Where are you located? Directions, landmarks.
- What type of therapy do you offer? Cognitive, Behavioral, Psychotherapy, Eclectic?
- What are your fees? Insurance?

- References?
- How long is the average time for a client to be in therapy?
- How long are the sessions?
- Any other questions you might think of.

The therapist you go to the first time is going to have some questions for you. Some common questions that therapists have for clients are:

- What brings you here? They probably will want to know if there is anything going on in your life that is not functioning well or anything you want to tell them that you want help with or anything that you need help with.
- Have you seen a therapist or counselor before? Be as general as you want or as explanatory as you want on all the questions.
- What seems to be the problem from your viewpoint? Everyone has a different perspective. The point of counseling is to find a way to change or assist you in finding a healthy viewpoint as quickly as you both can.
- How do you feel about this problem(s)? Do you feel mad, sad, hopeless, stuck?
- What makes the problem better? Along with that, the therapist will also ask what makes the problem worse?
- If you could wave a magic wand, what positive changes would you make to your life? There will be smaller questions if you get stuck on this one.

- Overall, how would you describe your mood? Are you in a good mood or bad mood more of the time? There are no right or wrong answers.
- What do you expect from the counseling process? These would be what goals or changes would you want to see being made?

There are many more articles on websites you can find on therapy and other topics, especially on PsychCentral. HealthyPlaces is another fabulous website. Another excellent tool is the book *The Courage to Heal,* and its companion, *The Courage to Heal Workbook.* I lived by the first book when I was dealing with my sexual abuse issues. It helped me normalize my thoughts and behaviors. I just wish I had the workbook back then. It is excellent, asking you questions and you fill in answers on the blank line. It has left-hand writing and drawing exercises. I don't think it has all the inner child tools and techniques, but it has exercises like making a collage of all your inner child's favorite things. Lots of cool stuff in it. Something to use and keep forever. To balance out the inner child work, I would read Lucia Capacchione's book, *Recovery of your Inner Child*, at the same time, along with Dr. Ellsworth's book, *How I Got This Way and What I'm Going to Do About It.* Those four books would be my sexual abuse self-help course, but if there is some money, therapy even every other week (preferably every week) would be a great accompaniment.

I had a woman counselor, Patricia, who made a strong impression on me after I remembered my abuse history. She was very soft and comforting and the opposite of my mother. She taught me that I was worthy of someone's love and time. She took me out to lunch on my birthday when I lived in Portland and gave me a small necklace and a card. She wasn't in a hurry and she was so loving. It really filled my love bucket and I felt good about myself. She helped me go from feeling like a bother to feeling like a joy to be with. She taught me how to meditate and do visualizations. She was my therapist when the Mormon Disciplinary Council was held on my father. We used Dr. Ellsworth's relaxation music tape while visualizing angels all around me. That was well worth it and it's responsible for getting me through the Council as well as I did and as peacefully as possible.

Pat did a couple of inner child exercises. We shared our stories together and at a good time, we all brought a small piece of paper with some therapy portion we wanted to get rid of, e.g., Mom not reading to me or Dad hitting me. We each tied this black helium balloon to our note and released it up, up, and away and we tried not to worry about that issue anymore. I tied the Church Court to it. I hardly worried about the Disciplinary Council.

Pat moved to Hawaii and I lost touch with her. I feel that each counselor came along at the right time, but didn't quite have the inner child piece, and I knew I should be back with Dr. Ellsworth and that is when I understood about getting a doll and starting to nurture the doll who represented my inner child work.

Whenever a patient of Dr. E's was ready and wanted to explore inner child work, he would tell them to buy a doll. One man found a little boy doll and brought it into Dr. Ellsworth's office for his appointment. Dr. E got him to lie down on the couch to do some visualizations. The patient held the doll and told Dr. Ellsworth how he wasn't treated very well as a child. He said, "No, I was abused, gosh darn it!" He then began to weep profusely and muttered, "My mommy didn't treat me right." Sob, sob. "In fact, she would never read me a story." Sob. Wah. He was just howling up a storm and Dr. E gave him lots of empathy and the man curled up in the fetal position and wailed the rest of his allotted time. Dr. Ellsworth said to me when he told me that story, "Don't ever feel embarrassed by crying. Crying is good for you. It's all about feelings and that's what your inner child is…feelings."

Another story he told me was that he had this woman patient and she wanted to do inner child work, so Dr. E told her as soon as she brought a doll in, they could start. Well, she complained about having to buy a doll. The expense would be wasteful and she would look silly in her suit, buying a doll. Her neighbors would see a bag from Toys R Us and think she lost her mind. Dr. Ellsworth told her to buy the doll. She came to the next appointment with a large tote bag and when he asked her what was in the bag, she muttered, "A doll." They spoke for a moment and then he wanted her to take out the doll and do visualizations with him. She stalled for a while and then finally took the doll out and Dr. Ellsworth remarked on what a pretty, but rather large, doll she was and he began visualizing about her childhood. She said she was three years old and her mom came into the room. Dr. E said, "What did she do?" The patient sat straight up and said, "She said, 'You stupid son of a bitch.' That's what she said." She smashed the doll down on the floor. She marched right out of Dr. Ellsworth's office and slammed the door. A few minutes later, she marched right back into his office and blurted out, "Might as well have the doll. Paid for it. It's large because I was a large little girl. See you next week?" And all Dr. Ellsworth could say was, "Right, next week." She was gone like a leaf in the wind. By the way, she brought the doll back with her the next week.

Dr. Ellsworth's stories are always good, but he never gives names or real identifying clues as to who the patient is. I also live out of his area so we do telephone visits, which are good also. It really took me a long time to accept the inner child theory, and it wasn't until I started seeing other books and other people doing inner child work that I could commit to doing it. Dr. Ellsworth has been professing this type of therapy for several decades and he feels strongly that he is committed to helping individuals with this type of program and he enjoys his work.

There is one piece of information Dr. Ellsworth and I discussed at the end of this book. Just like there are stages for the death of a loved one, there are stages for going through the therapy process. You may not experience these steps chronologically—everyone is different—or you may not experience them one at a time. I experienced them in a chaotic fashion with one stage one day and by evening, I'd be in a completely different stage. These stages include the following:

1. Recognizing the effects of the abuse
2. Dealing with the memories
3. Overcoming feelings of guilt
4. Developing self-trust
5. Grieving for loss
6. Expressing anger

I would also add coming to acceptance and peace with one's abuse, which is very hard to do; at least, it was for me and still is at times. I asked Dr. Ellsworth, "Are all fathers, uncles, or brothers who molest or rape a child sociopathic?" He told me no because with most men, it is a sick love substitute, usually from a harsh or absent mom or parent. Little children can't or usually don't say no and, therefore, the adult doesn't get rejected. Dr. Ellsworth says that's what they tell him, but I think it is a weakness in their character as well.

There are a few studies I reviewed that speak to the recovery process that those with sexual abuse often have while healing from this disastrous effect. Both studies had several points in common with characteristics that survivors seem to have that end up helping them heal or heal sooner. They both agreed that more individuals with a child abuse background usually suffer from some type of mental illness, such as depression, anxiety, bipolar, or even borderline personality disorder (BPD). Don't worry about the BPD condition;

that's what I was diagnosed with in my thirties and I have improved my situation ever since with a lot of great self-help books and a lot of good therapy. But one thing I had going for me is my immense desire for control of the disorder and an earnest effort to reduce symptoms. Both studies speak to the resilience of our spirits to go on, even in the darkest of days.

Resilience is what makes one person give up and the same situation makes the other person say, "How do we survive another way?" We each had to survive as children with our difficult sexual abuse situations. I believe it's resilience that helps one person to survive and another person to commit suicide or end up a prostitute on the streets. Let's say a student at college gets an F or a D in philosophy. That's a pretty difficult class, I have heard. Another student in the same course also gets an F. One student that is resilient goes to the instructor and asks for help and the teacher spends one day a week helping the student and giving him resources. The other student that got an F tears up his grade slip and drops out of the class when maybe he had better insights into philosophy than the other person did. One sought another way than the kid who dropped out and changed careers. Resiliency helped us cope with our horrible childhoods.

There were all types of emotions that come to mind about our abuse. Anger, fear, rage, injustice, helplessness, guilt, and shame, just to name a few. These are enduring negative emotions that caused me to find various ways to cope. How do we now cope and heal from nightmares and flashbacks, the anger and injustice? Not everyone goes to years of therapy. How did they heal? It was found in these two studies and many more like them that "the following cognitive coping styles were used in a sample of female survivors: deliberate suppression [this is what my sister does], reframing the abuse—seeing it from a different viewpoint, working through the abuse experience, seeking support, and coping on one's own" (Perrott; Morris, Martin, and Romans, 1998). Morrow and Smith tallied their study of 213 female survivors and found two main coping strategies:

1. Strategies aimed at preventing a person from being overwhelmed by threatening feelings.
2. Strategies aimed at dealing with helplessness, powerlessness, and lack of control.

Below is a list of things that contribute to your recovery and things that do not assist your recovery. It is important to do as many as you can under the RECOVERY TOOLS list to ensure your healing process. This list came from many of the books I have recommended and from my own journey through recovery. The thing I most regret is losing my journal. I kept a detailed journal and with a divorce, a move across states, and five moves over the past twelve years, I lost it. I do have a set of CDs from Dr. Ellsworth's lecture seminars and they have been very helpful, not only in my journey through recovery, but also with this book.

RECOVERY TOOLS	NOT A RECOVERY TOOL
Attending therapy	Not keeping therapy appointments
Taping your sessions	Not listening to your tapes
Keeping a journal	Not sharing your journal in therapy
Sharing honestly with others	Lying or distorting the truth
Leisure time and hobbies	Keeping busy and overworking
Quiet time and meditation	Drinking alcohol or drugs to relax
Discover spirituality	Blaming God for the abuse
Talking to people you trust	Isolation and loneliness
Setting boundaries	Remaining nonassertive
Supportive relationships	Damaging relationships
Honesty with yourself	Denial of abuse or other problems
Slowing down your life	Rushing around in a stressful state
Making choices about your time	Over-committing yourself
Using short-term coping skills	Responding with survival skills
Using your voice	Keeping silent

The studies that I researched both stated that doing good deeds, such as volunteer work and being an optimistic person, was also mentioned by many of the participants. I think hospice is one thing I had going for me when I was dealing with my abuse issues. I volunteered for two hospices when I lived in Portland and it gave me great joy to do so. Whether it was putting programs and flyers together for an upcoming event or working directly with the patient or families, both were enjoyable and uplifting. I always came away from each experience knowing I helped in some way. I also knew my problems were bad regarding my abuse, but that other people were dealing with bad or life-threatening situations. It helped put my abuse issues into perspective. I wasn't the only person in the world dealing with extreme emotional problems.

I also found my spirituality through hospice. I saw all walks of life and all religious and non-religious people and I was able to be very open to others' belief systems. I saw people who cursed God for their disease and their pending death and I saw people so close to God, it was as though they could reach up and touch him. I did volunteer work for ten years and then I got my master's degree and worked another ten years as a medical social worker and I liked being a volunteer more than a professional employee. Less paperwork!

However, I am not an optimist. I am a pessimist and look at the worst scenario of all situations. It has not served me well. I am terrible at looking at things from different viewpoints, but my friend, Karin, and my hospice experiences cured me of that. Can you believe I went all those years praising Dr. Ellsworth and his therapy skills, but it took me writing my own book to read his book from cover to cover? I was familiar with his techniques and methods, but I would say things like, "I already know everything about his theory and the exercises he professes. Why do I need to read his book?" Now having read the book, I can see how the whole theory comes together and I could kick myself for not having read it before.

Right now, I'm trying to stay positive and optimistic about a situation in our family that I could be very pessimistic about. My sister

Rebecca has seven children. Her oldest boy was not abused sexually, but was abused emotionally and physically by his dad. He recently had a harder and harder time breathing and we discovered that he has congestive heart failure at the age of thirty-five. My sister is beside herself. I had been very pessimistic about his condition when he saw his first doctor. "Oh, he is not going to make it, I just know it," I said as I sobbed. He was so sick that doctors and nurses wrung their hands and shook their heads when in the room and out in the hallway, they said, "It doesn't look good," to his mother.

Well, after some time, I was trying to stay optimistic, but he was not getting better until he found the right doctor. Why is it the greatest doctors have no bedside manners? Joshua's started breathing a little easier now that he is on a good medication regimen, so I let a little light in and started telling my sister, "I think he's going to be okay. His breathing is easier now and his color is good. So I think he's going to be fine." He is now with the best cardiac department in town and Dr. Greenburg thinks he'll be fine at least in the near future.

The question is, "Can I remain optimistic and help my sister through this and not give her false hope?" I choose to try and remain optimistic and give my sister hope. It doesn't do any good to be the town crier and say, "Hear ye, hear ye, Josh is going to die." So I'm doing something new and deciding to remain optimistic. Hospice taught me that there is plenty of time to grieve. As I do a final edit on this book, it turns out Joshua is fine and they are healing his heart with multiple medications. His breathing is easier and he doesn't need the heart pump or a transplant at this time. Even though it looked grim, our prayers and optimism paid off.

Coping mechanisms develop for a reason, serve a purpose, and can be highly effective in the short term. But some methods of coping, such as alcohol abuse, can be risky themselves. Addictions to food, sex, or drugs, avoidance of seeing others, which reinforces isolation and compulsive behaviors, are all ways people try to cope. Recognizing that current behavior can be an attempt to solve past unresolved trauma can be the beginning of recovery. This is because you see the logic of your actions and that you are not "mad" or "bad" for wanting to escape the unbearable sensations which come with childhood sexual abuse trauma.

Replacing unhealthy coping mechanisms with healthy coping mechanisms is challenging and requires a lot of support. Understanding is important, but it is not enough, and you cannot recover thoroughly on your own. Research shows that childhood trauma affects a wide range of functioning. You cannot use "willpower" to resolve the trauma and you cannot move on without appropriate assistance.

Recovery is not denial, a magic wand covering the cracks, living in the past, and feeling restricted, nor doubting your self-worth. Recovery is confidence, freedom—from obsessive thoughts or the need to achieve or escape—self-acceptance, a sense of options and choices, opportunity, wider viewpoints, a sense of letting go of what used to be consuming. Putting supports in place when entering the recovery process is crucial.

I will end this chapter with some words from a dear friend I met on this journey. She wrote, "It must be noted that we did nothing wrong in order to survive, though we might feel we did and may have been told we did. In many cases, we were literally taught we were the one doing the wrong when the truth is anything but that. The fact remains we did what God gave us the job to do. To protect ourselves is to protect His creation, an act of self-love. From this point of realization, it is a small step to self-forgiveness for all wrongs, all misguided behaviors, all feelings, thoughts, words and deeds we did in order to survive. You can choose to forget this step, but know that it means you take your abusers with you and the consequence is you will not silence their voices."

CONCLUSION

Here we are at the end of the book and there are still things I haven't told you. I went to my family's house on Jepson Avenue in 1990 with my sister-in-law, Diana Hunter. It was much smaller than I remembered and the owners were the same people my father sold the house to in 1964. They knew much about the house. There was still no door on my bedroom and Linda, the daughter of the owner, who showed us around said it was once a bedroom for them also, but we saw it was now an office or study area. They didn't remodel much and the rest of the upstairs was pretty much the same, just smaller. The basement was remodeled and had three bedrooms instead of a makeshift one bedroom. No wonder we could roller skate down there. The wall on the right going down the steps to the basement was all sheetrocked. There were no spiders or mice anywhere in the house, and Linda told me they had to fix the brick around the fireplace to keep the mice out.

The barbeque area in the backyard was nicer and had been remodeled, but otherwise looked the same. The porch on the front of the house was the same and I could envision Mom on the middle of it, ironing sheets, pillowcases, and towels on the big roller ironer. Even the street looked smaller and I could imagine myself learning to ride a two-wheeler bicycle without training wheels up and down the street and what a wimp I was. We thanked Linda for showing us around and left, amazed and dazzled by the look of it, now that we were adults. Now that I have processed the experience of being raped by my father, I would like to go back and look at it again, but I probably never will.

The car lot is completely gone and the area has become the lower economic area of Salt Lake City. There is just an empty field where the car lot once was and the building was completely demolished and cleared away. The second car lot Dad had from 1963 to 1965 was now a carpet store and the building was still there with carpet inside.

I went to my father's grave in May 2012, on Memorial Day. We were in the tiny town of Manassa, Colorado, for a dear aunt's funeral. It was the year she lived near me and Rebecca in the assisted living facility in San Diego, California, and we took Mom out for her sister LeOra's funeral. We were very close to Aunt LeOra and we wanted to go and pay tribute to this aunt who meant everything to us. Mom begged to stay four extra days for Memorial Day to continue the tradition of setting flowers on the grave of family members, and there were a lot of family members who had died by 2012. I did not want to go because it meant "keeping peace" in the family by visiting and putting flowers on Dad's grave.

Well, I am not known in the family for "keeping peace," but I decided to go along with the crowd, which I never do, and just go. Well, when I got to Dad's grave, I got sick to my stomach and wanted to burn the grass on and around his grave to mark him as an evil man. I dissociated through most of it as Mom spoke about all of Dad's good qualities as her husband and our father. They were all lies. Rebecca wandered around other graves, so I was stuck hearing all this garbage about Dad which wasn't true. If I had it to do over, I would have said, "Mom, I'll be happy to go with you to all the graves except for Dad's. I'll bow out of that one, if you don't mind."

She would have asked why and I would have said, "Mom, you'll remember why if you just think about it for a while," or if necessary, I would also have said, "Remember, Dad raped me when I was nine years old." She would have flipped out on that statement. I don't hide what I'm feeling very well and I don't do it very often. If they told me when Dad died in 1995 that he was being buried as a member of the Mormon religion and having a Mormon type of funeral, I would have shown up and ruined all of their plans. I was relieved in some ways to not have had that information so I didn't do something bizarre.

Rebecca works as a nurse at Kaiser Permanente in San Diego. She spends her spare time with her seven children—all grown and on their own—and her eight grandchildren, ranging from one to thirteen years old. Her oldest son is still recovering from congestive heart failure at thirty-five years old. Rebecca will not take his death—should he die—very well and it could affect her relationship with God, she states. Rebecca feels we have had enough trauma in our lives. What with the childhood sexual abuse, an ugly divorce which almost took her life, and now her son gravely ill—it's all too much, I agree, but crisis hits everyone and you must go on.

As for Bethany and Alexander, they were not thrilled about being in this book, but I think they will grasp the importance of their story.

They both have long-term effects of childhood sexual abuse, but are handling it well. I cannot give specifics, but they have struggled to get where they are today and they have accomplished a lot in their lives. Bethany has her master's in accounting and has a good job. Alex has traveled all over the United States while working in the construction industry and his boss depends on him to help with each project that comes his way.

I guess that just leaves me, and I do the best I can. I would never have written this book if it wasn't for my medical condition. About eight years ago in 2007, I had a knee replacement due to my knee dislocating really badly and not being able to walk. I had to leave my hospice job behind, not knowing if I would ever walk normally again. About one percent or even less get RSD—Regional Sympathetic Dystrophy—which is a very painful chronic nerve disease affecting my legs, primarily the operated leg. I have struggled with the pain for eight years now. Sometimes, the pain is excruciating and some days, it's not very bad. There is no rhyme or reason for what affects it. I will have it for the rest of my life with grim predictions that it will continue to get worse with each year that passes. I walk with a walker now and if we have to go to a doctor's appointment and my legs hurt very badly, I have to go in a wheelchair.

I have many losses and I feel very sorry for myself some days. I talk with my inner child and I remind her that I wouldn't have written this book if I could walk or clean the house or cook. It is very important to me that I am useful. That I serve some purpose here on this earth is vital. If I can give to mankind and serve others, then I am happy. So I was praying one day about being able to do something with my limited life and I thought and thought about it and prayed some more and one night in a dream, I was typing a book and dreamed that I was an author and I remembered my dream the next morning.

At first, I said, "You could never be a writer; you just don't have the skills to do something like that. It would take classes and I would have to get a degree in writing and I cannot get to classes, so that's out." That was my negative Self talking so I started by reading a book on how to write your memoir. The author mentioned a school that gives Internet classes for writing. I looked *Writer's Digest* up on the Internet and saw they had classes that were quite expensive, but my fiancé, Pierre, encouraged me to take one or two to just try it and see if that's what I wanted to do. Everything went smooth as clockwork from then to now with the conclusion. With a few classes under my belt and a lot of emotional support from my fiancé, Pierre, and Rebecca, and a lot of help from my writing coach, Kathie Giorgio from AllWriters' Workplace & Workshop, I now have a book about some of the darkest days in my life. Dr. Ellsworth continued to work with me long distance and was instrumental in helping me with the book, but more in finding my inner child and getting "shrunk," as he puts it. Let me tell you, this man is eighty years old and can really work hard. He sees anywhere from twenty to thirty patients a week and gives great therapy and consults with large companies, helping individuals or giving workshops.

This is very important: if you think something is going to happen, dream about it, envision it, meditate about it, and pray about it. I do believe taking the right steps and doing these other important things will help you in your journey. If I can write, you can have your dream come true. It took a year and a half to make it happen, but that's a year and a half that I would have shopped from catalogs and watched TV. If you see it, you can be it. I may not write the next Great American Novel, but I have chronicled my deepest, darkest secrets of my life into a book which will hopefully help others.

I have a confirmed bachelor for a boyfriend and we have been together for twelve years now. His name is George Hody, but he goes by Pierre. He was born in France so a bunch of his friends in medical school nicknamed him Pierre and he stuck to that nickname. We met on Match.com twelve years ago and started by e-mailing each other. This was when I received my divorce from Steve and moved to California from Portland, Oregon. Steve died two years after I moved and my children took over and gave their father a beautiful memorial.

When I met Pierre, I was 5'2" and 105 pounds. I worked out at the gym four or five days a week, had long blonde hair, and was hot for forty-nine. Now I weigh a lot from not being able to move around enough and have short blonde hair, and I am no longer tan.

Pierre is my dream come true. That's not to say we don't have any difficulties in the relationship because we do. But far fewer than I ever thought possible. I dread the day he dies (he's fourteen years older than me) because with my being disabled, Pierre and Rebecca do everything for me and I would be lost without him. I love him so very much!

As far as my spiritual life goes, I know beyond a shadow of a doubt that there is a heaven. I do believe there is a higher power, whether that is God or whomever you name your higher power to be. I believe he is a gentle, loving being and I know there is a hell or, as Dr. Ellsworth calls it, a giant, not very nice "therapy room."

I believe there are good people and bad people and I don't have time to waste hearing about or worrying about the pedophiles, the terrorists, the politicians, and other bad guys. I get my spiritual needs met by prayer, meditation, nature, and reading. I will never get to Ireland, but I am grateful for my Irish heritage and my ancestors that sacrificed so much to get to America. I believe that all people in America should be treated fairly and equally. I pretty much believe in the American dream of having everyone's dream possible.

This book was very hard for me to write. I thought I was at peace with my childhood sexual abuse, but having it all come up again like it did in writing this book, I was not completely healed. And I don't believe anyone gets over their childhood abuse, but you do need to come to certain terms with it. You should deal with it as best as you can. If you just remember a little or have a body memory, that's a start. I encourage you to take your journey whatever you can handle and if it keeps coming up for you, trust me, there is more work to do. My last suicide attempt was in January 2011 when a bad person told me a lie about Pierre, something she told me was true but was not true. Whenever I feel completely abandoned or betrayed is when suicide seems to crop up. I feel much more stable than I have ever felt because I did my inner child work this time around. I hope when Pierre dies, I can handle it well, even though we are close. I hope if Rebecca dies before me that I can also handle it well. I hope when Dr. Ellsworth dies at 105 years old, he can handle me not being a patient anymore.

Pierre and I would go sailing in his boat before my RSD and weight became an issue. We loved leaving the bay behind and going out to the ocean. We usually had another couple with us, Tony and Maria, and I felt pretty safe if there were two men handling the sails as the wind wrapped us in her crosswinds, and yet I wondered how they kept control of the sails and kept us going where we wanted to be. Dr. Ellsworth also sails and he gives an analogy about the wind and the sails which I believe to be so true. He says, "While you can't control the wind, you can always adjust the sails." This is true about life. We cannot change the trials and tribulations that come to us (the storms), but we can adjust our attitude toward them. We only have control over our responses toward new or recurring problems in our lives. We can't avoid the storms that hit us, but we can adjust our attitude toward them. Instead of freaking out at each problem that comes our way, we can say, "Why, look, here's another opportunity to grow and accept that this has happened," no matter what it is. Can we fix it? Maybe. Remember, you catch more bees with honey than with vinegar. Can we respond to it well? You bet you can. If you change your normal response to a positive response, at least you won't be the one causing any negativity. Like Dr. Ellsworth and I have found, you solve your own problems more positively (in your real Self) than you do in your negative Self. I have done this frequently and I must say it works, in most cases. Even if the other person stays in their negative Self, you'll be glad you rose to the occasion and ended up positively. "You cannot control the wind, but you can always adjust your sails."

This poem was written for me by another dear friend I met online who lives in France and who is writing her own book on her experiences as a preteen and the childhood sexual abuse she endured by her stepfather. Pauline, thank you for this poem:

SO YOU SAY YOU LOVE ME

At times when I lay alone in bed at night I often think did I make it up or did I dream of someone else's nightmare, you were there and then I heard myself say . . . so you think that you love me

But then . . .

I remember, that first time as if it were yesterday, that place, your breath, your smell, your touch . . . so you think that you love me

But then . . .

I recoil back into my shell, the shame, the guilt, and the fear

I'm all alone now living my hell because for so long now no one I dare to ever tell . . . so you say that you love me

But then . . .

I see them all look at me, I think they can all see
just exactly the sordid abuse that you have done to me
try as hard as I might to be good and to be kind
I feel that in my heart real love nowhere will I find . . . so you say that you love me

But then............

I want to break free, fly around this universe like a butterfly
But what you did has for so long crippled me
Hush I hear you say now, this is our secret which I must contain
No one would understand therefore a secret forever to remain
But this caterpillar is beginning to stir . . . so you say that you love me

But then . . .

My mind, my body and my soul has had enough now
I am stretching out now and beginning to feel bold
OK so let's just see, because now I'm ready to tell the whole world now and my story will unfold
Just exactly dear daddy what it is that you did to me . . . so you say that you love me

But then . . .

What's that I hear you say dear daddy, oh I see
"please don't tell, I am sorry and now I am so old"
Oh really dear daddy then please tell me this
why was it OK then daddy when I was so young
for you to violate and steal my innocence my childhood and most of my life . . . so you say that you love me

But then . . .

You beg and you plead and really I no longer care
Because the simple words of sorry you really not dare
But then I've even surpassed that because daddy I've just realized . . . so you say that you love me . . .

But then . . .

Get a bloody dictionary and look up what that actually means!
I am over it now, I now understand that that was not love . . . love is pure, joyful, peace and happiness all things that you are not.
I have grown, I am a butterfly I can now fly, I am alive, truly happy, joyous and blessed and to you all I sing . . . so you say that you love me . . . and I say then love all of mankind! Take care and God bless all you survivors.

Dear Reader: Remember that reviews are golden, especially yours.

I wish you Godspeed in your journey out of the darkness as you learn to forgive the perpetrator(s) who ravaged your spirit as well as your body. I hope you will learn to forgive these abusers and forgive yourself from anything you did in the name of survival. May you always have angels lighting the way for you. Thank you for coming along on my ride with me. May God bless each and every one of you so you can find your way home to yourself again.

THE END

APPENDIX

The following words are frequently encountered when reading or listening to discussions about The Church of Jesus Christ of Latter-day Saints. Entries marked with an asterisk have a separate article in the Encyclopedia at BYU.

Abomination Something that is loathing, disgusting, or hating someone for something.

Active in the Church* Refers to regular attendance at meetings, observance of the principles of the gospel, and acceptance of Church callings.

Angels* Literally, messengers; usually referring to messengers from God.

Baptism An essential ordinance in receiving forgiveness of sins and church membership. Baptism is by immersion, meaning that the person being baptized is briefly submerged in water. Baptism shows our willingness to follow Christ's example and to make covenants with God. Baptism may be performed in the font provided in many meetinghouses or in any body of water that is suitable.

Bishop* A priesthood office whose bearer has been ordained and set apart to preside over a ward.

Bishopric* A bishop and his two counselors.

Bishop's Storehouse A warehouse or large building of supplies for the poorest members of the church. They must have a bishop's recommendation. It is to satisfy a member's temporary need for food.

Branch Generally the smallest organized congregation of the Church (normally fewer than two hundred members).

Brethren (1) All male members of the Church; (2) "The Brethren," a designation of the General Authorities of the Church.

Callings* Invitations to accept an office or assignment; offices or assignments themselves.

Chapel The room or hall in a Church meetinghouse used for worship services.

Child of God The Latter-day Saint belief that all persons are spirit children of God in the premortal existence and that this parent-child relationship continues on this earth and through eternity.

Church of Jesus Christ of Latter-day Saints, The* The official name of the Church.

Church credentials Being able to give credit to or trust to another person, usually a member of the church or a church leader.

Church Disciplinary Court It does take courage and a deep conviction of right and wrong to call into question and condemn the behavior of someone. Twelve men being high counselors, stake presidency, and bishops, all congregate to accuse a woman or a man of a sin, e.g., an affair, and deciding if he or she should have their church membership taken away until certain conditions can be met.

Companion missionary A missionary's partner. Missionaries in the Church always work in pairs.

Confirmation* The bestowal of the gift of the Holy Ghost to newly baptized members by holders of the Melchizedek Priesthood; also official recognition of Church membership.

Congregation The members of an area, i.e., ward, stake, or group of people.

Convert A person who has just become a member of the Church of Jesus Christ of Latter-day Saints. Ex: "They are new converts to the Church."

Counselor A person called to serve as an adviser, assistant, and occasional substitute for an officer or leader in the Church.

Disciplinary procedures* The process of bringing a Church member before a priesthood officer or disciplinary council to account for alleged transgressions against Church standards and to take necessary steps toward repentance.

Disfellowshipment* A disciplinary action against a Church member that severely restricts participation in Church activity but falls short of excommunication.

Divine intervention A spiritual or Godly intervening between two causes, people churches, etc., in order to have some influence on the situation at hand.

Elder* An office in the Melchizedek Priesthood; a title designating a holder of this priesthood, a General Authority, or a male missionary.

Eternity A synonym for "endless" as contrasted to things of mortality.

Excommunication A disciplinary action against a Church member in which membership is withdrawn.

Garments* Sacred ceremonial undergarments associated with temple covenants.

Genealogy A record of lineage showing the descent of a person or family from an ancestor or ancestors.

General Authorities* Members of the presiding lay leadership of the Church: the First Presidency, Quorum of the Twelve Apostles, Quorums of the Seventy, and Presiding Bishopric.

God Latter-day Saints declare, "We believe in God, the Eternal Father, and in His Son, Jesus Christ, and in the Holy Ghost."

Gospel* The "good news" of redemption through Jesus Christ; the principles and ordinances of the plan of salvation.

Heaven* (1) The dwelling place of God; (2) any kingdom of glory.

Heavenly Father Also known as God the Father or Elohim.

Hell* (1) The condition of misery one may feel after sinning; (2) the temporary dwelling place of the unrepentant till the judgment day.

High council (high councilor)* A group of twelve high priests (and sometimes alternates) who help direct the affairs of a stake and speak in different wards once a month.

Holy Ghost* The third member of the Godhead, a personage of Spirit.

Hymns Mormon songs that are sung in meetings.

Indian student placement* The practice of bringing LDS American Indian children to live in LDS homes during the school year.

Jesus Christ The central figure in the doctrine of the Church of Jesus Christ of Latter-day Saints.

LDS - Latter-day Saint* A member of the Church of Jesus Christ of Latter-day Saints.

Laying on of hands* The placing of hands by those holding priesthood authority on the head of a member to confer authority, office, calling, or blessing.

Mia Maids A group of young girls ages 14-16 who do young women's activities, have class, and who do projects sometimes alone as a group or with joining other boys or girls of other ages, all teenagers.

Mission A certain area of the world where boys who are 18 and girls who are 19 can go and teach the gospel to the native people who live there, but are not yet members of the Church. A mission calling is sent by the leaders of the Church in Salt Lake City to the address of the boy or girl who wishes to be sent on a mission.

Missionary discussions Basic gospel lessons missionaries use to teach interested people about the Church and its doctrines.

Mission fields The particular area that the elder or sister is serving in.

Mission President The leader of a mission area over anywhere from 120 to 250 missionaries to teach, counsel, and watch over the health, well-being, and spirituality of each elder and each sister serving a mission for the church.

Modesty A standard of dress, behavior, or speech that is in line with good Church standards.

Mormon Headquarters Salt Lake City, Utah.

Mormonism, Mormons* Unofficial terms for the Church of Jesus Christ of Latter-day Saints and its members; members prefer to use the official name of the Church and to be referred to as Latter-day Saints.

Mutual The Church's auxiliary organization for youth ages 12 through 18, for many years called the Mutual Improvement Association, or MIA.

Nursery leader An adult who helps care for children during Sunday School and other instructional meetings for babies ages 6 months to 18 months.

Ordinances* A performance or prescribed ceremony related to the reception of a blessing, covenant, or ordination, such as baptism, confirmation, endowment, marriage, etc., performed by one who has been ordained to the priesthood and authorized to perform the ordinance.

Parishioner A person who goes to church.

Pioneer Day* July 24, celebration of the anniversary of the arrival of the Latter-day Saints in Salt Lake Valley in 1847.

Prophet The current and past Leaders of the Church of Jesus Christ of Latter-day Saints who are inspired to be the prophet of the church.

Priesthood* (1) The power of God; (2) the authority to act in God's name; (3) the right and responsibility to preside within the Church organization; (4) a term referring to the men of the Church in general.

Priesthood blessings* Blessings of counsel and divine influence conferred by the authority of the priesthood.

Primary* The auxiliary organization in the Church for children from ages 18 months through 11 years.

Prophet* (1) When capitalized, often refers to Joseph Smith; (2) when not capitalized, it can refer to the President of the Church, or any authorized spokesman for God; (3) one who has a testimony of Jesus Christ by the Holy Ghost has the "spirit of prophecy."

Proselyte (verb) An LDS variant of "proselytize"; that is, to invite others to convert to the Church of Jesus Christ of Latter-day Saints.

Relief Society* The adult women's auxiliary organization of the Church.

Returned missionary One who has completed a full-time mission for the Church.

Sacrament* The water and bread blessed and distributed as emblems of the body and blood of Jesus Christ to Church members in ward or branch meetings.

Sacrament meeting* The principal worship meeting of the Church, during which the sacrament of the Lord's supper is blessed and distributed to members of the Church. The members also pray, sing, and hear sermons.

Sacred Connected to God or dedicated to a religious purpose; same as holy, hallowed, blessed, or special.

Scriptures These include the King James Bible, The Book of Mormon, The Doctrine and Covenants, and The Pearl of Great Price for Mormons.

Sermon Anyone in the church giving a talk a group of people about an understanding of their duties and obligations. It also introduces them to the fullness of the gospel that Jesus established among them.

Sick, blessing the* An ordinance in which ill persons are anointed with consecrated olive oil and blessed by Melchizedek Priesthood holders, to the end that healing may take place (anointing).

Single adults* Adult Church members who are not married.

Social Services* A separate corporation from the Church (called LDS Social Services) which serves as a resource for meeting special social and emotional needs of Church members.

Soul* The united spirit and body. All living things on earth are souls, meaning they consist of a spirit body and a physical body.

Spirit body* A being formed of refined element, with which a physical body of earthly element. unites to form a soul. Human spirits are literally children of God.

Stake* A geographical-ecclesiastical unit of the Church, composed of several wards and sometimes branches. Boundaries are the large area that makes up a stake.

Stake president* The presiding authority of a stake, which is a number of congregations.

Sunday School Held weekly in each local ward or branch. It lasts about an hour. Each Sunday, ward members assemble at the meetinghouse chapel for prayer and hymn singing, following which those twelve years and older attend age-group classes for religious instruction.

Temple* A sacred building, the "House of the Lord," in which Latter-day Saints perform sacred ceremonies and ordinances of the gospel for themselves and for the dead.

Temple ordinances* Sacred ceremonies performed in Latter-day Saint temples.

Testimony* A personal expression of one's convictions or beliefs about the gospel of Jesus Christ.

Trials and tribulations A person who is suffering or going through hard times.

War in heaven* The conflict between Lucifer and Jesus Christ, and their followers, in the premortal existence.

Ward* A geographic ecclesiastical unit in the Church, consisting of several hundred members presided over by a bishop.

Young adult The program in the Church for young single members.

Young men* The instruction and activity program in the Church for young men ages 12 to 18.

Young women* (Mia Maids) The instruction and activity program in the Church for young women ages 12 to 18.

Made in the USA
San Bernardino, CA
18 November 2015